Middle East Imbroglio: Status and Prospects

Middle East Imbroglio: Status and Prospects

P.S. Link
Editor

Nova Science Publishers, Inc.
New York

Art Director: Maria Ester Hawrys
Assistant Director: Elenor Kallberg
Graphics: Eddie Fung, Kerri Pfister,
        Max Dutton and Barbara Minerd
Manuscript Coordinator: Gloria H. Piza
Book Production:Tammy Sauter, Gavin Aghamore
Circulation: Irene Kwartiroff and Annette Hellinger

Library of Congress Cataloging-in-Publication Data
available upon request

ISBN 1-56072-391-2

        ©1996 Nova Science Publishers, Inc.
        6080 Jericho Turnpike, Suite 207
        Commack, New York 11725
        Tele. 516-499-3103 Fax 516-499-3146
        E Mail Novasci1 @aol.com

Printed in the United States of America

CONTENTS

Hamas and Palestinian Islamic Jihad: Recent Developments, Sources of Support, and Implications for U.S. Policy[*]

Clyde Mark and Kenneth Katzman

Background[1]

On December 8, 1987, a traffic accident at the Gaza Strip-Israel crossing point resulted in the deaths of several Palestinian Arabs, and triggered a series of increasingly violent demonstrations aimed at revenge against the Israeli occupying forces. Over the next few days, the rebellion, of "intifadah" in Arabic, spread to the Wet Bank, and eventually to some Arab areas of Israel. The Muslim Brotherhood, a branch of the Islamic reform movement founded in Egypt in 1928 and transplanted to Jerusalem in 1945, wanted to participate in the uprising, but reared damaging its non-political image as a religious, educational, and social organization. To avoid the military-political connection, several Muslim Brotherhood leaders, Shaykh Ahmad Yasin and Mahmud Zahhar among them, formed the Islamic Resistance Movement, Harakat al-Muqawama al-Islamiyya in Arabic (since known by its Arabic acronym Hamas, which also is the Arabic word for zeal).[2] Hamas issued leaflets in December 1987, encouraging continued participation in the uprising against the Israeli occupation but without using the Muslim Brotherhood or Hamas names. In February 1988, Hamas began using its name on leaflets and communiques, and identified itself as a militant branch of the Muslim Brotherhood. The Hamas Charter, adopted on 18 August 1988, states in Chapter One, Article 2, that Hamas is a branch of the Muslim

---

[*]Excerpted from *CRS Report 94-993 F.*

[1]For additional background, see: Wooten, James. Hamas: the Organization, Goals, and Tactics of a Militant Palestinian Organization. CRS Report to the Congress 93-511F, 19 August 1993.

[2]Some observers believe Hamas was formed earlier: see for example Ahmad J. Rashad, Hamas: the History of the Islamic Opposition Movement in Palestine, Washington Report on Middle Eastern Affairs, vol. XI, no. 8, March 1993: 37-38.

Brotherhood.[3] But more recently, Hamas leaders rarely equate Hamas with the Muslim Brotherhood.

In the early 1980's, a group of Muslim Brotherhood members, led by Dr. Fathi al-Shaqaqi and Abd ad-Aziz Audah, dissatisfied with the Brotherhoods' reluctance to confront Israel, formed the Islamic Jihad for Palestine. Islamic Jihad called for the removal of Israel through armed warfare, and the establishment of an Islamic state of Palestine. The Islamic Jihad maintains its militant opposition to Israel and to a negotiated agreement that recognizes two states in Palestine. During the same period, the 1980's, some members of Fatah, dissatisfied with the secular nature of the mainstream resistance movement, sought a more activist Islamic foundation for their attacks on Israel. Some of these dissatisfied Fatah members, depending on the degree of their commitment to Islam, joined Islamic Jihad or formed the more secular "Fatah Hawks." Both Islamic Jihad and the Fatah Hawks joined in the December 1987 intifadah.

Other Palestinian organizations, such as Fatah, the Popular Front for the Liberation of Palestine, or the Palestine Liberation Organization, were caught off guard by the sudden popularity of the spontaneous and spreading rebellion, and quickly began to organize support for the growing numbers of young Palestinians in the street and their families sequestered by Israeli curfews. The PLO and affiliated groups formed the Unified National Leadership of the Uprising (UNLU) to coordinate secular Palestinian support for the intifadah.[4] Militant Islamic groups, including Palestinian Islamic Jihad and Hamas, joined Fatah and other groups, both secular and religious, in forming a loose confederation called the Unified National Command (UNC) to coordinate operations and support for those participating in the intifadah.[5]

Structure

Hamas follows, in general, an organizational structure similar to its parent Muslim Brotherhood. The general membership, which may number in the tens of thousands, is divided into areas, which are subdivided into sectors, which in turn are subdivided into regions and branches. Hamas has separate units for administration, intelligence, information, political affairs, and commando operations. Only the political and information units operate openly outside the occupied territories, maintaining offices in Amman, Damascus, Teheran, and other capitals. There is a Director-General to administer the day-to-day operations, and a Majlis al-Shura (advisory council) to set policy and advise on operations.

---

[3]See Journal of Palestine Studies, vol. XXII, no. 4, Summer 1993: 122-134.

[4]Abu-Amr, Ziad. Hamas: a Historical and Political Background. Journal of Palestine Studies, vol. XXII, no. 4, Summer 1993: 5-19.

[5]Some observers say there was only one organization and do not distinguish between the UNC and the UNLU.

According to one Israeli source, the Hamas structure underwent some changes after Israel deported 415 Hamas leaders in December 1992.[6] Following the December 1992 kidnapping and murder of an Israeli policeman, Israel arrested some 1,000 Hamas and Islamic Jihad supporters. Israel deported 415 of the Islamists to Lebanon on 16/17 December 1992. The deportee case became the focus of international attention because the deportees languished on the slopes of southern Lebanon's hills through the winter and summer of 1993 before being repatriated to Israel and the occupied territories in December 1993. The Israeli arrests and deportations forced Hamas to reorganize and promote new leaders while the old Hamas leaders were detained in Lebanon. The Israeli sources also claimed that the Hamas military wing was all but destroyed at the time of the December 1992 deportations.

The military commando wing of Hamas is known as the Izz al-Din al-Qassim Brigades, names after a Palestinian nationalist killed fighting the British in the early 1930;s, and probably numbers around 100 members at any given time.[7] Hamas military activities appeal to many Palestinians who want to confront the Israeli occupiers, but at a continuing cost of constant Israeli military engagement and a growing cost of confrontations with the Palestinian police.

The Islamist Program

Hamas and Islamic Jihad assert that the area of the West Bank, the Gaza Strip, and Israel is a Muslim trust and should be a single Islamic state; that to accept any compromise solution that allows Israel to exist is a violation of the Muslim trust; that the Muslim Palestinian state to be formed will tolerate Jews and Christians among its citizens; and that Sharia (Islamic law) should be the law of the land in the Palestinian state. Hamas and Palestine Islamic Jihad use armed force against Israel in their attempt to create a Palestinian state. Hamas provides food, medical treatment and supplies, and education to the Palestinian Arabs of Gaza and the West Bank.

Recent Developments

In April 1994, Hamas spokesmen offered what appeared to be a modified policy. Khalid al-Hindi, dean of the Islamic University in Gaza and reportedly a Hamas leader, said on 21 April 1994 that Hamas would have accepted the 13 September 1993 Declaration of Principles if it had included full Israeli withdrawal from the West Bank and the Gaza Strip, and a dismantling of all Israeli settlements. A leaflet issued by the Izz al-Din al-Qassim group the same day, 21 April 1994, said the Hamas

---

[6]Yaari, Ehud. The Metamorphosis of Hamas. The Jerusalem Report, 14 January 1993: 24-26; Also see the interview with Ehud Yaari by Roni Daniyel, broadcast over Qol Israel (Voice of Israel) radio, 31 January 1993, printed in Foreign Broadcast Information Service, 31 January 1993.

[7]One Israeli source states that the number of Izz al-Din al-Qassim members is between 40 and 50, organized into 5 or 6 operational squads or cells. Horovitz, David and Ehud Yaari. Can Hamas Blow Up the Peace Process? The Jerusalem Report, Nov. 17, 1994: 20-24.

military wing would stop fighting the Israelis when Israel withdrew from the occupied territories. Also on 21 April, Hamas leader Musa Abu Marzuk was quoted as saying the Hamas would accept a truce if Israel withdrew from the West Bank, including east Jerusalem, and Gaza, if Israel dismantled all its settlements and evacuated all settlers, and if free elections were held in the territories.[8]

The change of policy, if indeed it was a change, followed three incidents that contradicted peace overtures, and appeared to fit a Hamas vow to revenge five-fold the February 1994 incident at Hebron, in which an Israeli settler killed some 30 Palestinians. Hamas was implicated in the car bomb explosion that killed 8 and wounded 50 Israelis on a bus at Afula on 6 April, the explosion that killed 6 and wounded 25 on a bus at Hadera on 13 April, and the ax attack against Israelis in a Jerusalem bus on 18 April.[9]

Islamist Relations With Other Palestinian Groups

The Islamist groups and the PLO agree on the need for a Palestinian state, but do not agree on all particulars about the hoped-for nation. The PLO wants the Palestinian state to be secular, not governed according to Sharia as advocated by the Palestinian Islamist groups. The PLO accepted and the Islamist groups rejected a two-state solution to the Arab-Israeli problem (sharing the territory between an Israeli state and an Arab state). The Muslim Brotherhood differs from some other Islamist groups and from the PLO in that it pursues a non-military path to Palestinian statehood.

The December 1992 deportations triggered a meeting between Hamas and the PLO that temporarily ended the near open warfare between the two groups, but the truce did not last.[10] Tensions between the radical Islamist groups and the PL remain high and clashes between Hamas and the Palestinian police continue because of differences over the secular-religious nature of the Palestinian state they hope to form, control of areas and facilities, competition for members, and cooperation with the Israelis. The most recent incident, on 18 November 1994, began when the Palestinian police seized loudspeakers that Hamas members set up for a rally following Friday prayers. Hamas members responded with stones, and the police responded with gunfire. Fourteen died and 150 were wounded in the confrontation. In the days after the Friday clash, Arafat used the Fatah Hawks as irregular police to keep order, perhaps in a effort to lower the Palestinian police profile. Hamas claims

---

[8]The al-Hindi statement appeared in an interview published in the Jerusalem Arabic newspaper al-Nahar, the Izz al-Din al-Qassim leaflet was reported in the Hebrew language newspaper al-Hamishmar, and the Abu Marzuk statement was broadcast over Monte Carlo radio; all three are reported in Foreign Broadcast Information Service, Daily Report on the Near East and South Asia, 22 April 1994. Not all Hamas sources agreed with the apparent shift in policy; al-Quds clandestine radio reported on 21 April that the "jihad" and military operations against Israel would continue until Israel no longer occupied the Palestinian homeland; also reported in FBIS, 22 April 1994.

[9]All reported in FBIS, on 6 April 1994, 13 April 1994, and 18 April 1994.

[10]Kershner, Isabel. Hope and Fear. The Jerusalem Report, 14 January 1993; 27-29.

that the Palestinian police, under direction of Arafat and the PLO, were cooperating with the Israeli authorities by arresting and detaining Hamas and Islamic Jihad members accused of attacking Israelis during October 1994.

Israel and Islamist Groups

Israel considers Hamas and Palestinian Islamic Jihad illegal terrorist organizations. Israel expects the Palestinian police, who began operating in Jericho and the Gaza Strip in May 1994, to pursue Islamist or other terrorists who attach Israelis or the occupied territories.

The Muslim Brotherhood, prior to 1987, limited its activity to religious and welfare issues, and did not engage in military or political confrontations with the Israeli occupation forces. Israel tolerated the non-threatening, service oriented Brotherhood. Hamas, with its more militant approach and its commando unit, was a threat to Israeli troops and settlers, and drew Israeli attention and enmity. But, there is some evidence that prior to intifadah or in the early days of Hamas formation, late 1987-early 1988, the Israeli government offered Hamas the same tolerance that it had offered to the Muslim Brotherhood, hoping that the Islamists would provide a counter to Fatah and the PLO.[11] After it became clear that Hamas was a more active political organization and that the military unit was acting against the Israeli occupying forces and Palestinian Arab collaborators, the Israeli support ended, and Israeli forces began attacking Hamas and its military wing. Israel used the same tactics against Hamas as it used against other Palestinians: detention, arrest, imprisonment, deporting known leaders, destroying houses and crops of activists' families, and, in some cases according to some evidence, harsh physical treatment.[12]

Support for the Palestinian Islamist Groups

Hamas and Palestinian Islamic Jihad derive financial and political support from a wide range of sources, both from supporters in the West Bank and Gaza Strip and from countries and supporters in and outside the region. The financial aid takes many forms, ranging from small private contributions raised in mosques to large grants from wealthy contributors and some governments in the region. Israeli sources reportedly estimate Hamas' total annual budget to be about $30 million.[13]

---

[11]See Wilkinson, Paul. Hamas: an Assessment. Jane's Intelligence Review. July 1993: 313-314. Hamas and Friends. Economist, vol. 331, 23 April 1994:43.

[12]U.S. Congress. House of Representatives. Committee on Foreign affairs. And Senate. Committee on Foreign Relations. Country Reports on Human Rights Practices for 1993. Submitted by the Department of State. 103rd Congress, 2nd session, Joint Committee Print. Washington, U.S. Gov't. Print. Off., February 1994, pgs. 1203-1205.

[13]Ibrahim, Youssef. Palestinian Religious Militants: Why Their Ranks Are Growing. New York Times, November 8, 1994. p. A12.

LOCAL SUPPORT

The radical Palestinian Islamist groups appear to attract significant popular followings in their home bases in the West Bank and Gaza Strip. However, it is difficult to gauge precisely this support, in part because it fluctuates with the ebbs and flows of the peace process. At times when progress in the peace process has been slow, Hamas has often drawn as much as 35 to 45 percent of the vote in races for positions in local professional associations, unions, chambers of commerce, and student councils.[14] However, its underlying base of support throughout the West Bank and Gaza may be somewhat lower than that. A recent poll by the Center for Palestine Research and Studies reported in November 1994 that 17.4% of Palestinians in the West Bank and Gaza Strip claim political affiliation with Hamas, and 3.7% with Palestinian Islamic Jihad.[15]

Many Palestinians of all social classes are attracted to the Palestinian Islamist groups' ideological opposition to territorial compromise with Israel. Others, particularly the lower classes, are attracted to the Islamist groups for their ability to deliver social services (schools, medical clinics, sports clubs, religious community centers, food and money for orphans and poor families) that the Palestinian national authority or Israeli administration do not provide. This may explain why the Islamist groups are more popular in the poorer Gaza Strip than in the more affluent West Bank. Many supporters of the Palestinian Islamist groups provide funds in the form of contributions or levies; Hamas reportedly imposes a religious tax (zakat) of 2.5 percent on the wages of its members in the territories, but allegedly it sometimes uses threats of violence to compel payment.[16] Some observers contend that support for the radical Palestinian Islamic groups could drop if and when self-rule successfully is extended throughout the occupied territories and if the Palestinian Authority is able to accelerate economic development in the areas under its control.

The radical Palestinian Islamist groups' militia arms have a core of zealous, committed volunteers to carry out violent operations against their Palestinian enemies and against Israeli soldiers and civilians. The State department estimates the strength of Hamas as an "unknown number of hardcore members and tens of thousands of supporters and sympathizers," but says the strength of Palestinian Islamic Jihad is "unknown."[17] Israeli and Palestinian security authorities reportedly believe that Hamas' militia (the Izz al-Din al-Qassim Brigades) numbers fewer than 100 at any given time.[18] Hamas and Palestinian Islamic Jihad militiamen are drawn

---

[14]Greenberg, Joel. Self-Rule Pact Is Major Challenge to Islamic Militant Group in Gaza. New York Times, November 7, 1993. p. 10.

[15]The poll was conducted by the Nablus-based Center for Palestine Research and Studies during November 17-19. The poll was sponsored and published by the International Republican Institute: Washington, DC, November 30, 1994.

[16]Wilkinson, Paul. Hamas-An Assessment. Jane's Intelligence Review, July 1993. p. 313.

[17]U.S. Department of State. Office of the Coordinator for Counterterrorism. Patterns of Global Terrorism: 1993. Released April 1994. pp. 45, 56.

[18]Ibrahim, Youssef. Palestinian Religious Militants: Why Their Ranks Are Growing. New York Times, November 8, 1994. p. A12.

from overpopulated, impoverished neighborhoods that support the radical Palestinian Islamic groups and offer protection from Israel and Palestinian security authorities. According to John Cooley, a well-known observer of Islamic movements, some of these militiamen served as volunteers in the war against Soviet forces in Afghanistan, as did many Islamic guerrillas now fighting secular regions in Algeria, Egypt, and other countries.[19]

EXTERNAL SUPPORT

The October 11, 1994 kidnapping of an Israeli soldier and the October 19, 1994 bombing of a Tel Aviv bus -- for which Hamas claimed responsibility -- have focussed greater attention on the external sponsorship of Hamas and Palestinian Islamic Jihad. In some cases, the Palestinian Islamist groups receive outside financial aid from private contributors, although in other cases the groups may receive aid directly from sympathetic governments in the region. Some regional governments may be acting as unwitting or reluctant hosts for efforts by Iran to provide assistance to its Islamist Palestinian allies.

Iran

Iran, Hamas, and Palestinian Islamic Jihad all oppose compromise with Israel, and Iran is the most vocal governmental sponsor of the radical Palestinian Islamic groups. Iran argues that territorial compromise with Israel by the Palestine Liberation Organization (PLO) and its Palestinian allies represents a sellout of Muslim rights. For the most part, Iranian leaders have been open about their support for Hamas and Palestinian Islamic Jihad, and these groups, especially Palestinian Islamic Jihad, similarly have been public in acknowledging their affinity for Iran. During a visit to the United Nations in New York in April 1994, Iran's Foreign Minister Velayati said Iran would continue to provide "political and emotional" support for Palestinian groups that rejected the September 1993 Israel-PLO Declaration of Principles on Interim Self-Government, though he denied Iran provided military aid to those groups. Since the accord, several Iranian officials, including the Commander-in-Chief of Iran's Revolutionary Guard, have met with Hamas and Palestinian Islamic Jihad leaders in Damascus, lauding these organizations and their goals.[20] There have been press reports that the Revolutionary Guard is training Hamas and Palestinian Islamic Jihad activists in Lebanon (where the Guard maintains a contingent of troops) and in

---

[19]Presentation by John Cooley at a Middle East Institute-sponsored briefing for congressional staff. November 19, 1994.

[20]Iranian Official Discusses Ways to Foil Peace Pact. Reuters, November 17, 1993. Hamas and Palestinian Islamic Jihad are part of a ten member, Damascus-based front of Palestinian rejectionist groups, which includes some extreme nationalist and leftist Palestinian organizations.

Sudan, where Revolutionary Guards reportedly also are present.[21] It should be noted that hard evidence of Iranian military training of Palestinian Islamic militants is lacking. For their part, Hamas leaders have said that Hamas and Iran share an "identical view in the strategic outlook towards the Palestinian cause in its Islamic dimension,"[22] and Palestinian Islamic Jihad leaders have acknowledged Iranian political support.

It is increasingly clear that Iran provides funding to the Islamic Palestinian groups, although the funding levels are not precisely known. In the aftermath of the Tel Aviv bus bombing, Israel's Ambassador to the United States, Itamar Rabinovich, said "I think that speaking in state or government terms, Iran is the address [the main source of external funding for Hamas]."[23] The State Department's Office of Counter-terrorism supports the Israeli allegations of Iranian funding, noting in its report on international terrorism for 1993 that Hamas and Palestinian Islamic Jihad receive funding from Iran.[24] On the other hand, some dispute the implication that acceptance of Iranian funding means that Iran somehow controls the radical Palestinian Islamist movements or that it drives actions these groups commit. Hamas receives funding from a wide range of sources, and it is not necessarily beholden to Iran as a sole benefactor. Some analysts of Iranian affairs have noted that, despite its rhetoric, the clerical regime has taken, as far as is known, little direct action to derail the peace process,[25] and that sectarian differences between the Sunni Muslim Palestinian groups and Shiite Muslim Iran limit their potential to remain allies.

The Israeli and U.S. assessments have been confirmed indirectly by some Palestinian Islamic leaders, including Fathi al-Shaqaqi, the Secretary General of Palestinian Islamic Jihad. In April 1993, he told a New York newspaper that Palestinian Islamic Jihad has received Iranian funds since 1987 and that "Hamas and four other groups are likewise funded by Tehran."[26] Hamas' representative in Iran said in 1993 that "there were forms of assistance from the Iranian people to help the steadfastness of the Palestinian people in the occupied territories," but he denied that Hamas had received as much a $30 million from Iran, as alleged by PLO leader Yasir Arafat.[27] A Lebanese newspaper that often has proved reliable on Iranian affairs reported in December 1993 that Hamas, as of January 1994, would receive $10 million (presumably per year) from Iran, to be derived from spot sales of Iranian oil stored in Rotterdam, the Netherlands.[28]

---

[21]Horowitz, David, with Ya'ari, Ehud. Can Hamas Blow Up the Peace Process? Jerusalem Report, November 17, 1994. pp. 23-4.

[22]Hamas Says It Sees Iran as Strategic Ally. Reuters, February 28, 1993.

[23]Itamar Rabinovich Press Conference, Washington, DC. Reuters, October 19, 1994.

[24]U.S. Department of State. Office of the Coordinator for Counterterrorism. Patterns of Global Terrorism: 1993. Released April 1994. pp. 45-6, 56.

[25]Amirahmadi, Hooshang. The Islamic Republic and the Question of Palestine. Middle East Insight, May-August 1994. pp. 50-54.

[26]Jihad Leader Acknowledges Iranian Funding. London Al Sharq Al Awsat, quoting Shaqaqi's interview with New York Newsday. April 12, 1993. p. 4.

[27]Hamas Says It Sees Iran as Strategic Ally. Reuters, February 28, 1993.

[28]$10 Million Reportedly Granted to Hamas. Beirut Al-Shira,' December 1993, p. 9.

Lebanon/Hizballah

Following fifteen years of civil war, the government of Lebanon is trying, with mixed success, to extend its control throughout Lebanon, but Israeli, Syrian, and Iranian forces and their local allies continue to maintain a presence in Lebanon. The most important militia operating in Lebanon is the radical Shiite Islamic Hizballah organization, a close ally of Iran, and there appear to be growing links between Hizballah and the radical Palestinian Islamist groups.[29] Hizballah and the Palestinian Islamic groups have organized demonstrations in Beirut denouncing the September 13, 1993 Israel-PLO accord and the October 26, 1994 peace treaty between Jordan and Israel. When Israel returned the last of the 415 Hamas and Palestinian Islamic Jihad deportees in December 1993, Hizballah and Iranian Revolutionary Guard officials helped the deportees dismantle their tent camps in the no-man's land between Israel and Lebanon.[30] As further evidence of the growing bonds between the Palestinian Islamic groups and Hizballah, the Hamas militants who kidnapped Israeli soldier Nachshon Waxman in October 1994 demanded the release not only of Palestinian Islamic leaders, but also of Hizballah leaders kidnapped by Israel (Shaykh Abd al-Karim Ubayd and Mustafa Dirani).[31] There are some unconfirmed reports that Hizballah, along with Iranian Revolutionary Guards based in Lebanon, is training Hamas (and presumably also Palestinian Islamic Jihad) fighters in Lebanon.[32]

Syria

According to the State Department, Syria may be providing some funds to Palestinian Islamic Jihad.[33] There are no official U.S. allegations of Syrian funding for Hamas, but some Members of Congress have alleged that there is Syrian support for Hamas. The Secretary-General of Palestinian Islamic Jihad, Fathi al-Shaqaqi, is based in Damascus and Syria allows Hamas and Palestinian allies -- to operate in Damascus as a rejectionist front. Syria probably hosts these groups, at least in part, as potential leverage in negotiations with Israel, and as a means of preserving Syria's alliance with Iran, from which Syria reportedly gets some oil and political support. Perhaps more significant is Syria's tacit approval of cooperation between the Palestinian Islamic groups and Hizballah and Iran in Lebanon. Hizballah and Iran's Revolutionary Guard operate in Lebanon in areas, such as the Bekaa Valley, that are under the direct control of Syria's approximately 35,000 troops in Lebanon. On the

[29]For further information on Hizballah, see U.S. Library of Congress. Congressional Research Service. Hizballah: A Radical Militia in Lebanon. CRS Report 93-905 F, October 7, 1993, by Kenneth Katzman.

[30]Hoffman, David. Palestinian Militants' Exile in Lebanon Ends. Washington Post, December 16, 1993. p. A35.

[31]Gellman, Barton. Hamas Kidnaps Israeli, Threatens to Kill Him. Washington Post, October 12, 1994. p. A27.

[32]Background on Hamas, in Middle East Week. Center for Near East Research. December 29, 1992. p.5.

[33]Patterns of Global Terrorism: 1993. p. 56.

other hand, Syria has often acted to rein in Hizballah or other groups when their clashes with Israel have escalated to the point at which the Arab-Israeli peace process is in jeopardy. Syria is believed willing to expel Hizballah's militia, Iranian forces, and radical Palestinian elements from Lebanon in conjunction with a peace settlement with Israel that leads to a full return of the Golan Heights to Syria and an Israeli withdrawal from southern Lebanon.

Jordan

Until recently, Jordan had tacitly supported the Muslim Brotherhood in the West Bank and, through it, Hamas, believing that building up Hamas would help weaken the influence of the PLO in the West Bank. (The PLO and Jordan have vied for support among Palestinians in the West Bank.) Jordan has aided Hamas through Jordan's Islamic endowments ministry, which maintains mosques and funds Islamic clerics in the West Bank.[34] In the last few years, however, Jordan increasingly has become concerned that Hamas' militancy might radicalize its sister organization in Jordan, the Muslim Brotherhood, which is now a key bloc in the Jordanian parliament. In April 1994, reportedly with some U.S. urging, King Hussein declared Hamas illegal in Jordan.[35]

There is some circumstantial evidence to suggest that Jordan unwittingly or reluctantly is hosting a potential Iranian conduit to Hamas. Iran has no presence in the West Bank or Gaza Strip, where Hamas operates, but, in 1992, Iran reopened its embassy in Jordan, from which Hamas activists can gain relatively easy access to the West Bank. In 1993, Iran appointed Ahmad Dastmalchian as its Ambassador to Jordan. Dastmalchian had served during 1987-1990 in Lebanon where he helped funnel Iranian assistance to Hizballah; Jordan reportedly had hesitated to accept his appointment in Amman because of concerns that he would seek to back Islamic extremists in Jordan.[36] In January 1994, Jordan demanded Iran cut its embassy staff in Amman from forty persons to nine; Dastmalchian remained in place.[37] That month, King Husayn said that Dastmalchian was "acting as an Ambassador should," but that Jordan was watching the Iranian embassy closely.[38] Based on Dastmalchian's background and the circumstances of his appointment in Amman, it is possible that he might aid Hamas through Iran's embassy there, if assertions of Iranian aid to Hamas are true.

---

[34]Bailey, Clinton. Hamas: The Fundamentalist Challenge to the PLO. Washington, DC: Washington Institute for Near East Policy. Research Memorandum Number 19, April 1992. pp. 16-17.

[35]Sabbagh, Rana. Jordan Says Hamas Is Illegal. Reuters, April 16, 1994.

[36]Sabbagh, Rana. Jordan Tells Iran to Reduce Diplomats in Amman. Reuters, January 22, 1994.

[37]Iran to Cut Staff at Amman Embassy by 31. Reuters, February 5, 1994.

[38]Boustany, Nora. Jordan Expels 31 Iranian Diplomats. Washington Post, February 4, 1994. p. A26.

Persian Gulf States -- Private Contributors

The State Department believes that Hamas is receiving some funding from private contributors in Saudi Arabia and other moderate Arab states.[39] Saudi Arabia is a conservative Islamic state that has supported Islamic movements throughout the Middle East. In addition, Saudi Arabia and the other Persian Gulf states were angered by the PLO's support of Iraq during the 1990-91 Gulf crisis, and have backed the radical Palestinian groups as an expression of their displeasure with the PLO. Exact estimates of aid from Gulf state contributors are difficult to obtain, but one report, quoting Western intelligence sources, says Hamas gets "millions" of dollars annually from private contributors in the Gulf states.[40] Hamas reportedly has an office in Saudi Arabia and, in April 1993, a Hamas delegation visited Qatar to discuss aid to Hamas and the Palestinian people from that Gulf state and the opening of a Hamas political office there.[41] On the other hand, the Saudi and other Persian Gulf governments have been supportive of the Arab-Israeli peace process. Their reluctance to block private contributions to Hamas and Palestinian Islamic Jihad may stem from the unwillingness of the Gulf regimes to offend their wealthy and powerful constituents, or provoke terrorist attacks within their own countries.

Sympathizers in the United States and Europe

A debate over Hamas linkages in the United States began in February 1993 when Israel alleged that Hamas was directing its operations in the occupied territories from U.S.-based command centers. Israel based the charges on information obtained in the January 1993 arrest of two naturalized Arab-Americans (Muhammad Jarad and Muhammad Salah) allegedly for carrying money and instructions from the United States to Hamas activists in the occupied territories. At the time, a State Department spokesman acknowledged that Hamas has sympathizers in the United States but that there was "no evidence to prove that Hamas terrorist operations are working out of the United States."[42] Shortly after these allegations surfaced, some Members of Congress called for investigations of suspected Hamas activity in the United States.[43] The issue flared again following the October 19, 1994 bus bombing in Tel Aviv. That day, some Israeli officials reiterated concerns of private U.S. funding for Hamas, although Israel's Ambassador to the United States acknowledged that U.S. law enforcement agencies had worked diligently to curb Hamas activity.[44] On October 24, 1994, Secretary of State Christopher promised a major U.S. effort to cut off

---

[39]Patterns of Global Terrorism: 1993. p. 46.

[40]Sieff, Martin. U.S. Aims at Hamas' Pocketbook. Washington Times, October 26, 1994. p. 1.

[41]Fouad, Ashraf. Hamas Team in Qatar for Political, Financial Aid. Reuters, April 3, 1993.

[42]Elan, Bruce. Hamas and the Heartland. Time, February 15, 1993. pp. 37-8.

[43]See Congressional Record, daily edition, February 2, 1993. p. H320; and February 18, 1993. p. S1931.

[44]Itamar Rabinovich Press Conference. Reuters, October 19, 1994.

private U.S. funding for Hamas, including support for the passage of new legislation, if necessary.[45]

No one is certain how extensive Hamas fundraising activities are in the United States. State Department officials reportedly have said Hamas is receiving "millions" of dollars each year from donors in the United States.[46] Some press reports suggest that Hamas may be receiving one third to forty percent of its budget (estimated by Israeli sources at $30 million per year, see above) from private fundraising in the United States and Britain,[47] but free lance journalist Steven Emerson believes Hamas may get as much as 80 percent of its money from contributors in the United States.[48] Emerson presented his allegations of extensive Hamas fundraising and political activity in the United States on CBS' November 13, 1994 edition of "60 Minutes" and in a Public Broadcasting Service special entitled "Jihad in America," on November 21, 1994. A former Federal Bureau of Investigation (FBI) official, Oliver Revell, has reported that Islamic organizations in the United States publish and distribute radical Islamic literature in this country and engage in terrorist training operations, and that radical Islamic clerics frequently visit the United States on fundraising drives.[49] The Justice Department position is that fundraising is legal as long as the contributions are not for acts of terrorism. Many Arab-Americans and others contend that the vast majority of the funds raised to toward helping poor Palestinians in the West Bank and Gaza Strip, and are not diverted to any terrorist activity.

---

[45]Worsnip, Patrick. U.S. Hints at Laws to Stop Hamas Funding. Reuters, October 24, 1994.

[46]Greenhouse, Steven. U.S. Hints at Better Ties if Syria Signs Peach Pace With Israel. New York Times, October 24, 1994. p. A8.

[47]Sieff, Martin. U.S. Aims at Hamas' Pocketbook. Washington Times, October 26, 1994. p. 1.

[48]Winer, Todd. Hamas's Chicago Connection. Chicago Jewish News, October 28, 1994.

[49]U.S. News and World Report, October 31, 1994. p. 44; Schweid, Barry. Ex-FBI Official Says U.S. Provides Sanctuary for Muslim Militants; Reuters, November 17, 1994.

Terrorism: Middle Eastern Groups and State Sponsors*

Kenneth Katzman

Middle Eastern terrorism is a complex issue that involves many different groups and state sponsors, and is widely considered a threat to U.S. interests. Currently, the Administration and Congress are paying particularly close attention to terrorist groups and state sponsors that oppose the Arab-Israeli peace process, a major U.S. foreign policy initiative. Some Middle Eastern groups are apparently trying to scuttle the peace process directly, by undermining the positions of the negotiating parties. Others threaten the process indirectly, by striving to overthrow pro-U.S. regimes that have been supportive of the process. A key target is the government of Egyptian President Hosni Mubarak.

Middle Eastern terrorist groups and state sponsors sometimes have relatively narrow objectives. Iran, Iraq, and Libya have recently employed terrorism to strike at their domestic political opponents located abroad. The Iranian opposition People's Mojahedin, although considered a terrorist group, is working to overthrow the clerical regime in Iran, which is described by the State Department as the mot dangerous state sponsor of terrorism. Although U.S. policymakers oppose all terrorism, the above uses of terrorism are probably not as threatening to U.S. foreign policy interests as those of such peace process rejectionist groups as Hamas, Palestinian Islamic Jihad, Hizballah, and Egypt's Islamic Group and Jihad. Successful terrorist attacks by these groups could fundamentally undermine U.S. strategic interests in the Middle East.

Introduction

Middle Eastern terrorist groups and their state sponsors have been the focus of U.S. counter-terrorism policies for several decades.[1] Since the 1970s, many of the major acts of terrorism against Americans and U.S. targets have been conducted by Middle Eastern groups or states. According to the State Department's 1994 terrorism

---

*Excerpted from *CRS Report 95-872 F.*

[1]This report will analyze those Middle Eastern groups discussed in the State Department's report on international terrorism, Patterns of Global Terrorism: 1994. State Department Publication 10239, Released April 1995.

report, terrorist violence in the Middle East continued at a high level, even though the number of terrorist attacks worldwide -- 321 for 1994 -- was 25% lower than the 431 recorded in 1993. In addition, five out of the seven states currently on the U.S. "terrorism list" are in the Middle East -- Iran, Iraq, Syria, Libya, and Sudan.[2] (The other two are Cuba and North Korea.) In the February 1993 bombing of the World Trade Center in New York, Middle Easterners demonstrated a willingness and ability to strike within the United States itself. Bombings of Israeli and Jewish targets in Buenos Aires in March 1992 and July 1994, which appeared to be the work of Lebanon's Hizballah, showed that Middle Eastern groups can strike elsewhere in the Western hemisphere.

Middle Eastern terrorism involves groups and state sponsors that differ in their motivations, objectives, and ideologies. For example, some radical Islamic groups are trying to derail the Arab-Israeli peace process, while others state their main objective as the overthrow of secular governments in their countries of origin. Recent writing on Middle Eastern terrorism gives prominence to radical Islamic organizations, but many of the older groups, founded in the 1960s and 1970s, are leftist and nationalist in orientation. Some of the leftist Palestinian groups share with their Islamic allies opposition to peace with Israel. Other leftist groups fight for much different causes, such as the formation of separate ethnically based states or the overthrow of incumbent regimes.

The five Middle Eastern states on the terrorism list, like the groups they reportedly sponsor, differ in their objectives or their degree of involvement in terrorism. The State Department's report on terrorism for 1994 again referred to Iran as the most dangerous state sponsor of terrorism, but, in contrast, the report characterizes Sudan as primarily a harbor of terrorist groups and training camps rather than an active perpetrator of terrorism. Iran and Sudan use paramilitary and terrorist groups to promote radical Islamic ideology. Syria, in contrast, is led by an authoritarian nationalist and secular government that appears to support terrorist groups as levers in its negotiations toward a peace settlement with Israel and other regional issues. Iraq uses terrorism to strike at people or institutions, such as international relief workers, that symbolize international sanctions imposed on Iraq for its invasion of Kuwait.

Groups

Organizations that conduct terrorist operations may not have much, if any, state sponsorship. Those that do often fall out with their state patrons or reject their guidance. Terrorist operations sometimes end up embarrassing their state sponsors, causing them to expel or distance themselves from client groups. Alternately, the focus can be on the state sponsors, which provide arms, documentation, large sums of money, and free movement across borders, as well as overall guidance and safehaven.

---

[2]Each year, under the provisions of Section 5(j) of the Export Administration Act of 1979, as amended [P.L. 96-72], the Secretary of Commerce, in consultation with the Secretary of State, provides Congress with a list of countries that support international terrorism.

State sponsors, when they have chosen to do so, have often been able to restrain terrorist organizations. The Administration and Congress are increasingly trying to formulate policies against individual groups, as well as their more easily identified and sanctioned state patrons.

RADICAL ISLAMIC GROUPS

Since the 1979 Islamic revolution in Iran, and particularly the seizure of the U.S. Embassy in Tehran in November of that year, radical Islam has attracted widespread press attention as the driving ideology of the most active Middle Eastern terrorist groups and state sponsors. Of the twelve terrorist groups opposed to the Middle East peace process, identified in President Clinton's Jan. 23, 1995 executive order (12947) on Middle Eastern terrorism, five are radical Islamic organizations (Hamas, Palestinian Islamic Jihad, Hizballah, and Egypt's Islamic Group and Jihad). Of these groups, Hamas, Palestinian Islamic Jihad, and Hizballah are working directly to undermine the Arab-Israeli peace process, which they see as overwhelmingly favorable toward Israel and incapable of producing an equitable settlement. Their activities have not altered the parties' commitment to the peace process, but these groups appears to have succeeded in making all sides hesitant to offer concessions, sometimes leading to long periods in which little progress in the peace process is achieved.[3] Although the Egyptian radical Islamic groups are not believed close to toppling President Mubarak, the threat posed by them has been sufficient to hurt Egypt's tourist trade and prompt Mubarak's allies and critics to urge him to make much needed economic and political reforms, and to appoint a vice president who would succeed him. These groups killed Mubarak's predecessor and came close to assassinating Mubarak himself in Addas Ababa in June 1995.

The following provides information on the objectives, activities, external ties, and strength of the Islamist groups mentioned above.

HIZBALLAH (PARTY OF GOD)[4]

Lebanese Shiite clerics, many of whom subscribed to the Islamic revolutionary ideology of Iran's Ayatollah Khomeini, founded Hizballah in 1982, in the wake of the Israeli invasion of Lebanon in June of that year. The organization's initial goal was to establish an Islamic republic in Lebanon as part of a broader region-wide Islamic republic. More recently, perhaps in recognition that such a goal may be

---

[3]Presentation of Itamar Rabinovich, Israel's Ambassador to the United States, before the Washington Institute for Near East Policy. June 21, 1995; Haberman, Clyde. Goal Missed, Israel and P.L.O. Vow To Revive Talks Soon. *New York Times*, July 3, 1995. p. 3.

[4]For further information on Hizballah, see *Hizballah: A Radical Militia in Lebanon*, by Kenneth Katzman, RS Report 93-905, Oct. 7, 1993. An updated version of that report was included in: U.S. Army War College, Strategic Studies Institute. Terrorism: National Security Policy and the Home Front. May 15, 1995, edited by Stephen Pelletiere. pp. 1-30.

unattainable, Hizballah has focused on attempting to derail the Arab-Israeli peace process. To fulfill that objective, Hizballah is trying, through attacks on Israeli and Israel's proxy forces, to force Israel to end its control over a six mile deep "security zone" in Shiite Muslim-inhabited southern Lebanon. By attacking Israel militarily, Hizballah may be trying to create opposition within Israel to further participation in the peace process or, possibly, to provoke direct conflict between Israel and the 35,000 - 40,000 Syrian troops in Lebanon. It should be noted that the United States does not consider Hizballah's military operations against Israeli or Israel's proxy forces in southern Lebanon as terrorism, but rather as military action. The State Department's report on terrorism for 1994 places the strength of Hizballah's military wing at "several thousand." However, some sources believe Hizballah's militia consists of a hard core of about 400 fighters, which can be expanded up to 3,000 within several hours as a battle with Israel develops.[5]

Hizballah also maintains -- and according to some interpretations, has expanded -- an active international terrorist arm. During the 1980s, Hizballah was a principal sponsor of anti-Western, and particularly anti-U.S., terrorism. It is known or suspected to have been involved in suicide truck bombings of the U.S. Embassy (April 1983), the U.S. Marine barracks (October 1983, killing 241 Marines), and the U.S. Embassy annex (September 1984), all in Beirut. It also hijacked TWA Flight 847 in 1984, killing a Navy diver, Robert Stethem, who was on board, and it was responsible for the detention of most, if not all, U.S. and Western hostages in Lebanon. Elements of Hizballah claimed responsibility for the bombing of Israel's embassy in Buenos Aires in March 1992, in retaliation for Israel's killing of the group's Secretary General, Abbas Musawi, one month earlier. The State Department's 1994 terrorism report says Hizballah "could well have been responsible" for the July 18, 1994 bombing of the Argentine-Israel Mutual Association building in Buenos Aires that left nearly 100 dead.[6] A wide variety of press reporting indicates that Iranian diplomats posted in Lebanon, Syria, Sudan, and elsewhere abroad provide logistical or other support to Hizballah's foreign cells; some of these diplomats were captors of the U.S. Embassy in Tehran in 1979.[7] Iran also is said to grant Hizballah about $50 million to $100 million per year,[8] although Iran reportedly wants Hizballah to become more self-sufficient financially.

Hizballah apparently is positioning itself to survive politically if there is a peace agreement between Israel and Syria and Lebanon. Israel will undoubtedly demand that any peace settlement include the dismantlement of Hizballah's militia. Hizballah has been trying to integrate into the legitimate political process in Lebanon, and it now holds eight seats in Lebanon's 128 seat national assembly; with Hizballah's allies, this is the largest single bloc in the assembly. When Prime Minister Rafiq Hariri reshuffled the Cabinet in May 1995, there were reports that he was considering including some Hizballah members in the new government, a level of official participation Hizballah

---

[5]Tarnowski, Andrew. Guerrilla 'Mini-Army' Winds Israel's Respect. Reuters, Sept. 30, 1994.

[6]Patterns of Global Terrorism: 1994. p. 21.

[7]Iran Hostage Takers Now Hold Key Posts. Newsday Wire Service, printed in Roanoke Times and World News. Sept. 8, 1994. p. A11.

[8]Middle East Mirror, Aug. 12, 1993. p. 19.

had previously ruled out.[9]   Hizballah also has been meeting with members of Lebanon's other sects and factions, including traditionally dominant Christians, whom it previously shunned. Other reports indicate that Hizballah is increasingly involving itself in tourism businesses as a means of earning revenue and softening its terrorist image.

HAMAS AND PALESTINIAN ISLAMIC JIHAD[10]

Hamas (Islamic Resistance Movement) and Palestinian Islamic Jihad[11] are Sunni Islamist Palestinian groups based in the West Bank and Gaza Strip. Palestinian Islamic Jihad, which was formed in 1979 and remains almost purely a guerrilla organization, appears internally united in its opposition to territorial or political compromise with Israel. Hamas, which grew out of the Palestinian uprising in 1987, generally opposes the peace process, but an increasing number of Hamas leaders appear open to compromise and to participation in the governing structure of the Palestinian Authority.[12] Hamas has a military wing, the Izz ad-Din al-Qassam Brigades, but it also possesses a component that provides social services, charity, and education to needy Palestinians. Hamas, unlike Palestinian Islamic Jihad, has engaged in some peaceful political activity, such as running candidates in West Bank Chamber of Commerce elections.

The precise political strength of the Islamist groups among Palestinians is not known, but the few independent polls conducted in Palestinian-controlled areas suggest that the two groups (combined) have a support base of about 15-20% of the population.[13] The State Department characterizes Hamas' strength as "an unknown number of hardcore members [and] tens of thousands of supporters and sympathizers." The 1994 terrorism report says that Palestinian Islamic Jihad's strength is unknown.[14]

Unlike Hizballah, Hamas and Palestinian Islamic Jihad have not targeted the United States directly, although some American citizens have died in attacks for which they were responsible. The two Palestinian Islamist groups have generally confined their terrorist attacks to Israel, the occupied territories, or areas now under Palestinian control, although both groups reportedly have representation in neighboring Arab countries., in Iran, and in Sudan. According to the State

---

[9]Hizballah To Decide Position on Cabinet Role. FBIS-NES-95-101, May 25, 1995. p. 43.

[10]For further information on these two groups, see *Hamas and Palestinian Islamic Jihad: Recent Developments, Sources of Support, and Implications for U.S. Policy,* by Clyde Mark and Kenneth Katzman, CRS Report 94-993, Dec. 12, 1994.

[11]Palestinian Islamic Jihad should not be confused with Islamic Jihad, which is a name often used by elements of Hizballah in the conduct of terrorist or military operations. The group that is referred to here is the dominant faction of Palestinian Islamic Jihad led by Fathi al-Shiqaqi.

[12]Shriteh, Taher. Hamas Ready To Dive into Palestinian Politics. Reuters, June 8, 1995.

[13]Results of recent opinion polls conducted by the Center for Palestine Research and Studies. The polls were commissioned by the International Republican Institute. Other polls have yielded similar results.

[14]Patterns of Global Terrorism: 1994. p. 41, 54.

Department's 1994 terrorism report, Hamas attacks in 1994 resulted in the highest number of Israeli casualties inside Israel since the Palestinian uprising began in 1987.[15] Among the most noted recent attacks were Hamas' bombing of a bus in Tel Aviv in October 1994 (22 killed, 48 wounded); the Jan. 22, 1995 bombings of a bus stop at Beit Lid, for which Palestinian Islamic Jihad claimed responsibility (21 killed, 60 wounded); and Hamas's bombing July 24, 1995 bombing of a bus outside Tel Aviv that killed 6 (including the bomber) and wounded 32. The latter bombing came the day before Israeli and Palestinian negotiators were to have reached an agreement on extending Palestinian self-rule to much of the West Bank. An American student, Alison Flatow was killed along with seven Israelis in a Palestinian Islamic Jihad suicide bombing in Gaza, Apr. 9, 1995.

U.S. officials say Palestinian Islamic Jihad is politically closer to Iran than is Hamas, although both groups are said by the State Department to receive funds, and possibly military training, from Iran. Press reports quoting U.S. intelligence reports say that the bombers involved in the Jan. 22, 1995 Beit Lid bombings were trained in Iran.[16] In testimony before the Senate Intelligence Committee on Jan. 10, 1995, Director of Central Intelligence James Woolsey said that Iran had provided over $100 million to Hamas, without giving a time period over which those funds were provided. State Department counterterrorism officials believe that figure might be high, however. Hamas reportedly also receives funding from wealthy benefactors in the Persian Gulf monarchies and, U.S. officials say, from residents of the United States, mostly Arab and other Muslim Americans. Most individual donors, however, appear to believe their contributions are charity to poor Palestinians served by Hamas' social services network, and are not being used for terrorism.

In July 1995, the United States detained in New York a suspected Hamas leader, Musa Abu Marzuq, who had lived in Falls Church, Virginia until early 1994. He has had permanent resident alien status since 1990, and might have been involved in fundraising for Hamas in the United States. Israel is seeking extradition of Abu Marzuq under a 1962 U.S.-Israel treaty. Jordan had expelled him in June 1995 for his reported efforts to promote opposition to Jordan's peace treaty with Israel. He also reportedly helped build ties between Hamas and Iran.[17]

Hamas and Palestinian Islamic Jihad are members of a 10 group anti-peace process front, based in Damascus. The other members of the alliance are: the Democratic Front for the Liberation of Palestine (DFLP) of Nayif Hawatmeh; the Fatah Uprising of Col. Abu Musa; the Palestine Liberation Front (PLF); the Palestinian Popular Struggle Front; the Palestinian Revolutionary Communist Party; the Popular Front for the Liberation of Palestine (PFLP); the PFLP-General Command, led by Ahmad Jibril, and the Popular Liberation War Vanguards Organization (al-Sa'iqah).[18]

---

[15]Patterns of Global Terrorism: 1994. p. 12.

[16]Iran Said to Escalate Anti-Mideast Peace Efforts. Reuters, May 9, 1995.

[17]Thomas, Pierre and Hall, Charles. Palestinian with Local Ties Is Detailed as Suspected Hamas Leader. *Washington Post* July 28, 1995. p. A31; Lancaster, John and Hall, Charles. U.S. Is Asked To Turn Over Terror Suspect. *Washington Post*, July 29, 1995. p. A15.

[18]Palestinian Organizations and Officials. FBIS-NES-95-030-S, Feb. 14, 1995. p. 2.

THE ISLAMIC GROUP AND JIHAD

The Islamic Group and Jihad seek to replace Egypt's pro-Western, secular government with an Islamic state. According to the State Department's 1994 report on terrorism, both groups recognize Shaykh Umar Abd al-Rahman, an Egyptian cleric, as their spiritual leader.[19] Abd al-Rahman is on trial in New York for an alleged plot to blow up U.N. headquarters and several tunnels in the New York City area. Both groups formed in the early 1970s as offshoots of the Muslim Brotherhood, which opted to work within the political system after being crushed by former President Gamal Abd al-Nasser. The primary focus of the Egyptian radical Islamist groups -- in their statements and their actions -- is to replace what they perceive as a corrupt government with an Islamic Republic. The leaders of these groups, particularly Abd al-Rahman, have said relatively little about how they would conduct Egypt's relations with Israel if they were to come to power. However, the Clinton Administration and most observers are operating under the assumption that the Egyptian-Israeli peace treaty and the Arab-Israeli peace process would be set back severely if the radical Islamist groups came to power in Egypt.

The Islamic Group recruits and builds support openly in poor neighborhoods in Cairo, Alexandria and throughout southern Egypt, running social service programs and distributing charity. Tactically, the Islamic Group conducts attacks against local security officials and Western tourists and other symbols of Western culture. It occasionally tries to assassinate high ranking officials, killing, for example, the People's Assembly Speaker in October 1990 and wounding the Minister of Information in April 1993. The Islamic Group claimed responsibility for the failed June 25, 1995 assassination attempt against Mubarak in Ethiopia. Jihad is primarily a clandestine organization that focuses almost exclusively on assassinating high ranking Egyptian officials. It was the group responsible for the assassination of President Anwar Sadat in October 1981. A reborn version of the group claimed responsibility for the Aug. 18, 1993 bombing in Cairo in which Egypt's Interior Minister was wounded, as well as a November 1993 car bomb attempt against Prime Minister Atif Sidky. Sidky was unharmed.

According to the State Department's 1994 terrorism report, sources of external aid for both groups are not precisely known. However, the report cites Egyptian government assertions that Iran, Sudan, and "militant Islamic groups in Afghanistan" support the groups.[20] Several followers of Shaykh Abd al-Rahman, some of whom were convicted in the February 1993 World Trade Center bombing, fought on behalf of the Islamic guerrillas in Afghanistan or raised money for that cause (see below).

---

[19]For more information, see *Shaykh Umar Abd al-Rahman and His followers*, by Kenneth Katzman, CRS Report 93-709, July 29, 1993. This report includes information about Abd al-Rahman's entry into and immigration status in the United States.

[20]Patterns of Global Terrorism: 1994. p. 46.

THE ARMED ISLAMIC GROUP

The Armed Islamic Group (GIA, after its initials in French) is the most significant of a group of radical Islamic factions fighting to establish an Islamic state in Algeria.[21] The GIA and other Islamic guerrilla groups formed breakaway factions of the Islamic Salvation Front (FIS) in 1992, after the regime cancelled the second round of parliamentary elections on fears of an FIS victory. In contrast to the FIS, which is the largest Islamic opposition group, the GIA rejects any compromise with the Algerian government. Unlike the FIS, which relies primarily on open political action (although it does have a military wing), the GIA believes that violence against regime targets, as well as civilians and foreigners in Algeria, will help it achieve its objectives. The GIA would mot likely continue fighting if the FIS entered into a governing coalition with the regime. According to the State Department's report on terrorism for 1994, the GIA has killed almost 90 expatriates in Algeria (mostly Europeans) since announcing its terrorist campaign against foreigners in Algeria in September 1993. In December 1994, four GIA terrorists hijacked an Air France flight in Algiers, killing three passengers before being killed by French anti-terrorist forces in Marseille.

The State Department's 1994 terrorism report says that the GIA's strength is unknown, and that it probably varies from several hundred to several thousand. Many within the GIA reportedly fought with the mujahedin in Afghanistan (see below). According to the report, the GIA receives financial and logistical aid from Algerian expatriates, many of whom reside in Western Europe. As has Egypt, Algeria has accused Iran and Sudan of supporting the GIA from training camps in Sudan. Press reports quoting Western intelligence sources say that Sudan is assisting the Algerian guerrillas by permitting Iran to use Sudanese territory as a transit point for smuggling weapons to them.[22] However, most observers believe that any Iranian and Sudanese aid to the GIA has probably not been decisive in the GIA's development or its activities, although both countries would probably wield influence in a radical Islamic Algerian regime.

VETERANS OF THE AFGHAN CONFLICT

Many attach increasing significance to the activities of Arabs and other Muslims who fought in the war in Afghanistan, although they are not an organized terrorist group. Although the veterans may come in contact with -- or even receive some arms or funding from -- regional governments and state sponsors of terrorism, a National Security Council counter-terrorism official has described them as a "free floating network" rather than surrogates or proxies of any one state sponsor.[23] Recruited

---

[21]For more information on the Islamist challenge to the Algerian government, see *Algeria in Crisis: Situation Update*, by carol Migdalovitz, CRS Report 94-21, Mar. 15, 1994.

[22]Hedges, Chris. Sudan Linked To Rebellion in Algeria. *New York Times*, Dec. 24, 1994. p. 5.

[23]Presentation by Richard Clarke, Senior Director, Office of Global Issues and Multilateral Affairs, National Security Council, before the Washington Institute for Near East Policy. May 25, 1995.

within or outside their countries of origin, these volunteers helped the Afghan mujahedin expel the Soviet occupation forces from Afghanistan, and received religious indoctrination and paramilitary training. Many of them apparently returned to their countries of origin and became active in indigenous anti-regime Islamic movements, such as Egypt's Islamic Group or Algeria's Armed Islamic Group. The veterans are reportedly most active in Egypt and Algeria, but the Jordanian government has also accused "Afghans" of participating in radical anti-regime activities in Jordan.[24] Some reportedly are serving as trainers and fighters for Muslim forces in Bosnia. According to press reports, many of the veterans returning to their countries of origin are stopping, at least temporarily, in Sudan, where they undergo additional indoctrination by Iranian Revolutionary Guards based in Sudan.[25] Sudan's location facilitates their infiltration into Egypt, Algeria, Tunisia, and Libya.

According to the State Department's terrorism report for 1993, several thousand non-Afghan Muslims fought in the war against the Soviets and the Afghan Communist government during 1979 to 1992.[26] They were recruited from Egypt, Turkey, Jordan, Sudan, India, Algeria, Malaysia, several European and North American states, Kuwait, Saudi Arabia, and Pakistan. Some veterans of the Afghan war remain at base camps in Afghanistan or in Pakistan, near the Afghan border. Some might contend that the number of total volunteers in Afghanistan is too small for the volunteers, alone, to constitute a significant opposition force in the countries where they are believed to be operating.

In addition to their reported involvement in radical Islamic movements, veterans of the Afghan conflict -- of those associated with them -- have been connected to a number of recent acts of terrorism. For example, Shaykh Umar Abd al-Rahman and several of his followers -- including several of those convicted in the World Trade Center bombing and reputedly involved in the alleged plot to bomb U.N. headquarters and other structures in New York -- were associated with or raised money for the Afghan rebels.[27] Ramzi Ahmad Yusuf, a suspect in the Trade Center bombing and in other attempted terrorist acts in east Asia, reportedly was associated with Afghan veteran groups still in Pakistan, where he was arrested.[28] Tow of Abd al-Rahman's sons reportedly fought in Afghanistan, as did another Abd al-Rahman follower -- the brother of the leader of the assassination plot against Egyptian President Anwar Sadat.

RADICAL JEWISH GROUPS

Some radical Jewish groups are as opposed to the Arab-Israeli peace process as are radical Islamic groups, and they have been willing to engage in terrorism to try to derail the process. Two movements, Kach and Kahane Chai ([Rabbi Meir] Kahane

---

[24]Report on Court Sentencing of Jordanian 'Afghans.' FBIS-NES-94-246, Dec. 2, 1994. p. 21.

[25]Hedges, Chris. Sudan Linked to Rebellion in Algeria.

[26]Patterns of Global Terrorism: 1993. Released April 1994. p. 4.

[27]Ottaway, David. Retracing the Steps of a Terror Suspect. *Washington Post*, June 5, 1995. p. A1.

[28]Ibid.

Lives) state their objectives as the restoration of the biblical state of Israel. Kach was founded by the radical Rabbi Meir Kahane, who was assassinated in the United States in 1990; Kahane Chai was founded by Kahane's son, Binyamin, following his father's assassination. On Mar. 13, 1994, the Israeli Cabinet declared both to be terrorist organizations under the 1948 Terrorism Law. The declaration came after the groups publicly stated their support for a Feb. 25, 1994 attack on a Hebron mosque by a radical Jewish settler, Baruch Goldstein, himself a Kach affiliate and an immigrant from the United States. The attack killed 40 worshippers and wounded about 150. The groups, many members of which live in Jewish settlements in the West Bank and Gaza, organize protests against the Israeli government and they harass and threaten Palestinians. They also claimed responsibility for several shooting attacks on West Bank Palestinians, in which four persons were killed and two wounded in 1993. According to the State Department's 1994 terrorism report, the first of the Department's annual reports to analyze the groups, they receive support from like-minded Jews in the United States and Europe. Both groups are named in President Clinton's Jan. 23, 1995 executive order on Middle Eastern terrorism.

LEFTWING AND NATIONALIST GROUPS

Middle Eastern terrorist groups differ in ideological outlook. Some groups, such as the Popular Front for the Liberation of Palestine (PFLP), profess radical Arab nationalism or Marxist-Leninism. However, ideological differences do not prevent the non-Islamist Palestinian groups from working with the Islamist organizations against the peace process.[29] Despite such cooperation, however, according to recent annual State Department reports on terrorism, the leftwing and nationalist groups such as the Abu Nidal Organization appear to be less active in international terrorism than they were in the 1970s and 1980s, and less active than the radical Islamist groups. Thus, the older, non-Islamist groups have not had as important an adverse effect on the peace process as have the Islamist groups.

The apparent decline of the leftwing and nationalist terrorist groups might be attributed to decreased support from some state sponsors, particularly Libya and Syria, as well as the rise of Islamic political ideology more generally. The collapse of the Soviet Union apparently led Libya and Syria, among other countries, to conclude that there was no military solution to the Arab-Israeli dispute and that the ideology of the leftwing Palestinian terrorist organizations was probably unattractive to most Palestinians. The Islamist groups, to a greater degree than the leftist and nationalist groups, have developed extensive social service networks to attract popular support to their movements, making them somewhat more self-sustaining than other groups.

Some of the more important leftwing and nationalist groups in the region are analyzed in the following sections. With the exception of the PLO, whose chairman

---

[29]For more information on the Palestinians and the Arab-Israeli peace process, see *Palestinians and Middle East peace: Issues for the United States*, by Clyde Mark, CRS Issue Brief 95052 (updated regularly).

had renounced terrorism, all the Palestinian groups below are named in the Jan. 23, 1995 executive order on Middle Eastern terrorism.

PALESTINE LIBERATION ORGANIZATION (PLO)

Yasir Arafat rode his Fatah guerrilla organization to the chairmanship of the PLO, an umbrella of many Palestinian organizations, in 1969. Fatah was formed by Palestinian exiles in Kuwait in 1957, and began armed raids into Israel in January 1965. After the Arab defeat in the 1967 Six Day War, Fatah grew rapidly and eclipsed to a considerable degree other Palestinian organizations. After Fatah/PLO and other Palestinian guerrillas were forced out of Jordan in 1970 and 1971, after which cross border attacks on Israel became difficult, it resorted to international terrorism.[30] In September 1972, eight guerrillas reportedly linked to Fatah seized the dormitory of Israeli athletes at the Olympics in Munich; eleven Israeli athletes were killed in that incident.[31] In the wake of the 1973 Arab-Israeli war, U.S. and other Western efforts to achieve a comprehensive peace settlement caused Arafat to limit terrorist operations largely to targets within Israel, Lebanon, and the occupied territories. In 1988, Arafat renounced the use of terrorism as part of an effort to initiate an official dialogue with the United States. The dialogue lasted until 1990, when Arafat refused to denounce an attempted attack by a small PLO-affiliated organization, the Palestine Liberation Front, on a Tel Aviv beach (see below). On Sept. 9, 1993, in letters to Israeli Prime Minister Rabin and Norwegian Foreign Minister Holst, Arafat committed the PLO to cease all violence and terrorism and, four days later, signed the Declaration of Principles with Israel in Washington.

According to the State Department's report on terrorism for 1994, there has been no authorized PLO/Fatah terrorist operation since the September 1993 agreements.[32] The latest (June 1, 1995) Administration report to Congress on PLO commitments compliance reiterates that assertion.[33] Most of the debate over the PLO's post-agreement record centers on whether or not the PLO, as the power behind the new Palestinian Authority (PA), is taking sufficient steps to prevent other groups from conducting terrorist attacks against Israelis, especially those attacks in or launched from areas under PA control. According to the June 1, 1995 compliance report, PLO leaders have denounced the terrorist attacks as they have occurred and, during the period under review, initiated prosecutions of those involved in terrorism. The reports said there is "evidence that the PA is making a serious effort to prevent terrorist attacks..." For example, Arafat quickly denounced the July 24, 1995 Hamas suicide bombing of a bus near Tel Aviv.

Some critics, including House International Relations Committee Chairman Benjamin Gilman and Senate Foreign Relations Committee Chairman Jesse Helms,

---

[30]Department of Defense. Terrorism Group Profiles. Washington, G.P.O., November 1988.

[31]Ibid. p. 13.

[32]Patterns of Global Terrorism: 1994. p. 35.

[33]U.S. Department of State. Report Pursuant to Title VIII of Public Law 101-246 Foreign Relations Authorization Act for Fiscal Year 1990-91, As Amended. June 1, 1995.

contend that the Administration reports have deliberately overlooked some unkept PLO commitments in order to justify continued aid to the PA under the Middle East Peace Facilitation Act of 1993 and is extensions (P.L. 103-125; P.L. 103-166, Part E of Title V of P.L. 103-236, and P.L. 104-17).[34] According to PLO critics, the PA has not been sufficiently vigilant in trying to disarm suspected militants before they commit acts of terrorism against Israelis, although Arafat also has had to take care not to appear as an Israeli puppet. Critics also note that the Palestine National Council (PNC) still has not convened to amend the PLO Covenant calling for the destruction of Israel, possibly because Arafat does not have the votes in the Council to repeal the relevant clauses in the Covenant. Senator D'AMATO, for example, has introduced legislation (S.915) that would cut U.S. aid to the PA unless the PLO strictly and completely fulfills all obligations under the Declaration of Principles, as well as other conditions.

POPULAR FRONT FOR THE LIBERATION OF PALESTINE – GENERAL COMMAND (PFLP-GC)

The PFLP-GC is an offshoot of the Popular Front for the Liberation of Palestine (PFLP), a hardline Marxist group that has been part of the PLO. Ahmad Jibril, a former captain I the Syrian army, formed the PFLP-GC in October 1968 because he considered the PFLP too moderate and potentially willing to compromise with Israel. He also disagreed with the PFLP's emphasis on Marxist ideology, and believed the organization needed a conventional military arm to complement terrorist operations. The PFLP-GC is a staunch opponent of the PLO. The State Department report for 1994 places Jibril's strength at several hundred fighters, but his organization has tried to maximize its effectiveness by experimenting with conventional military and unconventional terrorist tactics. For example the PFLP-GC units in Lebanon reportedly are equipped with Russian SA-7 anti-aircraft missiles, heavy artillery, light aircraft, motorized hang gliders, ultralight aircraft, and hot air balloons. It has successfully used motorized hang gliders to cross the Israeli border from Lebanon.

Probably because of Jibrils' service in the Syrian military, Syria reportedly remains the chief backer of the PFLP-GC and reportedly provides logistic and military support, safehaven in Damascus, and approval for PFLP-GC units to operate in Lebanon. However, in the late 1980s, the PFLP-GC apparently began entering into a close relationship with Iran. In southern Lebanon, the PFLP-GC has fought alongside Iran's chief ally, Hizballah, against Israeli forces. It also reportedly attacked U.S. Marines participating in an international peacekeeping force in Beirut during 1982-83. There were also reports that Iran approached the PFLP-GC to bomb a U.S. passenger jet in retaliation for the July 1988 U.S. downing of an Iranian airbus.[35] The PFLP-GC allegedly pursued such an operation and abandoned it or, according to other speculation, handed off the operation to Libya in what became a successful effort to

---

[34]Lippmann, Thomas, Rabbis Urge End of Aid to the PLO. *Washington Post*, June 14, 1995. p. A32.

[35]Closing In on the Pan Am Bombers. *U.S. News and World Report*, May 22, 1989. p. 23.

bomb Pan Am flight 103 in December 1988. The State Department reports that the PFLP-GC receives some financial support from Libya.

POPULAR FRONT FOR THE LIBERATION OF PALESTINE (PFLP)

The Popular Front for the Liberation of Palestine is a Marxist-Leninist organization founded in December 1967 by George Habash, following the Arab defeat in the war with Israel that year. After Yasir Arafat's Fatah faction, it has been the largest Palestinian organization within the PLO umbrella, although the PFLP's influence within the Palestinian movement may be weakening. It strongly but unsuccessfully opposed the decision to join the Madrid peace process and suspended its participation in the PLO after the September 1993 Israel-PLO Declaration of Principles, which the PFLP viewed as a sellout of Palestinian interests. Despite the collapse of the Soviet Union -- and the decline of Marxist ideology more generally -- the PFLP has held on to its goal of establishing a Marxist secular government in all of the land that was British Mandata Palestine. Its more immediate objective, however, is to scuttle the peace process. On Oct. 15, 1993, Habash announced in Damascus the formation of the ten group coalition opposed to the peace process. The State Department's 1994 terrorism report fixes its strength at 800.

The PFLP was active in international terrorism during the 1960s and 1970s, responsible for several hijackings and international airport attacks. On Sept. 6, 1970,[36] it simultaneously hijacked three airliners; the plane flown to Egypt was blown up. All 400 passengers were released at the end of the episode on the 29th of that month. Since the death in 1978 of its primary international terrorist planner, Wadi Haddad, the PFLP has concentrated on attacks against Israelis inside Israel and the occupied territories. On a few occasions in recent years, PFLP guerrillas have infiltrated into Israel's security zone in southern Lebanon. According to the 1994 terrorism report, the PFLP receives most of its financial and military assistance from Syria and Libya, but the report does not indicate which is the more significant donor to the PFLP. However, the PFLP is based in Damascus and it reportedly has training facilities in Syrian-controlled areas of Lebanon.

DEMOCRATIC FRONT FOR THE LIBERATION OF PALESTINE (DFLP)

Like the PFLP, the DFLP advocates Marxist revolution and class struggle within the Palestinian movement. However, it split from the PFLP in 1969 and considers itself more pragmatic than harder line Palestinian groups, like the PFLP, which call for the liberation of all of what was Palestine. The DFLP was the first group to take the public position that a Palestinian state could be formed on any land liberated from

---

[36]At that time, PLO guerrillas in Jordan were engaged in preliminary phases of a major confrontation with Jordanian forces subsequently ordered to expel the Palestinian guerrillas. Jordan's King Husayn had decided that the PLO had assumed too much autonomy and authority inside Jordan, and he moved against the organization. This confrontation has come to be known as "Black September."

Israel, and that the destruction of Israel need not be the Palestinians' ultimate goal. The issue of peace with Israel aggravated tensions within the DFLP. Several months before the October 1991 Madrid conference, a DFLP faction led by deputy leader Yasir Abd al-Rabbuh split with elements led by DFLP leader Nayif Hawatmeh; the Abd al-Rabbuh faction supported negotiations with Israel, the Hawatmeh faction wanted to set stringent conditions for Palestinian participation. Abd al-rabbuh later dropped the DFLP name and denounced Marxist-Leninism, but Hawatmeh steered his DFLP faction into closer relationships with other peace process rejectionist groups. Hawatmeh's faction is a member of the ten group rejectionist front based in Damascus. Like the PFLP, Hawatmeh's DFLP was affiliated with the PLO but suspended its participation in the PLO following the September 1993 Israel-PLO accord. The split in the DFLP has undoubtedly left it less influential than it was previously; the State Department estimates the total strength (for both factions) at 500.

When it has used terrorism, the DFLP historically has attacked within Israel or territory under Israeli control. Its most noted attack was the May 1974 takeover of a school in Maalot, in northern Israel, in which 27 schoolchildren were killed and 134 people wounded. Since 1988, it has been involved in small-scale border raids into Israel and attacks on Israeli soldiers, officials, and civilians in Israel and the occupied territories. The DFLP receives assistance from Syria and Libya, according to the State Department's 1994 report. It has headquarters in Syria and Lebanon.

PALESTINE LIBERATION FRONT (PLF)

The PLF was founded in 1976 when Muhammad Abbas, commonly known as Abu Abbas, failed in his attempt to gain control of the PFLP-GC, which itself was an offshoot of the PFLP (see above). At the time of the split, Abu Abbas was serving as Ahmad Jibril's representative in Lebanon; he opposed Syria's military intervention in Lebanon that year, while Jibril supported it. The PLF was established with support from Iraq and it obtained seats on the Palestine National Council in 1981. In 1983, the PLF itself split into a pro-PLO, pro-Iraqi faction led by Abbas, and a pro-Syria faction led by Talat Yaqub. (Yaqub died of natural causes in 1988.) Abu Abbas and his supporters left Damascus and went to Tunis to align with Yasir Arafat and the mainstream of the PLO. (Following the 1985 Achille Lauro incident, discussed below, Abbas relocated to Baghdad at the request of the Tunisian government.) The pro-Syrian faction further split in January 1984, with one faction subsequently moving to Libya. Abu Abbas, despite his personal loyalty to Yasir Arafat, has disagreed with Arafat's willingness to negotiate with Israel and is a member of the ten group rejectionist front in Damascus. Abbas resigned from the PLO Executive committee, a position he acquired in 1984, following the PLO decision to support the Madrid peace process in 1991.

Even if it were unified, the PLF would be one of the smallest of the major Palestinian rejectionist organizations. The State Department estimates the strength of Abu Abbas' faction at abut 50; other sources indicate that each of the other factions have about 100 hardcore activists. Abu Abbas reportedly receives assistance from Iraq, Libya, and the PLO. The PLO aid is probably due to Abbas' past loyalty to Arafat. Although Abbas is based in Iraq, his faction of the PLF reportedly places most of its fighters in Sidon, Lebanon, where Arafat's Fatah organization has a significant presence. Abbas supported Iraq in the Persian Gulf war, as did Arafat. The other PLF factions receive aid, or at least safehaven, from the countries where they are based (Syria, Libya).

Although it is small and has committed relatively few terrorist attacks, but Abbas' faction of the PLF has had a significant impact on U.S.-Palestinian relations. Its most noted attack was the October 1985 hijacking of the Italian cruise ship Achille Lauro, in which the group murdered disabled U.S. citizen Leon Klinghoffer and held the other passengers hostage for two days. Abu Abbas and his team surrendered to Egyptian forces in exchange for a promise of safe passage. They were apprehended at a NATO airbase in Italy after U.S. aircraft forced down the Egyptian airliner flying them to safehaven. Abu Abbas was released by the Italian government but was later sentenced in Absentia (a warrant for his arrest is outstanding in Italy). The four other PLF hijackers were tried, convicted, and sentenced in Italy. On May 30, 1990, PLF members unsuccessfully attempted a seaborne landing on a Tel Aviv beach. The militants were delivered from Libya by a Libyan ship and then used speedboats to reach the beach. Arafat refused to condemn the attempt and, as a consequence, the United States broke off its dialogue with the PLO, which had begun in 1988. the PLF is not believed to have undertaken a major terrorist operation since a failed raid on the Israeli sea resort town of Eilat in May 1992.

ABU NIDAL ORGANIZATION (ANO)

Also known as the Fatah Revolutionary Council, the Abu Nidal Organization was created in 1974 when its founder Abu Nidal (his real name is Sabri al-Banna) broke with the PLO after PLO leader Yasir Arafat restricted PLO terrorist activities to targets within Israel or the occupied territories.[37]   Abu Nidal believed that there should not be limits to the PLO's use of terrorism or any compromise in its commitment to achieving the destruction of Israel. Abu Nidal has targeted any who accept compromise, whether they are Israelis, Palestinians, PLO officials, or moderate Arab states. The Abu Nidal Organization apparently has been less active in the 1990s than it was in the 1970s and 1980s, possibly because of Abu Nidal's reported health problems (cancer), splits within the organization, friction with state sponsors, and clashes in southern Lebanon and elsewhere with Arafat loyalists. The ANO is not a member of the 10 group Damascus-based coalition opposed to the Arab-Israeli pace process. The State Department estimates its current strength at several hundred members, plus an unknown number of militiamen in Lebanon and support cells overseas.

Since its formation, the Abu Nidal Organization has carried out over 90 terrorist attacks in 20 countries, killing or injuring almost 900 people. One of its most well-known operations was a Dec. 27, 1985 attack at airports in Rome and Vienna, in

---

[37]Department of Defense. Terrorist Group Profiles. p. 5.

which 18 died and 111 were injured. ANO members assassinated a Jordanian diplomat in Lebanon in January 1994 and conducted other attacks against Jordan in early 1985, apparently as at Syria's behest. Abu Nidal's high profile international attacks have often embarrassed the organization's state sponsors and led to tensions between them and the group. U.S. pressure contributed to Iraq's decision to expel the organization from Baghdad, its first headquarters, in 1983. In 1987, Syria expelled Abu Nidal, although Abu Nidal militiamen maintain a presence in Lebanon's Bekaa Valley, an area largely controlled by Syrian troops. According to the State Department's report for 1994, the group currently is headquartered in and receives financial assistance from, Libya. It also reportedly has a presence in Sudan.

OTHER NON-ISLAMIST ORGANIZATIONS

Two significant groups are not concerned with the Arab-Israeli peace process, but rather with influencing the domestic politics of their countries of origin. The Kurdistan Workers' Party (PKK), established in 1974, is a Marxist-Leninist group composed of Turkish Kurds.[38] Its objective has been to establish an independent, Marxist state in southeastern Turkey, where there is a predominantly Kurdish population, although in 1993, PKK leader Abdullah Ocalan proposed a federal Turkish state. With a reported 10,000 to 15,000 full-time and 60,000 to 75,000 part-time guerrillas, the PKK has recently moved beyond rural insurgent operation to somewhat increased use of urban terrorism. The PKK has generally targeted government forces and civilians in eastern Turkey but, in May 1993, it began directing attacks against the tourism industry. It also has attacked Turkish diplomatic and commercial facilities in Europe. The PKK has received safehaven in Syria and Lebanon's Bekaa Valley, which is controlled by Syrian forces. It also reportedly receives aid from Iraq and Iran.

The People's Mojahedin Organization of Iran (PMOI), the largest organization within a broader National Council of Resistance (NCR) has similarly leftwing roots but, unlike the PKK, it is not composed of an ethnic minority. It is working to try to overthrow the clerical regime in Iran, just as it previously sought to bring down the Shah of Iran. Group representatives, however, assert that the organization now is committed to free markets and democracy, should it achieve power in Iran, and it publicly supports the Arab-Israeli peace process. In October 1994, the State Department issued a congressionally-mandated report on the organization, asserting that the organization's assets in Iran and Iraq-based military wing do not pose a threat to the regime in Iran.[39] Further official U.S. mistrust of the group is

---

[38]For more information on the PKK, see *Turkey's Kurdish Imbroglio and U.S. Policy*, by Carol Migdalovitz, CRS Report 94-267, Mar. 18, 1994. The PKK is distinct from Iranian and Iraqi Kurdish organizations which the State Department does not consider terrorist and which, in some cases benefit from U.S. support.

[39]U.S. Department of State. People's Mojahedin Organization of Iran. Oct. 31, 1994. See also *Iran: The People's Mojahedin Organization of Iran*, by Kenneth Katzman, CRS Report 94-683, Aug. 24, 1994.

engendered by its killing of several U.S. military officers and civilians during the struggle against the Shah, and its support of the takeover of the U.S. Embassy in Tehran in 1979. The PMOI disputes those allegations; in particular it says that the killings of the Americans during the 1970's were conducted by individuals outside the PMOI leadership's control. The State Department has included the PMOI in its last two annual reports on terrorism because of attacks on Iranian diplomatic facilities abroad that it attributes to the PMOI and its anti-regime operations inside Iran. Some Members of Congress disagree, and believe the PMOI could constitute a viable opposition to the Iranian regime.

Middle Eastern State Sponsors

The Administration and Congress have devoted substantial time and attention to trying to pressure state sponsors to end their support for terrorist groups. The Administration and Congress view the provision of funds, safehaven, and weapons and logistic support to terrorists by sovereign states as crucial to the operation of many international terrorist organizations. In some cases, the state sponsor might be directly involved in planning and executing terrorist attacks, often using its own agents. In other cases, the state sponsor might work through surrogate groups, with little or no direct involvement of its own. The following sections analyze the activities and objectives of the five Middle Eastern countries designated by the Secretary of State as sponsors of terrorism.

IRAN

According to the State Department's report for 1994, Iran is still the most active state sponsor of international terrorism. Some of the groups it reportedly sponsors, Iran's objectives, and the methods of assistance are discussed above. Iran reportedly is directly involved in terrorist operations directed against Iranian dissidents abroad. Iran's primary targets are PMOI officials and Iranian Kurdish leaders. According to a wide variety of press reports, Iran uses its diplomatic missions and personnel abroad to plan, conceal, and carry out anti-dissident operations,[40] as well as monitor the opposition. More significant for U.S. foreign policy is Iran's reported funding, arming, and training of radical Islamist groups working to undermine the Arab-Israeli peace process and to establish Islamic regimes in Lebanon, North Africa, and areas under Palestinian control. Of the peace process rejectionist groups, the State Department report links Iran most closely to Hizballah, Hamas, and Palestinian Islamic Jihad, as well as the non-Islamist PFLP-GC. On the other hand, some observers believe Iran's actions against the peace process are limited in comparison

---

[40]U.S. Asserts Iranians Plotted to Disrupt Rally in Germany. *New York Times*, June 25, 1995. p. 12.

to its public condemnations.[41] They add that Iran's role in supporting Islamist groups battling the Egyptian and Algerian regimes is limited, and that the governments of those countries are purposely overstating the degree of Iranian involvement.

Iran's death sentence against author Salman Rushdie is of concern to the United States and its European allies. Iran maintains it cannot lift Ayatollah Khomeini's 1989 death sentence against Rushdie, Author of "The Satanic Verses," a novel deemed blasphemous by Khomeini. According to Iranian officials, only the cleric who issued the ruling can retract it, and Khomeini is dead. Signalling a willingness to compromise after the United States, on May 6, 1995, imposed a trade ban on Iran, Iranian officials, including Majlis Speaker Ali Akbar Nateq-Nuri, said Iran had no intention of sending assassination squads to Europe to implement the sentence. However, at a June 22, 1995 meeting with European Union representatives, Iran refused to make a written pledge to that effect. A private Iranian foundation (with links to the regime), the 15th Khordad Foundation, continue to offer a $2 million reward for the murder of Rushdie.

Many observers see growing tensions within the Iranian regime on such issues as support for terrorism and export of the Islamic revolution. President Rafsanjani has said on several occasions that Iran should "end foreign adventurism" and normalize its relations with other countries. As he did in a July 2, 1995 interview with Cable News Network, he frequently sets out conditions or circumstances under which relations with the United States might improve.[42] Some in the clerical community and the military and security services want to maintain the "purity" of the Islamic revolution, and believe that exporting the Islamic revolution is crucial to maintaining the regime's essential character. A major concern for the United States is that it is primarily the hardliners who dominate major institutions, including the Revolutionary Guard and the Ministry of Information and Security that carry out terrorism and export of Islamic revolution. Rafsanjani's ability to restrain these elements is uncertain.

Iran was placed on the terrorism list on Jan. 19, 1984, following determination of its involvement in the October 1983 bombing of the U.S. Marine barracks in Lebanon. The United States has blocked $22.4 million in Iranian assets in the United States, mostly diplomatic property. This property is separate from the issue of military equipment paid for by the Shah but not delivered because of his overthrow. That issue is being negotiated in the U.S.-Claims Tribunal at the Hague, as are certain standby letters of credit issued prior to the Islamic revolution.

---

[41]Amirahmadi, Hooshang. The Islamic Republic and the Question of Palestine. Middle East Insight, May-August 1994. pp. 50-54.

[42]Text of interview with CNN, July 2, 1995. Distributed by Permanent Mission to the United Nations of the Islamic Republic of Iran, July 7, 1995.

IRAQ

According to the State Department's 1994 terrorism report, Iraq is rebuilding its ability to mount terrorist attacks abroad, despite strict U.N. sanctions imposed after the Kuwait invasion. Unlike Iran, Iraq is not seeking to use terrorism or terrorist groups to promote a particular ideology, but rather to gain revenge for or disrupt the implementation of international sanctions against it. Iraq tried to gain revenge against President Bush, architect of the successful coalition war against Iraq, by organizing a failed assassination plot against him during his April 1993 visit to Kuwait. Iraq is believed responsible for at least 16 reported attacks in 1994 on international relief workers and journalists operating in Kurdish controlled northern Iraq, and the Iraqi Government reportedly has offered monetary rewards to anyone who assassinates U.N. and other relief workers. Iraqi intelligence also has resumed sending agents outside Iraq to track regime opponents. Iraq was reportedly responsible for attacks in 1994 against a prominent oppositionist in Beirut (Lebanon subsequently broke relations with Iraq) and against members of the family of the late Iraqi Shiite cleric Ayatollah Abol Qasem Musavi-Khoi.

Iraq provides safehaven and assistance to some non-Islamist Palestinian groups opposed to the Arab-Israeli peace process, including the Abu Nidal Organization, and Abu Abbas' faction of the PLF (Abbas reportedly enjoys sanctuary in Baghdad). Terrorist bomb-maker Abu Ibrahim also is based in Iraq. However, disrupting the peace process appears to be a secondary concern for Iraq. On many occasions, Iraqi officials, including Saddam, have said that any peace deal acceptable to the PLO would be acceptable to Iraq, and Saddam has traditionally had good relations with Arafat. Despite denials from both Israel and Iraq, there have been repeated reports since 1993 of some unofficial contacts between the two.

Iraq continues to provide backing for the Iranian opposition PMOI, and the PMOI's army, the National Liberation Army (NLA) has bases in Iraq, near the border with Iran. Iraq appears to maintain a degree of control over PMOI activities in Iraq, unleashing the organization when Iraq's relations with Iran deteriorate, and reining in the group when it wants to signal an improvement in ties with Tehran. Iraq suffers from severe shortages of hard currency as a result of international sanctions, and it is unclear to what degree Iraq can financially assist the PMOI. However, since the war with Iran, Iraq apparently has given the NLA a significant amount of surplus or captured military equipment.

Iraq was placed on the terrorism list when that list was started on Dec. 29, 1979. In March 1982, Iraq became the only country ever to be formally removed from the terrorism list.[43] It was restored to the list on Sept. 13, 1990 following its invasion of Kuwait and reports that Iraq was planning terrorist operations against the nascent allied coalition. The United States has blocked $1.66 billion in Iraqi assets in the United States, mostly bank deposits.

---

[43]After it merged with North Yemen in 1990, South Yemen was no longer on the terrorism list, on the grounds that South Yemen no longer existed.

SUDAN

Many observers view Sudan as a passive sponsor of terrorism or, according to some, as a surrogate for Iran. The State Department's 1994 terrorism report notes that there was no evidence that Sudan conducted or sponsored a specific act of terrorism in 1994. The report says Sudan allows Iran to use Sudan as a transit point for weapons shipments to Islamic extremist groups and as a meeting site for Iranian-backed groups. There are a reported several hundred Iranian Revolutionary Guards in Sudan helping in the government's war against southern Sudanese rebels, as well as training militants from other countries.[44] Iran's Navy reportedly uses Port Sudan as one of its resupply ports and Iran's Air Force reportedly has landing rights in Sudan.[45] Sudan provides safehaven for the Abu Nidal Organization, Hamas, Palestinian Islamic Jihad, and Egypt's Islamic Group. Sudanese officials see these organizations as legitimate freedom fighters and says there is no reason to expel them from Sudan. Sudan refused to investigate information supplied in September 1994 by the U.S. Ambassador in Sudan about the alleged training of terrorists at the Merkhiyat Popular defense Camp northwest of Khartoum. On the other hand, in August 1994, Sudan turned over the aging terrorist Carlos (Ilyich Ramirez Sanchez) to France, possibly in an effort to counter U.S. charges that it harbors terrorists.

The actions of Sudan's chief Islamic leader Hasan al-Turabi further complicate efforts to interpret Sudan's involvement in terrorism. Turabi sees himself as a guide for Sunni Islamists in and outside Sudan, and he does not want to be overshadowed by the Islamic revolution in Iran. He hosts major conferences on Islam in Khartoum, attended by members of radical Islamic organizations throughout the region. These conferences give the impression hat Turabi is trying to promote regionwide Islamic revolution. On the other hand, he has sometimes tried to broker reconciliation between radical Islamic movements and secular incumbents; for example, between Hamas and the PLO.

The assessment of Sudan as a relatively passive sponsor of terrorism might change if Egypt's assertions of Sudanese involvement in a failed June 25, 1995 assassination attempt in Ethiopia of Egyptian President Hosni Mubarak prove correct. Egypt's Islamic Group claimed responsibility for the attack but questions remain whether or not Sudan harbored the Group members responsible for the attack of helped them get into Ethiopia.

Sudan is the newest addition to the terrorism list; it was placed there on Aug. 12, 1993. The United States holds about $30 million in Sudanese assets in the United States, mostly liabilities to that country. These assets are not blocked or frozen.

---

[44]Hedges, Chris. Sudan Linked to Rebellion in Algeria. *New York Times*, Dec. 24, 1994. p. 5.
[45]Ibid.

LIBYA[46]

Libya has used terrorism to oppose Western interests in the Middle East. Having suffered U.S. retaliation and international sanctions, over the past few years Libya has been attempting to appear responsible to international condemnation of its alleged involvement in the bombings of Pan Am Flight 103 and UTA Flight 772. Three U.N. Security Council resolutions -- 731 of January 1992, 748, of March 1992, and 883, of November 1993 -- call on Libya to turn over the two Libyan intelligence agents (Abd al-Basit Ali al-Meghrahi and Al Amin Khalifah Fhimah) suspected in the bombings; prohibit air travel into and out of Libya, or arms transfers to that country; freeze Libyan assets; and prohibit the sale to Libya of certain petroleum equipment. Libyan compromise proposals have failed to satisfy the requirements of these resolutions. However, Libya has, over the past few years, tried to avoid direct association with acts of terrorism and terrorist groups, probably in an effort to relieve international pressure over the airline bombing cases and avoid further economic sanctions.

Some of Libyan leader Muammar Qadhafi's actions suggest he has not abandoned support for terrorism as an instrument of Libyan foreign policy. Qadhafi urged radical rejectionists of the Arab-Israeli peace process to use all necessary means to oppose it. He also hailed the Oct. 19, 1994 Hamas bus bombing in Tel Aviv as a "courageous operation." There are some indications Qadhafi views his regime as a target, rather than an ally, of radical Islamic groups and state sponsors.[47] Qadhafi has cooperated, to some degree, with Algeria, Tunisia, and Egypt in their attempt to curb radical Islamic groups in North Africa. Reflecting those concerns, Libya is closer politically to the leftwing nationalist Palestinian groups -- which also are closer to Libya ideologically than are the Islamist groups. Libya provides safehaven and some assistance to the Abu Nidal Organization, the PFLP-GC, the PFLP, and DFLP, and several PLF factions. Unrelated to the peace process, Libya reportedly was responsible for the disappearance of a prominent Libyan dissident, Mansour Kikhia, from his hotel in Egypt in December 1993.

Libya was placed on the terrorism list when that list was started on December 29, 1979. About $1.025 billion in Libyan assets are blocked by the United States. These assets consist mostly of bank deposits.

SYRIA[48]

Syria is the only Middle East terrorism list country that appears even close to being removed from the list by the Administration. Syria actively participates in peace negotiations with Israel, and, according to the State Department, it has not

---

[46]For further information on Libya and its involvement in terrorism, see *Libya*, by Clyde Mark, CRS Issue Brief 93109 (updated regularly.)

[47]Libya Cracking down on Militants. *Washington Times*, July 17, 1995.

[48]For further information on Syria and its support for terrorist groups, see *Syria-U.S. Relations*, by Alfred Prados, CRS Issue Brief 92075 (updated regularly).

been directly involved in planning or executing terrorist attacks since 1986. The State Department also credits Syria with helping to limit fighting between Israel and Hizballah in southern Lebanon. Syria apparently has concluded that it cannot actively work to try to derail a peace process of which it is a part, although Syria apparently still wants to replace Arafat with Palestinian leadership that is more pro-Syrian. Many observers speculate that the United States has, implicitly or explicitly, promised to remove Syria from the terrorism list once it signs a peace deal with Israel. U.S. officials have repeatedly denied such linkage, however, and they have publicly stated that Syria's sanctuary for terrorist groups must end.[49]

Although Syria says it deserves to be removed from the terrorism list, it apparently continues to view terrorist groups in Syria or Syrian-controlled territory as a lever it can use in negotiations with Israel. Damascus gives sanctuary to the ten member anti-peace process coalition of radical Palestinian groups. Syria grants a wide range of terrorist groups basing privileges in Syrian-controlled areas of Lebanon. These groups include Hamas, the PFLP-GC, Palestinian Islamic Jihad, the Abu Nidal Organization, and the Japanese Red Army. The PKK also trains in the Bekaa Valley and its leader spends time in Damascus. Although it has prevented Hizballah from derailing the peace process, Syria allows Iran to resupply Hizballah through the Damascus airport. Some in Congress have cited these and other Syrian policies in contending that Syria should remain on the terrorism list.[50]

The Syrian regime is secular and, like Libya, it has tended to favor the leftwing nationalist Palestinian groups. Syria's improving relations with the radical Islamist Palestinian groups might be attributed to their relative effectiveness in causing concern in Israel, their opposition to Arafat, and Syria's effectiveness in causing concern in Israel, their opposition to Arafat, and Syria's desire to preserve its alliance with Iran. Syria maintains that peace process rejectionist groups are fighting Israeli occupation of Palestinian land and of south Lebanon and are not violating any Syrian laws and will not be expelled. Syrian officials contend that when a comprehensive peace with Israel is achieved, terrorist groups will disband for lack of support.

Syria was placed on the terrorism list at the list's inception, Dec. 29, 1979. There are approximately $602 million in U.S. obligations to Syria. These assets are not blocked or frozen.

Controlling Middle Eastern Terrorism

There is no universally agreed strategy, either within the United States or between the United States and its Middle Eastern and European allies, for countering the Middle Eastern terrorism threat. There is not even agreement as to the nature of the threat. For example, the State Department's annual report on terrorism considers as

---

[49]Strobel, Warren. Syria Slams Door on Terrorism Issue. *Washington Times*, Nov. 23, 1992. P. A1.

[50]Removal from the list requires advance notification to the House International Relations Committee, the Senate Foreign Relations Committee, and the Senate Banking Committee. Each of the current chairs of those committees, Representative Benjamin Gilman, Senator Jesse Helms, and Senator Alfonse D'Amato, has been generally critical of many Syrian policies.

terrorism the assassination of regime dissidents, as well as terrorist operations against the Arab-Israeli peace process. However, most observers would probably agree that threats to the peace process are more significant for U.S. foreign policy than are anti-dissident operations by Middle Eastern governments. To many, anti-dissident operations can be regarded as an extension of internal politics.

Even for those terrorist groups fighting established regimes, the threats to U.S. interests are not equivalent. Egypt's Islamic Group and Jihad are regarded as major threats to President Mubarak of Egypt, who is probably the most important U.S. ally in the Arab world. Many fear the Arab-Israeli peace process -- a centerpiece of U.S. foreign policy in the Middle east -- would unravel if Mubarak were replaced by a radical Islamic regime. The Armed Islamic Group and other Islamist forces in Algeria pose a major challenge to a secular and relatively pro-Western regime, although the fall of the Algerian government could bolster the confidence and capabilities of the Islamist opposition in Egypt. The achievement of the PMOI's goals, on the other hand, might not prove detrimental to U.S. interests, because the regime in Tehran that it is fighting is identified as the most dangerous state sponsor of terrorism. Because the Kurds do not seek to control all of Turkey, the PKK is not a threat to replace the Turkish government, which is an ally of the United States, although the PKK is a major source of domestic instability.

POLICY TOWARD STATE SPONSORS

The U.S. approach to Middle Eastern terrorism has tended to vary with different circumstances and allied perceptions.[51] Although the United States has tracked and brought some individual Middle Eastern terrorists to justice, U.S. counter-terrorism policy has tended to focus on pressuring state sponsors of terrorism, in part because there are more policy levers available to use against states than against individual terrorists or terrorist groups. To pressure state sponsors of terrorism, the United States has employed a combination of unilateral and multilateral measures, which State Department officials say have succeeded in making state sponsors more cautious in their use or sponsorship of terrorism.

Military Force

On the few occasions when the United States has used military force in retaliation for state sponsored terrorism, such action has been generally unilateral. These U.S. actions have enjoyed strong congressional support. U.S. allies in Europe have provided some logistic and much diplomatic support for U.S. retaliatory attacks, but

---

[51]An extended discussion of U.S. counter-terrorism policy, policy options, and legislation is provided by two CRS issue briefs. See *Terrorism: Background and Issues for Congress*, by Elizabeth Bazan, Larry Eig, Suzanne Cavanagh, and Raphael Perl, Coordinator, CRS Issue Brief 95086 (updated regularly) and *Terrorism and U.S. Foreign Policy Options*, by Raphael Perl, CRS Issue Brief 92074 (updated regularly).

have tended to refrain from using this policy option themselves. Acts of Middle Eastern terrorism have often occurred in Europe and U.S. allies appear to believe that military retaliation will inspire a cycle of attack and reaction that might be difficult to control.

Major retaliatory attacks took place against Libya and Iraq. On Apr. 15, 1986, the United States sent about 100 U.S. aircraft to bomb military installations in Libya. The attack was in retaliation for the Apr. 2, 1986 bombing of a Berlin nightclub in which 2 U.S. military personnel were killed. President Reagan announced that there was considerable evidence of Libyan responsibility for that terrorist bombing. On June 26, 1993, the United States fired cruise missiles at the headquarters in Baghdad of the Iraqi Intelligence Service, which allegedly sponsored a failed assassination plot against former President George Bush during his Apr. 14-16, 1993 visit to Kuwait.

U.S. military action against state sponsors of terrorism has had some effect on their support for terrorism, although not necessarily long-lasting. Both Saddam Husayn and Muammar Qadhafi remained defiant of the United States even after U.S. military action against them. Libya was quiescent after the attack, but it apparently returned to the use of terrorism in the December 1988 bombing of Pan Am 103 and the UTA bombing the following year. Iraq continued to support terrorism after the 1993 U.S. strike, although not against high profile U.S. targets. However, both countries have tried to show some diplomatic flexibility in order to obtain relief from U.S. and international economic sanctions.

Unilateral Sanctions

The United States has tended to favor economic sanctions, even if unilateral, against the Middle Eastern countries that sponsor terrorism. The primary instrument for that policy option has been the list of state sponsors of terrorism; the listing of a country as a state sponsor of terrorism triggers a wise range of U.S. economic sanctions. Countries on the list are prohibited from receiving U.S. foreign aid, Export-Import Bank guarantees, and sales of items on the U.S. Munitions Control List. U.S. exports to terrorism list countries are subject to strict licensing requirements that generally prohibit exports of items, such as advanced sensing, computation, or transportation equipment, that can have military applications. In addition, U.S. Executive Directors of international financial institutions are directed to vote against any loan or other program for a country determined to be supporting international terrorism.[52] Foreign aid appropriations bills over the past several years have barred any direct or indirect assistance to most states on the terrorism list, thereby preventing these and other countries from benefitting from U.S. contributions to international relief programs.

---

[52]The above list of sanctions are under the following authorities: Section 6(j) of the Export Administration Act, as amended [P.L. 96-72; 50 U.S.C. app. 2405 (j)]; Section 40 of the Arms Export Control Act, as amended [P.L. 90-629; 22 U.S.C. 2780]; Section 620A of the Foreign Assistance Act of 1961, as amended [P.L. 87-195; 22 U.S.C. 2371]; and Section 6 of the Bretton Woods Agreements Act Amendments of 1978, as amended [P.S. 95-435; 22 U.S.C. 286e-11].

Unilateral U.S. sanctions have not, by themselves, forced major changes in the behavior of state sponsors of terrorism. Only Iraq hanged its behavior enough to obtain removal from the list (1982), and that removal was attributed more to the merging of U.S. and Iraqi strategic interests in the early 1980s than to U.S. pressure on terrorism issues. However, U.S. sanctions have been effective to the extent they have convinced other governments to join the United States in refusing to conduct "business as usual" with terrorism sponsors. Virtually all Middle Eastern terrorism list states have publicly protested their inclusion or continuation on the list, suggesting that these sanctions are hurting politically and/or economically. Some U.S. allies have tightened their export control laws. U.S. officials assert that U.S. sanctions, even if unilateral, have made some terrorism state sponsors "think twice" about promoting terrorism.

Multilateral Sanctions

In several cases, the United States has sought to make sanctions against Middle Eastern terrorism list countries multilateral, as a more effective means of forcing these countries to change their behavior. U.S. allies and others have often been reluctant to impose or rely on sanctions to the degree the United States has. Allied business interests in terrorism list countries, or philosophical differences over how to dissuade states from sponsoring terrorism, have often accounted for U.S.-allied splits on some terrorism-related sanctions issues. In the case of Libya, for example, the United States and its European allies worked together to obtain some United Nations Security Council sanctions on that country. However, U.S. allies, which buy substantial amounts of Libyan oil geared to certain refineries in Europe, have been reluctant to follow U.S. urging in 1994 and 1995 to enact a U.N. ban on purchases of Libyan oil. In the case of Iran, European countries and Japan have refused to join a U.S. trade ban on that country, imposed by executive order on May 6, 1995, preferring instead to maintain their policies of "critical dialogue" with Iran. U.S. allies believe there are elements within the Iranian regime that want to end Iran's support for terrorism, and that these officials can be strengthened through trade and dialogue.

Anecdotal evidence suggests that multilateral sanctions have a far greater effect on state sponsors of terrorism than do unilateral sanctions. Iran, a case in which sanctions are not multilateral, has shown little sign in 1995 of abandoning its support for international terrorism. U.S. officials have not formally proposed any U.N. Security council sanctions against Iran, tacitly acknowledging a lack of support on the Council for such sanctions. Libya, on the other hand, hoping to gain relief from or forestall stricter U.N. sanctions, has tried to demonstrate to the international community that it no longer supports international terrorism. Iraq, which is subject to stricter U.N. sanctions than is Libya, has been cooperating with U.N. weapons inspectors in the hopes of obtaining an easing of sanctions.

Selective Engagement

Although some observers believe the United States favors punishments over incentives in dealing with terrorism supporting states, the United States has conducted diplomacy with some state sponsors to curb their support for terrorism. The United States has no diplomatic relations with Iran, Iraq, or Libya, but it does have full relations with Sudan and Syria. The United States has engaged Syria in the Arab-Israeli peace process and has not moved to expand U.S. sanctions or persuade U.S. allies to impose sanctions on Syria. The United States has allowed U.S. private investment in Syria's oil and other industries to expand. As a by-product of its participation in the peace process, Syria agreed to conduct a dialogue with the United States on terrorism, and U.S. officials have occasionally praised what they describe as declining Syrian support for terrorism. Prior to placing Sudan on the list in 1993, U.S. officials presented Sudan with a list of specific terrorism-related requirements which, if they had been met, might have kept Sudan off the list.[53] Since then, the U.S. Ambassador in Khartoum has met with his counterparts in Khartoum in an effort, thus far unsuccessful, to persuade the Sudanese government to investigate U.S. charges of Sudanese support for terrorists.[54] The United States has, nonetheless, continued to provide humanitarian assistance to the Sudanese people suffering from the effects of the civil war.

In 1993, the United States, though reluctant to place Pakistan on the terrorism list, threatened Pakistan's inclusion on the list to encourage Pakistan to curb terrorists on its soil.[55] Pakistan has long been an ally of the United States, particularly in the battle against the Soviet occupation of Afghanistan. In January 1993, the State Department placed Pakistan under "active continuing review" for inclusion on the list because of its alleged assistance to terrorists in Kashmir and Punjab. (Pakistan acknowledges moral and political support to Kashmiri militants but denies allegations of other assistance.) As noted above, Pakistan also hosts several thousand Islamic militants who volunteered in the Afghan war. In July 1993, after it took several steps to curb Kashmiri and Punjabi militants, Pakistan was no longer strongly considered for inclusion on the terrorism list, although the State Department said it would continue to monitor Pakistani cooperation.

Since returning to power in October 1993, Prime Minister Benazir Bhutto has appealed for U.S. help in closing the religious schools and training camps near the Afghan border run by the veterans of the Afghan war. Pakistan has refused to extend the visas of many of those veterans. In 1994, it concluded an extradition treaty with Egypt directed against Egyptian militants staying in Pakistan. In February 1995, Pakistan cooperated with U.S. law enforcement agents in capturing, in Pakistan, Ramzi Ahmad Yusuf, allegedly a major figure in the February 1993 bombing of the

---

[53]Washington Demands Expulsion of Iranian Ambassador in Khartoum. Middle East Mirror, July 23, 1993. P. A1.

[54]Department Statement: Sudan's Support for International Terrorism. U.S. Department of State Dispatch, Vol. 5, No. 38, Sept. 19,. 1994. p. 631.

[55]For more information on U.S.-Pakistani discussions on terrorism, see *Pakistan-U.S. Relations*, by Barbara Leitch LePoer, CRS Issue Brief 94041 (updated regularly).

World Trade Center. The State Department has said Bhutto's government has been helpful in the search for Mir Aimal Kansi, who is sought in connection with the Jan. 25, 1993 shooting outside CIA headquarters in Langley, Virginia. Two CIA employees were killed and three were wounded in that attack.

Policy Toward Terrorist Groups

Effective policies intended to combat individual terrorists or terrorist groups are often difficult to construct. Individual terrorists or groups are relatively immune to economic sanctions policies and military or law enforcement forces must find terrorists before they can apprehend them. It is partly for these reasons that U.S. counterterrorism policy has tended to focus on pressuring state sponsors. However, over the past few years, groups that are less dependent on state sponsorship, such as Hamas, have become more prominent, as have Middle Eastern terrorists operating in the United States itself. There has, therefore, been increasing attention to formulating U.S. policies directed against terrorist groups and individual terrorists and strengthening laws that can be used against terrorists operating or basing themselves in the United States.

Even before policies against specific terrorist groups can be formulated, there is sometimes disagreement as to whether to engage or combat a particular group. For example, the United States had some low level Embassy contacts with Hamas and Egypt's Islamic Group, in an effort to gauge their intentions and capabilities;[56] these contacts angered the Israeli and the Egyptian governments, respectively. Especially in the Egyptian case, there were some inside the Administration who believed the United States should not repeat a mistake it made in Iran in not having had any contacts with the Islamic revolutionaries who eventually triumphed there. The contacts with Hamas and the Islamic Group accompanied public pronouncements by high ranking U.S. officials that the United States had great respect for Islam as a religion, but opposed Islamic extremists who used violence. However, the contacts were ended after the February 1993 World Trade Center bombing, even though Hamas members were not suspected of involvement in that incident.

Foreign Cooperation

U.S. law enforcement authorities generally depend on cooperation from host governments in order to be able to strike at terrorists or their groups. As noted above, it is unlikely the United States would have captured Ramzi Ahmad Yusuf if it had not had the cooperation of Pakistan, nor would France likely have captured "Carlos" in 1994 if Sudan had not decided he was expendable. Argentina has hosted U.S.

---

[56]Hedges, Chris. U.S. Aides in Egypt Said To Have Met With Group Tied to New York Blast. *New York Times*, Apr. 13, 1993. P. A3.

investigators looking into the 1992 and 1994 bombings of Israeli and Jewish facilities in Buenos Aires, in which Hizballah is suspected.[57]

U.S. counterterrorism officials say cooperation from U.S. allies in the Middle East is generally good. Saudi Arabia, for example, has responded to U.S. requests to stop its citizens from funding radical Islamic groups that use terrorism, although more steps are being sought. In April 1994, Saudi Arabia revoked the citizenship and froze the assets of Usama bin Laden, a Saudi believed to be financing and providing training facilities for radical Islamic elements in Sudan. The Persian Gulf states were helpful in preventing Iraq-sponsored terrorism during the Gulf war.[58] Kuwait cooperated with the United States in investigating the 1993 Iraqi attempt to assassinate President Bush. The United States also has urged Jordan's King Husayn to curtain Hamas activities in Jordan and to expel Hamas leaders.[59] Jordan declared Hamas illegal in April 1994 and, in May 1995, asked some Hamas officials to leave.[60] In July 1995, Jordan signed an extradition treaty with the United States and subsequently arrested and turned over to the United States a suspect in the World Trade Center bombing, Iyad Ismail.

On occasion, allies of the United States, probably for internal political reasons, have been uncooperative with U.S. efforts to capture terrorists. Egypt is a major supporter of U.S. policy in the Middle East, especially the Arab-Israeli peace process. However, as noted above, in 1985 Egypt gave safe passage in return for their ending the hijacking. In this incident, Egypt apparently did not want to offend Arab states that might have accused Egypt of "selling out" Palestinians to the United States. In April 1995, according to U.S. officials, Saudi Arabia refused to cooperate with a U.S. operation to capture a known terrorist when his plane landed in Saudi Arabia. The terrorist is believed to be Imad Mughniyah, a Hizballah leader who reputedly held some of the U.S. hostages in Lebanon.[61] Saudi Arabia might not have wanted to antagonize radical Islamist elements inside Saudi Arabia or cause further deterioration in relations with Iran, which supports Hizballah, both of which might have resulted from Saudi cooperation in the capture of Mughniyah. Saudi officials point out that there was very little time for them to react to the U.S. request for help.

A cornerstone of U.S. efforts to counter terrorist groups is to assist friendly groups and governments to combat terrorist groups themselves, without direct U.S. involvement. For example, the Clinton Administration has transferred to the Lebanese Armed Forces (LAF) lethal military equipment, including 175 excess M-113 armored personnel carriers, 16 UH-1 helicopters, and spare parts for M-48 tanks, in part to strengthen the LAF against Hizballah, should there be a conflict with that militia. However, Lebanon does not receive U.S. anti-terrorism assistance (training for law enforcement personnel to deter terrorists) because of the poor security

---

[57]Statement of Barbara Bodine, Coordinator for Counterterrorism, before the Subcommittee on International Security, International Organizations, and Human Rights, of the House Foreign Affairs Committee. Aug. 1, 1994, in U.S. Department of State Dispatch. Vol. 5, No. 33, Aug. 15, 1994. p. 558.

[58]Comments to CRS by State Department counterterrorism official. July 13, 1995.

[59]Sabbagh, Rana. Jordan Says Hamas Is Illegal. Reuters, Apr. 16, 1994.

[60]Sabbagh, Rana. Jordan Orders Two Hamas Leaders To Leave. Reuters, May 31, 1995.

[61]Hizballah Denies Mughniyah on Board Plane. FBIS-NES-95-079, Apr. 25, 1995. p. 44.

environment in Lebanon. Egypt and Jordan are among the largest Middle Eastern participants in the anti-terrorism program in which the United States provides training in airport security, explosives detection, and crisis management. State Department officials say the U.S. program of aid to the Palestinian Authority -- as well as the transfer thus far of 200 non-lethal excess military trucks to the PA -- is designed to help the PA establish its effectiveness and popularity in Palestinian controlled territory.[62] Some press reports indicate the PA is gaining greater control over the areas under its jurisdiction and it is increasingly placing Hamas and Palestinian Islamic Jihad on the defensive.[63] State Department officials add that there is intelligence cooperation between the United States and Israel and between the PA and Israel directed against Hamas and Palestinian Islamic Jihad. On the other hand, it is not certain that success in Arab-Israeli peace negotiations will, as hoped, lead to an end to Palestinian Islamist terrorism. Hamas and Palestinian Islamic Jihad might ultimately shift their emphasis from undermining the peace process to establishing a Palestinian Islamic Republic.

The Domestic Front

The World Trade Center bombing, coupled with Israeli allegations that month that Hamas was receiving funding and direction from Arab residents in the United States, placed greater focus in the Administration and Congress on domestic efforts to combat Middle Eastern terrorist groups. The Trade Center bombing exposed the vulnerability of the United States to Middle Eastern-inspired terrorism as did no other event previously, and demonstrated that terrorist groups can function outside the direct protective umbrella of state sponsors. The bombing also sparked much academic research and law enforcement investigation into the presence of radical Muslims in the United States and alleged fundraising in the United States for Middle East terrorism.

On Jan. 23, 1995, the Clinton Administration issued an executive order, mentioned above, intended to sever any connection between U.S. residents and acts of Middle Eastern terrorism. The executive order, taken under the authority of the International Emergency Economic Powers Act (50 U.S.C. 1701 et.seq., and the National Emergencies Act (50 U.S.C. 1601 et.seq.) froze the assets of twelve named Middle Eastern terrorist groups opposed to the Arab-Israeli peace process, as well as eighteen individuals. The executive order also prohibited financial transactions between U.S. nationals and the named terrorist organizations. To provide legislative backing for the executive order and for future counterterrorism policies, President Clinton submitted a draft bill to Congress, which was introduced in both chambers on Feb. 10, 1995. (H.R. 896 was introduced by Representative Schumer, and S.390 was introduced by Senator Biden.)

---

[62]Comments to CRS by State Department counter-terrorism official. June 8, 1995.

[63]Ibrahim, Youssef. Arafat's Forces Push Crackdown on Gaza Radicals. *New York Times*, July 10, 1995. p. A1.

In the aftermath of the Apr. 19, 1995 Oklahoma City bombing, Senator Dole introduced a Republican version of the comprehensive anti-terrorism bill, which incorporated many elements of the Administration bill. A revised version of the bill, S. 735, was substituted as an amendment on May 25, 1995, and passed the Senate on June 7, 1995. A similar measure in the House, H.R. 1710, was introduced by Representative Hyde on May 25, 1995, and reported out of the House Judiciary Committee on June 20, 1995. These bills, including a revised Administration bill introduced by Senator Daschle on May 5 1995, have many provisions in common but differ on measures involving domestic investigation procedures, tactics, and law enforcement authorities. S.735 and H.R. 1710 contain provisions that would curb fundraising in the United States for foreign terrorist groups and use special courts to determine if classified information could be used in the deportation of alien terrorists. These provisions have drawn substantial criticism from U.S. civil liberties groups and Arab-American organizations. An amendment to the Senate version prohibits arms sales to countries that do not cooperate with U.S. anti-terrorism efforts.

ALGERIA: FOUR YEARS OF CRISIS[*]

Carol Migdalovitz

Introduction[1]

For over four years, crises of inept democratization, reluctant economic transformation, and unrelenting Islamist terror and army counterterror have beset Algeria. While other Middle Eastern states may have similar problems, none has suffered comparable warfare and loss of life.

Some observers hope that the November 1995 presidential election and municipal elections will help to create a climate freer from violence and more conducive to political stability and economic growth. Others remain skeptical of the regime's willingness to make meaningful changes that might bring about real democratization by broadening political participation and depriving extremists of their following among the alienated. Nonetheless, with the November election, the Algerian people signaled a clear desire to end their beleaguered status.

Developments in Algeria are of keen interest in the Middle East, North Africa and Western Europe, and, thereby, affect U.S. interests. Algeria is located on the periphery of the Arab-Israeli arena and on the southern Mediterranean coast. Its domestic turmoil has increased concern about the spread of militant Islamism, possibly threatening the Middle East peace process in which the United States has invested considerable time, effort, and political and other capital. Algeria's next-door neighbors, Morocco and Tunisia, have long-established, cordial relations with the United States, have contributed to the peace process, and opened ties to Israel. They, too, are worried about events in Algeria, and about Islamist violence. Algeria's northern neighbors and U.S. allies, France, Spain, and Italy, depend on Algeria's energy resources and have large Muslim minorities. They likewise seek to contain Algeria's problems and to remedy them in order to attain greater stability to their south.

---

[*]Excerpted from *CRS Report* 96-392F

[1]Some information in this report is derived from background interviews with U.S., Algerian, and French officials, and others during the past two years.

While U.S. interests are not immediately engaged in Algeria, U.S. policy makers cannot ignore Algeria's regional strategic and historical significance and the concerns of friends and allies.

Background

The Algerian Revolution against France, 1954-1962, was the longest and bloodiest war for independence in Africa. The revolutionary movement, the Front de Liberation Nationale (National Liberation Front-FLN), adopted as its slogan "Islam is our religion, Arabic is our language, Algeria is our fatherland." After independence, the FLN took power as a single party and seemed to neglect parts of that theme. It openly adopted a secular culture and bred a political/economic elite who spoke French, not Arabic, and were influenced more by European ideologies, especially socialism, than by Islam. Houari Boumedienne and Chadli Bendjedid, products of the army and the FLN, headed the state from 1965-92, following the overthrow of revolutionary leader Ahmed Ben Bella (1962-65). During this time, the Ministry of Religious Affairs controlled and funded mosques and Islamic education, but the nation's leaders remained isolated from popular currents and, in retrospect, appear to have failed to achieve a national consensus on values and culture. The memory and myth of the war for independence served as the only common national bond.

In 1979, Islamists began to proselytize on university campuses, demanding a return to Islam and its moral values. One, Shaykh Abassi Madani, became well known for his eloquence. He was first arrested (and held without charge or trial) in 1982. In the 1980s, Mustapha Bouyali led an Islamist guerrilla movement, attempting armed insurrection against the regime. By 1987, Bouyali was killed and his movement suppressed. These stirrings of discontent, however, drew the regime's attention and it accommodated some Islamic sensitivities, promulgating a 1984 family code or set of laws regulating marriage and the family that conformed more closely to Islamic principles and abrogated many women's rights.

By the late 1980s, a deteriorating economy exacerbated social tensions: oil prices fell, birth rates soared, and unemployment and urbanization were out of control. In 1987-88, the regime began to dismantle the socialist economy and move, fitfully, toward a market economy, emphasizing efficiency and austerity. Such actions heightened people's anxieties, while party leaders, merchants, and former and present military officers continued to flaunt their affluence and, to some, their decadence and corruption. Mass demonstrations culminated in unprecedented riots in October 1988. The government declared a state of siege and harshly repressed the perpetrators. To redress and channel grievances, President Chadli Bendjedid decided on a course of political reform. A new February 1989 Constitution did not mention the FLN, consigned the army to a role in defense of nation, and allowed political associations.

The FLN had held a monopoly on political power and expression since before independence. For as long a period, there was no tradition of political opposition or outlet for dissent. In 1989, the FLN was challenged by over 50 parties, including the Front Islamique du Salut (Islamic Salvation Front-FIS) founded by Abassi Madani, Ali Belhadj, and others. Most new parties were narrowly centered on personalities or geographic regions, unable to coalesce, and lacking mass appear and organizational capability. The FIS had appeal and organization. Its followers had infiltrated government-controlled mosques and organized informal or street mosques, completely uncontrolled by authorities. Mosques became natural vehicles for opposition expression. The FIS argued that foreign, Western ideologies, particularly secularism and socialism, had failed Algerians, citing widespread shortages of staples and housing, rampant unemployment, especially among youth, and other deficiencies and inequities.

Chadli Bendjedid's decision to allow the formation of a religious party contravened the Constitution and has been criticized. Nonetheless, he may have been attempting to involve moderate Islamists in the political system and to isolate militants. Elections for local offices took place on June 12, 1990. Some 60 to 65% of those registered voted. FIS won 54% of the vote, control of over half of the municipal councils, and of almost 75% of the *wilayah* or state governments. It immediately called for parliamentary elections. A new electoral law intended to constrain FIS provoked a FIS-led general strike, martial law, the cancellation of the elections, and the temporary arrests of Madani[2] and Belhadj.

After the state of emergency ended in September 1991, parliamentary elections were scheduled for December 26, with a run-off to be held January 16, 1992. In December, turnout was about 60%. FIS obtained 47.5% of the votes and won 188 out of 430 electoral districts outright in the first round. It stood to gain control of two-thirds of parliament after a second round. Some analysts suggest that Chadli Bendjedid was prepared to proceed to the runoff and, thereafter, to work with a FIS-dominated parliament while relying on the overwhelming power of the presidency to keep it in check.

On January 11, however, military leaders (preeminently Defense Minister General Khalid Nazzar and Interior Minister Larbi Belkheir) forced the President to resign. The election results were voided and the second round was canceled. A five-member Haut Conseil d'État (High Council of State-HCE), including Nazzar and Belkheir, took over. Madani and Belhadj were arrested, tried for fomenting violence against the state, and sentenced to 12 years in prison. In the next two years, the HCE would appoint three presidents (Mohammed Boudiaf, Ali Kafi, and Liamine Zeroual) and four prime ministers.

The coup worsened Algeria's Islamist crisis. Militant Islamists took up arms against the army. Since 1992, an estimated 50,000 lives have been lost in a conflict characterized by extreme barbarity. Islamist terrorists attack, kidnap, assassinate, and bomb individuals and infrastructures that symbolize, to them, the establishment and its vices. They burn schools for allegedly disseminating foreign culture, kill foreigners, and attack women and girls for wearing secular dress and working outside the home. Journalists and teachers are frequent targets. The regime, too, has been charged with abuses. Security forces allegedly engage in torture, extrajudicial killings, disappearances, arbitrary detention, and excessive use of force;[3] they reportedly have

---

[2]Use of Madani as the shaykh's last name here conforms to common usage in reporting.

[3]U.S. Department of state. Country Reports on Human Rights Practices for 1995, Algeria, March 1996; also Amnesty International. Reports 1994 and 1995.

deployed death squads and "special" police units. Some observers conjecture that, in order to discipline those not adhering closely enough to an "eradicator" line[4] or to chill voices of free thinkers, security force *agents provacateurs* may even have been responsible for a few of the terrorist acts commonly attributed to Islamist militants. Thousands remain in prison. In February 1994, a prison riot at Serkadji where many Islamists were held was suppressed, at a cost of 98 prisoners killed and more than 100 injured. The violence continues; although, by the end of 1995, some observed greater army control over the countryside.

Islamists

From the beginning, FIS was an amalgam of several philosophical tendencies seeking a state governed by Islamic law and principles -- not a unitary party. After Madani and Belhadj were silenced by their arrests, FIS began to speak with several, conflicting voices. Since 1992, Head of the FIS Executive Abroad Rabah Kebir has lived in Germany, where he obtained refugee status in 1994. Kebir reportedly is in communication with FIS colleagues in Algeria and is believed to represent FIS positions accurately and authoritatively. He condemns terrorism. Anouar Haddam, who resides in the Washington area, was elected to parliament in the canceled election, and calls himself Chairman of the FIS Parliamentary Delegation Abroad. Haddam simultaneously claims to support armed struggle and to oppose terrorism. FIS statements increasingly deny Haddam's right to speak officially for FIS and accuse him of supporting the extremist Armed Islamic Group (GIA).

Smaller, somewhat more moderate, legal Islamist parties such as the Movement for an Islamic Society (HAMAS)[5] and An Nahdah (Renaissance Party)[6] did not fill the void left by the banned FIS, although they remained on the scene. Militant groups dominated events. The Islamic Salvation Army (AIS), led by Madani Mezrak, has ties to FIS and primarily targets the military. It is not known to attack foreigners or intellectuals and condemns GIA for doing so. The Armed Islamic Movement (MIA) was active in 1992-93, but faded following the death of its leader. Since fall 1993, the GIA has been the most violent. Now reportedly led by Abderrahmane Amine, GIA's organization divides Algeria territorially into disciplined, isolated cells ultimately headed by a *majlis* or council of leaders. It derives funds from Algerian expatriates in Western Europe and, reportedly, from "taxes" on local communities where it is strongest and from other illegal avenues. It obtains most weapons in raids on government forces. GIA's core members fought the communists in Afghanistan, therefore are called "Afghans," and are believed to be responsible for most atrocities perpetrated in Algeria and France. Some suggest that increased GIA terrorism in France in 1995 was a sign that GIA was less able to operate within Algeria; but terrorism continued at home. GIA was aligned with FIS at one time, but now

---

[4]*Eradicateurs* or eradicators believe that the solution to Algeria's civil war is to be found in the eradication of Islamists and advocate a military solution.

[5]Not connected with the Palestinian organization which has the same acronym.

[6]Not connected to the Tunisian party of the same name.

denounces FIS and refuses to recognize its leaders. FIS, in turn, condemns GIA attacks against foreigners and civilians.

Outside Support

The major sources of FIS, GIA, and other Islamist groups' funds and weapons are Algerian. That said, FIS's philosophy is derived partly from that of the Egyptian Muslim Brotherhood. It reportedly received early and substantial funding from Saudi Arabia; but Algerian Islamist publications now attack the Saudis for no longer providing support. Other support comes from a variety of alleged sources. The rich Turkish Islamist Welfare Party is said to tap benefactors at home and in Germany on its own behalf and for FIS with which it sympathizes. A few FIS leaders have fled to Turkey. Wealthy Algerian Islamists in Western Europe may have funded some arms purchases in Eastern Europe that transited Germany bound for militants at home. Madani's family has taken refuge in Germany. German authorities arrested Madani's sons in October 1994 and, in April 1996, charged them and two others with belonging to a criminal organization and explosives offensives. Prosecutors said that they "belonged to a group which organized the purchase of weapons, explosives and other war machinery, and procured false identity papers" for GIA and AIS. Some French analysts suggest that wealthy Indonesian, Malaysian, and Pakistani Islamists provide weapons and money to Middle Eastern Islamist groups, and imply that Algerians are among recipients.

The Algerian government charges that Iran and Sudan have interfered in its domestic affairs and that they support FIS. Algeria broke diplomatic relations with Iran in March 1993. Iranian officials claim that they give only political and moral support to Algerian Islamists and call for talks to meet "the demands of Muslim people."[7] The U.S. State Department report, *Patterns of Global Terrorism 1995*, does not mention Iranian support for any specific Algerian group. In April 1995, the Algerian army seized a caravan transporting arms from Sudan across the Sahara Desert. Soon thereafter, one journalist cited a U.S. official as claiming that Iran had delivered "several dozen tons" of small arms to Algerian militants via Sudan in small batches driven through other African Countries.[8] Algeria's Ambassador to the United States, Osmane Bencherif, charges that Sudan is a center for spreading arms and Islamist influence, and the U.S. State Department's terrorism report refers to Sudan as a "refuge, nexus and training hub" for international terrorist organizations, but cites no Algerian group as a beneficiary.[9] The State Department report for 1994 had agreed that the National Islamic Front (NIF), which dominates the Sudanese government, aids Algerian Islamic opposition groups. FIS delegates have attended Islamist conclaves in Khartoum and NIF leader Hassan al Turabi has praised the FIS struggle. Turabi denies having relations with GIA; but U.S. officials contradict him.

---

[7]Reuters, February 12, 1996.

[8]Robin Wright. U.S. Links Iran to Efforts to Torpedo Peace Process, *Los Angeles Times*, May 9, 1995, p. 1.

[9]U.S. State Department. *Patterns of Global Terrorism 1995*, p. 27.

The Algerian government is supported in its anti-Islamist crusade partly by Tunisia and Egypt, the latter supplying vehicles and training for police, and reportedly by France.

Sant'Egidio

The Sant'Egidio Community, a lay Catholic peace group, convened meetings of Algerian political parties in Rome in November 1994 and January 1995. The three major parties -- FIS, FLN, and FSS (Front des Forces Socialistes/Front of Socialist Forces) -- and several others, representing over 80% of the voters in the December 1991 election, participated. Never before had such diverse political currents found agreement. They issues "A Platform for a Peaceful Political Solution to Algeria's Crisis" on January 13 and referred to it as a national contract of covenant. By signing it, they committed themselves to reject violence as a means of reaching or preserving power, to respect human rights, to rotate power through popular ballot, to political pluralism, and to noninterference by the army in political affairs. All called for an end to the ban on FIS, the release of FIS officials, and guarantees that they would be able to meet freely. The parties agreed to condemn violence before negotiations.[10]

President Liamine Zeroual immediately issued a "categorical rejection" of the Sant'Egidio endeavor, saying that it "harms national sovereignty and invites foreign intervention in our internal affairs."[11] The regime never recognized FIS's rejection of violence and concessions to democratic principles or the Sant'Egidio document's constructive contribution to a possible solution. Some contend that despite Zeroual's public statements about wanting a dialog and reconciliation, the regime was resolved to follow a hard line. Others suggest that it had concluded that FIS could no longer influence or control events, such as GIA violence, and, therefore, did not have to be accommodated.

The United States and Western Europe took the Sant'Egidio document and FIS's signature thereto more seriously than the Algerian government. They viewed Sant'Egidio as a very important beginning in the search for a political solution and of the process of national dialog, and were chagrined that the junta chose to bypass the opportunity presented.

Reconciliation Efforts Under Zeroual

Although he repudiated the Sant'Egidio contract, President Liamine Zeroual undertook several publicized initiatives to achieve national reconciliation. The High State Council had named Zeroual, a retired general who had not taken part in the

---

[10]*Plateforme pour une Solution Politique et Pacifique de la Crise Algerienne*. Also, Foreign Broadcast Information Service, Daily Report, Near East and South Asia, (hereafter FBIS) NES-95-011, January 18, 1995, p. 11-12.

[11]FBIS, NES-95-005, January 9, 1995, p. 13.

1992 coup, defense minister in July 1993 and president on January 30, 1994. He was given a mandate to rule for a 3-year transition period during which economic reforms were to be carried out and stability restored. In his maiden speech, Zeroual called for a national dialog, without exception. In May 1994, he appointed and convened a 178-member National Transitional Council. The Council never became the forum for reconciliation that Zeroual said he desired because most political parties boycotted it, although a few participated, and many doubted the regime's sincerity. FIS had been banned in 1992 and was not included.

Zeroual attempted to negotiate with the FIS, but was said to be constrained by "eradicators" within the military hierarchy. Decision-making in the military elite is not transparent. Five or six senior generals appear to decide by consensus. Zeroual may be one, not first, among equals or he may follow the lead of others. Presidential advisor and former Chief of Intelligence, General Mohammed Betchin served as Zeroual's primary negotiator with FIS. Other important players, such as Chief of Staff Lieutenant General Mohammed Lamari, Chief of Military Intelligence Major General Mohammed Toufik Medienne and former Defense Minister Major General Nazzar may share veto power. Lamari was promoted to Lieutenant General in October 1994, the highest rank ever awarded in Algeria. When FIS insisted on talking to the real powers, it sometimes names Lamari, Nazzar, and others.

For over a year and a half, Zeroual seemed to tack publicly between eradication and conciliation. He could not get too far out in front of his peers for several reasons. Foremost, he may have agreed sincerely with objectors to conciliation or been prompted to agree with them by a strong desire to preserve the unity of the army. He also may have feared for his life if he dissented from the consensus view.[12]

In negotiations, FIS demanded release of all FIS prisoners, a lifting of the ban on the party, freedom for Madani and Balhadj to meet with FIS colleagues inside and outside Algeria (including representatives of armed groups), freedom for the FIS *majlis al shura* (consultative council) to meet, discussion with army leaders, and resumption of the electoral process. Zeroual and his representatives demanded that FIS disavow violence, ignoring FIS acceptance of the principles of Sant'Egidio. After an impasse, contacts resumed in June 1995. When they failed, the government blamed the FIS, while FIS rejected responsibility. Rabah Kebir accused the regime of using negotiations to divide Islamist ranks between pro- and anti-negotiation elements, meaning to divide Madani and Balhadj, and to give international financial institutions the impression that it was seeking a political solution.

Further dialog took place from August to October 1995. In September 1995, Madani and Belhadj were moved from prison to house arrest. On October 31, Zeroual accused them or reneging on undertakings to make a statement vowing to work to end violence. He claimed to have letters of encouragement from Belhadj to terrorists.

---

[12]Some analysts believe that hardliners in the military leadership may have been responsible for the Jun 1992 assassination of former President Mohammed Boudiaf and of others in the military and government who called for reform or dissented from the eradicators' conventional wisdom. The HCS called Boudiaf, a respected veteran of Algeria's struggle for independence, home from decades of self-exile in Morocco to lead the nation in 1992 because he was untainted by involvement in contemporary Algerian affairs. Boudiaf was particularly intent on rooting out official corruption and building an independent national following to support his program.

FIS spokesmen again said that FIS had refused to comply with the regime's demands as long as the leaders were in custody. One commentator suggested that the dialog had failed because the government discovered that, due to their imprisonment, the two FIS leaders no longer controlled militants.[13] Zeroual called for elections by the end of 1995.

November 16, 1995 Presidential Election

The November 16, 1995 election was the first contested presidential election in independent Algeria. The candidates were Zeroual, who ran as an independent; Shaykh Mahfoud Nahnah, a moderate Islamist of the Movement for an Islamic Society (HAMAS); Dr. Said Saadi, leader of the Rally for Culture and Democracy (RCD), an advocate of Berber cultural right and secularist; and Noureddine Boukrouh of the Algerian Renewal party, a centrist, Islamic reformist. Nahnah and Boukrouh had participated in government-initiated national dialog efforts, while Saadi had boycotted them. Nahnah, while not a signatory, supported the Sant'Egidio document and condemned the government for rejecting it. He appealed to voters who might have voted for FIS -- if it had been allowed to participate.

The limited field did not include the three parties which had won the most seats in the 1991 parliamentary election: the FIS, the FFS, and the FLN. They called for a boycott, arguing that the lack of security and stability in the country created circumstances unsuitable for elections. In a field of at least 40 announced candidates, former Prime Minister Redha Malek might have provided a real content for Zeroual by appealing to many of the same voters. Malek is an eradicator whom Zeroual had fired in April 1994. But the electoral commission declared that Malek and many others had failed to obtain sufficient signatures to be placed on the ballot.[14] Accepted challengers Nahnah, Boukrouh, and Saadi appealed to different constituencies than Zeroual and did not pose a comparable threat to his expected victory.

GIA threatened voters and labeled the election an act of infidelity. Violence escalated sharply before the election, but election day was relatively peaceful. Threats and violence did not dissuade voters who were weary of the war and sought to signal their desire for normalcy. A huge deployment of some 200,000 security forces gave added assurance. (If the regime was responsible for some of the violence, then it chose to desist during its own electoral exercise.) Official figures claim a turnout of 74.92% or about 12 million out of 16 million registered voters. Many observers, including the U.S. Embassy in Algiers, agree, that even if the government's figures were inflated, turnout was high. Officially, Zeroual won about 7 million votes or 61.3%. Nahnah took 25.38% or 2.9 million votes. Saadi won 9.29% or 1 million votes; and Boukrouh 3.78% or 433,000 votes. Only Nahnah challenged the result, alleging "irregularities;" but he also called the election a "celebration of democracy."

---

[13]FBIS, NES-94-244, December 20, 1994, p. 11.

[14]The electoral law required potential candidates to get 75,000 signatures in 25 out of 48 prefectures in the country. Malek claimed to have collected the required number.

The Islamists' share of the vote accurately reflected the level of support many analysts conclude they now have in the country.

Post-Election Developments

In the six months since the election, Zeroual has moved very slowly in all areas, including resolving Algeria's crisis. He waited until the end of the year to name a new Prime Minister and chose Ahmed Ouyahia, age 43, the youngest man ever to hold the office. Ouyahia had worked in government since 1976, latterly in the Ministry of Foreign Affairs as a mediator between the Mali government and rebel Tuareg tribesmen and as head of the cabinet. Some analysts suggest that the choice of Ouyahia and an equally youthful cabinet is a gesture toward the disaffected younger generation. Skeptics note that some new faces are those of scions of the elite and others are of recycled junior ministers from previous governments. Most observers agree that the selection of an unknown, government functionary, and not a more prominent figure, suggests that Zeroual will continue to dominate the government and politics -- a conclusion underscored by the constitutional prerogatives of the presidency. Zeroual also retains the defense portfolio. Although Ouyahia has negotiating experience, it is considered unlikely that Zeroual and the military would delegate responsibility for negotiations with Islamists, should they occur, to him. Ouyahia has taken charge of economic policy and other technocratic matters.

Zeroual requested the three parties that had competed in the presidential elections to suggest names for the new government. Nahnah of HAMAS and Boukrouh of the Algerian Renewal Party accepted; Saadi of the secularist RCD did not because the two Islamists did. Zeroual names a FIS dissident who had resigned from the party, Ahmed Merrani, Minister of Religious Affairs, HAMAS nominees to minor pasts as Ministers of Fishing and Small Industries, and Boukrouh's choice as Minister or Tourism and Crafts. This means that Islamists, albeit coopted moderates, are represented in a more visibly pluralistic government for the first time. This may be another reason why Zeroual may question whether outreach to FIS is still necessary.

By issuing a call for an election boycott that was ignored, FIS, FLN, and FFS marginalized themselves, at least temporarily. FLN Secretary General Mehri, who had signed the Sant'Egidio document and led the boycott, lost a vote of confidence at his party congress in January 1996. His successor, Boualem Benhamouda, a former finance minister, represents an FLN that had been part of the system and wants to reclaim its share of the spoils, not that of dissident reformers. Benhamouda declared that the Rome alliance had been overtaken by events and his party will participate in any dialog leading to parliamentary elections. In March, the FLN Central Committee issued a statement praising the presidential elections that its party had boycotted.

The FFS is a traditionally Berber party that favors secularism and cultural pluralism. In March 1996, FFS leader Hocine Ait Ahmed, a hero of the war of independence, returned from four years of self-imposed exile in Europe. Although he was overwhelmingly reelected president of the party, a new post of party first secretary was created in order to have someone in country to act during the president's absences. An emerging minority of dissidents reportedly questions Ait

Ahmed's participation at Sant'Egidio, his authoritarian style, and whether he is truly in touch with developments in the country. Some chose not to attend the party meeting.

On the militant Islamist side, fissures have become pronounced since the election. Immediately afterward, Rabah Kebir confirmed FIS's "permanent willingness to engage in dialog."[15] Some reports at the time intimated that FIS was preparing to call a truce. Anouar Haddam, on the other hand, said, "We are not ready to compromise with the military: and labeled Kebir's position a "betrayal."[16] More moderate FIS spokesmen repeatedly denounce Haddam as a toady of GIA. The message of this public debate in which FIS shows its peaceful side may be intended as much for Zeroual as for Haddam. FIS is said to have named a five-man negotiating team within Algeria in anticipation of a renewed dialog. GIA and the FIS-oriented AIS reportedly have engaged in open warfare and publicly disagree about tactics. AIS recently condemned GIA's kidnapping of French monks.

In his inaugural speech on November 27, 1996, Zeroual called on all political groups to engage in dialog. He specifically reached out to "misled" youths, blamed foreign plots for their actions, and vowed to continue the fight against terrorist violence.[17] He did not mention FIS, and he has not made other public overtures to Islamists or FIS or responded to its public debate. In December, he offered clemency in the form of shorter sentences and protection against former allies to those who "repent." On March 30, 1996, the President invited about 50 leaders of political parties and organizations, and other national figures to participate in bilateral talks to prepare for parliamentary elections that may be held in early 1997. This initiative I consistent with Zeroual's controlling style -- engaging each interlocutor independently of others. Preparations will include the drafting of new party and electoral laws. FIS was conspicuously not invited, indicating that Zeroual has decided to ignore it in planning for the future even though violence continues in the country.

Economy

After independence, the government grossly mismanaged the national economy, creating a vastly bloated public sector. Only the state-owned hydrocarbon sector was developed effectively and it still accounts for 97% of Algeria's foreign exchange earnings.[18] Low oil prices since the mid-1980s left Algeria unable to finance needed imports, producing a huge national debt, now nearly $30 billion. Official unemployment is 22%, U.S. figures peg it at 30%, and it is perhaps up to 60% among the youth. Official inflation in 1994 was over 22%; U.S. estimates place it at 30%,

---

[15]What Now n Algeria? *The Estimate*, Vol. VI, No. 24, p. 11.

[16]Ibid.

[17]FBIS. NES-94-228, November 28, 1995, p. 19.

[18]In January 1992, Algeria had 3,626 billion cubic meters of natural gas reserves, compared to Saudi Arabia with 5,170 b.c.m. In January 1995, its proven oil reserves stood at 9.2 million barrels, compared to 261.2 million barrels for the Saudis. *The Middle East and North Africa 1996*. Europa Publications Ltd, 1995, pp. 149, 156.

but project a decline. Gross domestic product growth rate was -2.5% in 1992, + 0.2% in 1994, and declared by the government to be +5% in 1995.[19]

In 1994, debt repayments were about to consume all of Algeria's hard currency earnings. In April 1994, it reluctantly signed an accord with the International Monetary Fund (IMF), recommitting Algeria to create a market economy -- to liberalize prices and imports, reduce subsidies, and exercise greater fiscal discipline. The government increased prices on staples and fuel, devalued the dinar, and raised interest rates. The IMF encouraged "structural adjustment" to restore growth, with heavy emphasis on labor intensive sectors such as housing both to ease a housing crisis and to create jobs. The IMF extended a $1 billion standby credit and called on creditors to provide $8-9 billion more. In May 1995, the IMF granted Algiers an additional three-year, $1.8 billion extended credit facility. The Paris Club of creditor countries agreed to reschedule about $5 billion of government debt (of which the United States rescheduled about $1 billion) and the London Club of commercial creditors to reschedule about $3.2 billion in debt. The European Union (EU) developed a generous, five-year assistance package, and pledged to proceed with talks on a trade association accord. These actions freed funds for more imports and shortages were said to diminish. IMF reforms may have short term negative effects (such as higher prices) as they bring long term benefits. The autocratic Algerian regime may weather short-term difficulties, such as the open manifestations of worker discontent that have occurred, more easily than a democracy.

Algerian officials try to disassociate the turmoil at home from economic problems. The strife, nonetheless, has been an unavoidable backdrop to their relations with the international financial community and a disincentive for investors. Aid and lending have continued because Western governments hope that if Algeria's economic problems can be remedied, then Islamism will decline. This view has led international financial institutions, prompted by France, to make an all-out effort to assist Algeria. These institutions provide optimistic economic assessments to support the effort. IMF Managing Director Michel Camdessus, a Frenchman, declared satisfaction with Algeria's implementation of accords with the IMF.

The government has reformed the investment code and announced an ambitious privatization program. The private sector accounts for only about 35% of production. After the election, investors' confidence was said to improve as they perceived increased possibilities for stability in Algeria. This confidence was reflected mostly in hydrocarbons. Several major deals to develop oil and gas reserves were announced, including British Petroleum's decision to spend $3.5 billion over 25 years, and French Total and U.S. Atlantic Richfield's decision to invest $3 billion. All the same, violence and insecurity have hampered the government's ability to attract foreign investment in the more risky non-energy private sector and, thereby, to translate IMF reforms into sustained growth.

---

[19]U.S. Central Intelligence Agency. *World Factbooks 1993, 1994, 1995.*

Morocco and Tunisia

There is some concern that the conflict in Algeria could spread to its neighbors, Morocco and Tunisia, which also have Islamist groups or parties. But many analysts regard Islamism in North Africa as largely home grown and intrinsic to each nation. The creation of an Islamist state in Algeria undoubtedly would give some impetus to movements in neighboring countries. But those neighbors would not necessarily become Islamist and their Islamist tendencies are not attributable to Algeria.

In Tunisia, President Zine al-Abidin Bin Ali has used autocratic rule, economic growth, and progressive social policies to repel Islamism. He harshly suppressed the Islamist An Nahdah Party and its leader, Rashid Ghannouchi, who has ties to FIS, took self-exile in Britain. Tunisia's emphasis on market reforms nurtures a strong middle class as a bulwark against extremism. Encouragement of women's rights and proactive population programs support the effort. Tunisia reluctantly grants refuge to Algerians fleeing violence at home, but limits the numbers allowed to stay and work and the length of their stays, and keeps them under tight surveillance. Several Tunisians were taken into custody for alleged involvement with GIA in Europe.

In Morocco, King Hassan II claims descent from the Prophet Mohammed, a status that he publicly claims to inoculate his country from Islamist contagion. Several political parties, including the oldest, the Istiqlal, hold traditional Islamic views. A stronger consensus about Islamic values does give Morocco greater state cohesion than Algeria and may preempt some of the field in which militant Islamists might otherwise operate. Morocco, too, is working to create a market economy. Yet, its demographic growth rate is similar to Algeria's and it has a large underprivileged class, including many unemployed and underemployed youths. Clashes between Islamists and secularists have occurred on university campuses, as in Casablanca in March 1996. Shaykh Abdessalem Yassine, leader of the Islamist Justice and Charity Movement, was under house arrest without charge for six years and only released with continuing restrictions on his political speech in December 1995. It is not known if FIS has contacts with Shaykh Yassine, his followers, or other Moroccan Islamists. Morocco closed the Moroccan-Algerian border in reaction to cross border arms smuggling and the killing of two tourists in Marrakesh by French-Algerians in summer 1994. This further strained poor relations between the two neighbors and debilitated the already weak Arab Maghreb Union.[20]

---

[20]The two nations are rivals for regional power, have different governing systems, and their ties are marked by mutual suspicion and antagonism. In particular, the dispute over the Western Sahara region, formerly Spanish Sahara located to the south of Morocco, pits an Algerian protégé or surrogate, the Popular Front for the Liberation of Saqiat al Hamra and Rio de Oro (POLISARIO) against the Moroccan government. The Arab Maghreb Union, a framework intended to ease regional cooperation, was formed in 1989 by Algeria, Morocco, Tunisia, Mauritania, and Libya.

Western Europe

West European governments have been alarmed about the situation in Algeria for several years. Algeria was a French colony for over 120 years and its fight for independence was bloody. Subsequently, France and Algeria developed multifaceted, complex, and ambivalent ties. French cultural and political influence over the Algerian elite was profound. France provides Algeria with $1.2 billion in economic aid a year, an unacknowledged amount of military aid, and is its largest trading partner. Yet, because of colonial and revolutionary history, the Algerian-French relationship also is one of mutual suspicion and ease of offense.[21]

France is alarmed by the prospect of an Islamist Algeria as a potentially destabilizing force in the region. (It draws an analogy to U.S. concerns about Cuba). Even more, the French are fearful because over 4 million Muslims, including about 1 million Algerians, live in France and might be susceptible to Islamism. Perhaps 2 million are French citizens. The French envision being inundated by hundreds of thousands of Algerians who would flee an Islamist state and take scarce jobs. So far, hordes of Algerians have not streamed northwards despite four years of bloodshed because strict immigration laws pose an impediment and because they are unwilling or cannot afford the move. Some suggest that French fears have an underlying racist of Islamophobic basis but note that, whatever the sources of its policies, France appears to have decided that the root causes of Algeria's Islamism are economic and that reform is the answer. France has served as an advocate for Algeria with international financial institutions and the EU. Thus far, France has refused to condition its own aid to Algeria on political reforms or heed criticism that its own and international assistance would be diverted to security. In addition to continuing economic aid, France supplied defense articles such as helicopters, night vision equipment, and training to the Algerian army for counterterror operations. French officials claim that such aid was marginal and has ceased aside from the provision of spare parts.

Algeria's Islamists are repelled by their country's French connection and threaten it. GIA has targeted France and the French, demanding that France end its support for the Algerian military. Most foreigners killed or victimized in Algeria since 1992 have been French. The kidnapping of French monks is but the latest in a series of incidents. In December 1994, GIA terrorists hijacked an Air France airbus in Algiers with 240 people aboard, killing 3. The plane was allowed to fly to Marseilles, where French police commandos stormed it, killing four terrorists. Between July and October 1995, GIA was blamed for eight bombings in France, targeting civilians. (Again, some suggest that Algerian security forces may have been behind some of the attacks in order to stiffen France's anti-Islamist resolve or as an expression of Algerians' ambivalence toward a former master to whom they resent being beholden.) GIA has recruited among disaffected, unemployed Algerian youth in France.

As violent incidents became more frequent, the French government detained alleged instigators, imposed stringent security measures, deployed thousands of troops

---

[21]For example, presidential candidate Zeroual used his abrupt cancellation of a meeting with French President Jacques Chirac for refusing to have joint photographs taken in the midst during the campaign to enhance his popularity at home. Both sides were insulted by the non-event.

on the streets, and encouraged other Europeans and the United States to act against Islamists. Recognizing the limits of their influence on Algiers, French officials focused instead on preventing the Algerian turmoil from influencing French and European domestic security. Suspected GIA militants have been arrested in Belgium, Sweden, Denmark, Germany, the Netherlands, and Britain. After the airbus incident, French officials adopted a more neutral public policy posture toward Algeria, distancing themselves from internal developments, while calling for dialog and elections at all levels. They reiterated this view after the November 16 Algerian election.[22]

The possibility of explosive migration following an Islamist takeover in Algeria also concerns Spain and Italy, which like France have large Muslim populations and strong economic ties to Algeria, especially for hydrocarbons. The three northern Mediterranean neighbors tried to get their EU partners to focus on the crisis on their southern flank. The December 1994 EU Summit at Cannes pledged $6 billion in aid for North Africa over five years, and proposed creating a free trade area with it by 2010. Spain, France, and Italy instigated a landmark November 1995 conference in Barcelona between the 15 EU member states and 11 Mediterranean countries to enhance economic and security relations and mutually address problems. Follow-up or working meetings have been held, but concrete results are as yet not evident.

U.S. Policy

The United States has more emotional and geographic distance from the Algerian crisis than its European allies, and fewer high priority or direct national interests. Algeria does not receive U.S. foreign aid, except for a small military education program. But it has benefited from sizeable Export-Import Bank and Department of Agriculture credits over the years, particularly for foodstuffs. For 1996, the USDA is providing a $265 million credit line. U.S. companies are heavily involved in Algeria's hydrocarbon industry, although Algeria is not a major supplier of these resources to the United States.[23] The United States supported and participated in international efforts to reschedule Algeria's debts and encourages economic reform as a foundation for a political solution.

Since 1992, U.S. officials have strongly believed that a military solution would not end the conflict, but would radicalize the opposition. The Administration has condemned human rights violations by all sides, encouraged the regime to reach out to moderate members of the opposition and have a dialog with those who renounce violence, and labeled the Sant'Egidio document a good starting point. U.S. officials

---

[22]A recently published book, *The second Algerian War*, by a French civil servant writing under the pseudonym Lucile Provost, suggests that such neutrality masks continuing and unconditional French support for the Algerian military aimed at preventing an Islamist state.

[23]In 1995, the United States imported approximately 235,000 barrels of oil from Algeria compared to 1,344,000 from Saudi Arabia, and 18 billion cubic feet of gas from Algeria compared to 2,711 billion cubic feet from Canada. U.S. Department of Energy, Energy Information Administration. *Monthly Energy Review*, March 1996, pp. 49-50, 75.

never openly recommended a specific dialog partner for the Algerian government, and particularly never named FIS as the primary potential interlocutor. However, they carefully distinguished between FIS and GIA, talking to FIS representatives and calling GIA a terrorist group. According to many reports, lower level State and Defense Department officials met with Haddam and Kebir until 1995, probably to learn more about FIS and to explore opportunities for a political dialog between the Algerian government and Islamists. Those meetings were not acknowledged officially and are said to have ceased.

Reported U.S.-FIS contacts created concern in Paris and Algiers and complicated U.S.-French relations. The French perceived an ominous American difference in policy about a country whose affairs are vital to French interests. Some French even suspected the United States of aiding Algerian militants and seeking to supplant France in Algeria. They saw evidence of this alleged collusion in the fact that none of the estimated 500-600 Americans in Algeria have been terrorist victims. (This also can be attributed to the remoteness of American oil, gas, and construction sites and heavy security precautions wherever Americans are located.)[24] The French and Algerians detect a recent change in U.S. policy, seen as cooler to FIS and warmer to the government. Some Algerians speculate that the Oklahoma City bombing and the bombings in Paris heightened American appreciation of the threat of domestic terrorism and produced a policy change.

Yet, the overall thrust of U.S. policy, advocating dialog and opposing force, has not changed.[25] It is the situation in Algeria that has evolved with the presidential election, and the State Department has responded positively to that change. Assistant Secretary of State for Near Eastern and south Asian Affairs Robert Pelletreau stated that the United States considered "the impressive turnout for the Algerian presidential election an important and positive development," signaling "the strong desire of the Algerian people for a peaceful resolution to the crisis." He said that "an opportunity now exists to move forward with a process of national reconciliation. The United States supports dialog among all Algerians who renounce violence as part of such a process." He added, "It is now clear that force alone cannot resolve the crisis in Algeria." Pelletreau affirmed that Zeroual's selection had reinforced his authority and given him greater legitimacy.[26]

Recently, the United States and Algeria appeared to find more common ground in the international fight against terrorism. Algerian Foreign Minister Ahmed Attaf participated in the "Summit of Peacemakers convened by President Clinton in March 1996 in Egypt to mobilize international outrage against Palestinian Islamist terrorist bombings that threatened the Arab-Israeli peace process. Attaf's speech drew a picture of the treat to encompass Algeria's own Islamist menace.

---

[24]GIA was probably responsible for setting fire to a U.S. Embassy warehouse on November 9 and threatening the life of an Algerian security guard because he was working for the United States. U.S. Department of State. *Patterns of Global Terrorism 1996*, ;. 17.

[25]In fact, since the airbus incident, France's public posture has moved toward that of the United States.

[26]Reuters, Pelletreau News Conference, December 5, 1995.

Shortly after the summit, Pelletreau became the first senior U.S. official since 1992 to visit Algiers, where he declared himself impressed by Zeroual's "commitment to national reconciliation through dialog and enlarging the political process through legislative and municipal elections."[27] On April 16, 196, testimony before the Senate Foreign Relations Committee, Pelletreau expressed "cautious optimism" about developments in Algeria, but also pressured Algeria to adopt a more democratic course in the coming parliamentary elections. He said that political parties should be free to hold meetings and campaign and the press should be able to operate without intimidation from extremists or censorship by the government. Early on, he noted that a high level of violence is still occurring, including 14 car bombs since the beginning of the year.

U.S. officials often have expressed concern about possible spillover of Algeria's strife to its neighbors and seek to contain radical Islamism by enhancing the stability of surrounding countries. They sometimes define U.S. national interest in the Algerian crisis in terms of regional stability or effects on others in North Africa (Morocco, Tunisia, and Egypt) and on Western Europe. The United States has stronger ties with all of the others, and sees Egypt, Morocco, and Tunisia -- all recipients of U.S. aid -- as moderate Arab states with important roles to play in the Arab-Israeli peace process. Islamist regimes would be unlikely to be similarly constructive.

Outlook

Many pending questions concerning Algeria may find answers in the next months or year. Until the 1995 presidential elections, obstacles to beginning a resolution included the inability or unwillingness of the major opponents to talk meaningfully to each other, to compromise,[28] and to make binding decisions required to reach an accord. Although the military did not splinter, it appeared divided between eradicators and conciliators, while Islamists split between politicians and militants. Neither side had control over all of its components. The election provided President Zeroual with more legitimacy, enabling him to speak more authoritatively for the government. Yet, Zeroual's definition of national reconciliation as a policy is limited. Even if he wanted to negotiate with FIS, and that is doubtful, he still may not be able to outmaneuver the eradicators. At the same time, the Islamists are splintered, with the eradicators. At the same time, the Islamists are splintered, with the FIS/AIS/GIA unable to unite. It is uncertain if FIS factions that are more willing to reconcile with the regime still represent the Islamist movement. The HAMAS factor complicates assessments of the Islamists. Its success in the presidential election could transform HAMAS into a more credible Islamist representative or taint it as a collaborator of an essentially unchanged regime.

---

[27]Reuters, March 20, 1996.

[28]Some observers suggest that Algerians have a national character flaw, evinced during the long war of independence, that is an inherent inability to compromise. Others might suggest that Sant'Egidio is evidence of the fallacy of such observations.

It also remains to be seen if the regime is sincerely ready to experiment with modest but real democratization. Zeroual, although regarded as honest, is also seen as the product of a corrupt elite whose vested interests lie in the status quo and who want neither power sharing nor dramatic political and economic reform. Many would probably prefer an unattainable status quo ante 1988 in which their positions and lucre were more predictably secure. Zeroual would have to separate from entrenched forces in order to take initiatives for real change. It is doubtful that status quo forces would permit him to do so and to survive. Those forces, however, need not fear Zeroual's methods. He is clearly a very deliberate man who might be better able to manage a more incremental and organized advance toward democracy than Chadli Bendjedid's rapid leap in that direction. In this regard, his controlling style might benefit his country. Zeroual has indicated that he wants parliamentary and local elections and the current bilateral dialogues may start the process. Parliamentary elections could lead to more representative government. Yet if Zeroual continues to ban FIS, then a significant segment of Algerians may still be denied their democratic choice.

On the other side, Sant'Egidio notwithstanding, past statements by FIS leaders validate questions about their commitment to democracy, which they appeared to disdain. Some, such as Anouar Haddam, have voiced only equivocal denunciations of violence. Others, perhaps the FIS mainstream, however, have repudiated such voices. With a likely new electoral law governing parliamentary elections, the number of seats that FIS could win might more accurately reflect its estimated 24% of popular following than the December 1991 election result produced by a flawed law. With an accurate system of representation, a legal FIS would probably not dominate the legislature and would have to cooperate and compromise with other parties in order to effectuate change. A FIS presence in parliament would symbolize real democratization in Algeria.

FIS parliamentary participation could provide the substance of democracy without necessarily bringing about an end to violence because FIS plainly cannot control GIA. Having let the genie out of the bottle when it canceled the 1992 election process, the Algerian military is likely to face varying levels of Islamist terrorist violence for some time to come. Neither the army nor the Islamists is likely to see complete victory.

While most observers agree that the possibility of an Algerian Islamist state has diminished, a worst case analysis could depict a FIS-dominated government spreading anti-Western propaganda and instability. Yet, a FIS government would not necessarily destabilize the region. Algerians are what the French call *auto-centriste*, self-centered, or strongly nationalistic. The FIS, like its military nemesis, appears to be strongly nationalistic.[29]

---

[29]This may be a reason that outside intermediaries my not have been appropriate for the all Algerian dispute between the FIS and the regime.

Selected Acronyms

AIS   Islamic Salvation Army
FFS   Socialist Forces Front (Front des Forces Socialistes)
FIS   Islamic Salvation Front (Front Islamique du Salut)
FLN   National Liberation Front (Front de Liberation Nationale)
GIA   Armed Islamic Group
HAMAS   Movement for an Islamic Society
HCE   High Council of State (Haut Conseil d'État)
MIA   Armed Islamic Movement
RCD   Rally for Culture and Democracy

Iran and Iraq:
Analysis and Chronology of Weapons Programs[*]
Kenneth Katzman

Introduction

The Clinton Administration came into office apparently determined to prevent crises in the Persian Gulf like those that had confronted previous administrations. In May 1993, it articulated a policy of "dual containment" of Iran and Iraq, under which the United States would seek to weaken and isolate both Gulf powers rather than play them off against each other. The pillars of the dual containment policy have been enforcement of comprehensive U.N. sanctions on Iraq, in place since the Persian Gulf crisis; and stepped up U.S. efforts to persuade its allies to deny Iran aid, investment, credits, and sales of advanced conventional arms or dual use technology.

The Clinton Administration has pressured Iraq by insisting that comprehensive U.N. sanctions be maintained until Iraq complies fully with all relevant U.N. Security Council resolutions that spelled out Iraq's obligations following the 1991 Persian Gulf war. The U.N. sanctions on Iraq included the formation of a special U.N. commission (UNSCOM) that worked in Iraq to uncover all weapons of mass destruction (WMD) programs and to prevent their restart.[1] All U.N. member states were banned from exporting arms to Iraq, and Iraq was prohibited from selling its oil until UNSCOM certifies that all Iraqi WMD programs have been uncovered and cannot be restarted.

As part of the dual containment strategy, the Administration sought to persuade its allies and other countries not to arm Iran, sell it militarily useful technology, or provide credits or investment in Iran's economy. However, the Administration did not initially impose major new sanctions on Iran and said it did not seek to ban all trade with Iran, or even prevent all arms sales to that country -- only those arms sales that were destabilizing. However, two years later, responding to intelligence reporting of Iranian support for radical Islamic groups opposed to the Arab-Israeli peace process and of Iranian attempts to acquire nuclear materials, the Clinton

---

[*]Excerpted from *CRS Report 96-57 F.*

[1]For further discussion of UNSCOM activities in Iraq, U.N. sanctions in force, and the requirements for the lifting of sanctions, see CRS Issue Brief 92117, *Iraqi Compliance With Cease-Fire Agreements,* by Kenneth Katzman. Updated regularly.

Administration hardened policy toward Iran further. On May 6, 1995, the Administration imposed a total ban on U.S. trade and investment with Iran, and called on its allies to follow suit.[2]

Iraq: Work Still To Be Done

Since 1991, inspectors from the U.N. Special Commission on Iraq (UNSCOM), established in U.N. Security Council Resolution 687 (April 8, 1991) and the International Atomic Energy Agency (IAEA) have been working to uncover all aspects of Iraq's WMD programs, including its foreign suppliers.[3] Conventional arms sales to Iraq are banned, but there is no mandated dismantlement of Iraq's existing conventional weapons inventory. UNSCOM/IAEA access to information and Iraqi WMD facilities has improved significantly since June 1993, when Iraq tried to limit the access of weapons inspectors. The United States and its allies strongly supported the inspectors' assertions of their rights and privileges in Iraq, and Iraq backed down. In November 1993, Iraq accepted Security Council Resolution 715, which provides for a long term monitoring program in Iraq to ensure that it does not restart its WMD programs. By June 1995, despite U.S. suspicions that Iraq was holding back information on its WMD programs, UNSCOM and IAEA reports suggested they were close to completing their mission in Iraq. UNSCOM's primary outstanding concern was in the field of biological weapons, where major questions remained.

In August 1995, Saddam's son-in-law, Husayn Kamil al-Majid, who had headed Iraq's WMD programs since 1986, defected to Jordan and threatened to reveal information to UNSCOM that Iraq had been withholding. He claimed that he defected because Iraq was not moving quickly enough to comply with all relevant U.N. resolutions, and thereby forestalling the lifting of sanctions that are hurting the Iraqi people. The defection apparently shook the regime politically (Saddam's two eldest daughters fled with their husbands) and prompted Iraq to reveal significant new information about its past WMD programs, especially the biological program. UNSCOM and IAEA officials are still evaluating the thousands of documents turned over and say that verification of the new information might take several months. The new revelations suggest that Iraq's past WMD programs were more advanced than UNSCOM and IAEA had believed, based on their first four years of work in Iraq, including over 130 total inspection visits.

The new revelations have not resolved some of the debates among experts about Iraq's capabilities. UNSCOM and IAEA do not believe Iraq has completely declared relevant information about its past programs. Continued uncertainty -- coupled with

---

[2]For a further discussion of U.S. policy toward Iran, U.S. sanctions, and pending sanctions legislation, see CRS Issue Brief 93003, *Iran: Current Developments and U.S. Policy*, by Kenneth Katzman. Updated regularly.

[3]Security Council Resolution 707 requires Iraq to reveal the foreign suppliers of its WMD technology. To protect its ability to gather information, as well as the privacy of foreign persons or companies that helped Iraq, UNSCOM and IAEA have been hesitant to release information on Iraq's foreign supply networks.

recent revelations that Iraq had been procuring components for and conducting research on prohibited programs since sanctions were imposed -- is likely to delay UNSCOM's certification to the Security Council that it has completed its work in Iraq.[4] Such a certification now appears unlikely in 1996. Even if UNSCOM makes such a certificate in the near future, the United States and others on the Security Council believe that Iraq's longtime withholding of the information indicates that it cannot be trusted sufficiently for U.N. economic sanctions to be eased.[5] Others on the Council, such as France and Russia, appear to believe that the new revelations represent a positive step by Iraq that brings UNSCOM and IAEA to a fuller understanding of Iraq's past WMD programs. They can be expected to support an easing of the sanctions if and when UNSCOM says it has accomplished its mission.[6]

All members of the Security council, as well as U.S. allies in the Persian Gulf, are concerned about hardships of the sanctions on the Iraqi people. In April 1995, to provide for additional humanitarian aid to Iraq, the Council passed a Resolution 986, intended to induce Iraq to participate in a temporary, U.N.-monitored sale of oil. The new oil sale plan significantly modified a 1991 temporary oil sale plan, outlined in resolutions 706 and 712, to take some Iraqi concerns into account. Iraq has thus far rejected the new plan as an unacceptable infringement on its sovereignty, as it did the previous plan. Nonetheless, the United Nations, France, Russia, and some Gulf states have urged Iraq to accept the new plan and it 'might do so if it believes that the full ban on oil sales will not be lifted any time soon.

Iran: Proliferation Threat Under Growing Pressure

In the aftermath of the 1991 Persian Gulf war, Iran appeared to benefit significantly as war damage and comprehensive U.N. sanctions eroded the military capability of its chief Gulf rival, Iraq. With no similar worldwide sanctions in place against it, Iran was able to freely export oil and other commodities, generating enough hard currency to fund about $2 billion per year in arms acquisitions during 1990-93, according to U.S. intelligence officials. The United States and its close allies remained sufficiently concerned about Iranian capabilities and intentions to refuse to sell Iran arms, but Iran was able to find other willing arms and technology suppliers less amenable to U.S. pressure. Iran turned primarily to Russia, China, and North Korea as willing suppliers of conventional arms, nuclear technology, ballistic missiles, and assistance in building a chemical weapons and missile production infrastructure.

---

[4]*U.N. Maintains Iraqi Sanctions at Regular Review.* Reuters, January 5, 1996.

[5]The recent revelations led the six Gulf Cooperation Council countries (Saudi Arabia, Kuwait, UAE, Qatar, Bahrain, and Oman), at their sixteenth annual summit in Muscat (December 4-6, 1995) to strongly denounce Iraq for deceiving UNSCOM and continuing to threaten the region. The final communique of the summit (attended by the author) also identified proliferation as a key threat to the Gulf region, referring primarily to Iraq but also hinting strongly about a potential WMD threat from Iran.

[6]*U.N. Maintains Iraqi Sanctions at Regular Review.* Reuters, January 5, 1996.
n

Iran has also sought and sometimes concluded arms deals with former Soviet republics, including Ukraine and Belarus, and former Soviet bloc countries, including Poland and the Czech republic.

The Clinton Administration was concerned in late 1994 by reports that Iran had accelerated its attempts to procure fissile material or other WMD technology. Central Asia appeared to be a major focus of Iran's procurement network, largely because Iran believed it could appeal to the Central Asian states as Muslims and because security of nuclear materials there was perceived as lax. Some observers fear Iran, following patterns established by Iraq and Pakistan, might be using its intelligence operatives of agents of its parastatal conglomerate, the Foundation for the Oppressed, to try to obtain advanced technology in Europe. The Foundation is headed by Mohsen RafiqDust, formerly the Minister and de-facto chief procurement officer for the Revolutionary Guard. It is, in part, RafiqDust's background that has made observers suspect that he is using his new role, and the large amount of funds under his control, to procure advanced technology for the Guard. According to observers in Dubai, interviewed by the author during a December 1995 visit there, the Foundation has a substantial presence in the emirate, from which it procures mostly consumer goods. (Dubai is believed to be a major center for the re-export of U.S. goods, including computers and computer chips, to Iran, although such re-export technically is banned by the May 6, 1995 Executive order.[8])

The reports of stepped-up Iranian procurement activity were followed, in early January 1995, by Israeli assessments that Iran might be closer to a nuclear weapons capability than previously thought, and, on January 8, 1995, by the signature of a Russian-Iranian contract to provide nuclear power reactors to Iran. These developments prompted U.S. officials to publicly focus on the Iranian threat. Although U.S. officials did not endorse the Israeli characterizations of Iran's nuclear progress, Secretary of State Christopher said, in congressional testimony and elsewhere, that Iran was engaged in a "crash program" to acquire a nuclear weapon. At the same time, U.S. military officials began publicly warning of an Iranian buildup of conventional forces, including anti-ship missiles, on islands in the Persian Gulf, some of which are fully or partially occupied by Iran but subjects of sovereignty disputes with the United Arab Emirates.[9] On March 22, 1995, Secretary of Defense Perry, during a visit to the Persian Gulf, said Iran had placed chemical weapons on one of the islands. On the other had, analysts were reporting that lower-than-expected oil prices had begun to slow Iran's conventional arms acquisitions.[10]

---

[8]U.S. officials in Dubai told CRS during a December 1995 visit there that the Bureau of Export Administration and the Customs Service were at various stages of considering setting up programs in Dubai to monitor and/or prevent the reexport of U.S. good to Iran. For further information on the effects of the U.S. trade ban on Iran, see CRS Report 95-909 F, *Iran: U.S. Trade Ban and Legislation*, by Kenneth Katzman. Updated January 4, 1996.

[9]For further information on the Iranian buildup and its implications, see CRS Report 95-572 ENR, *Iranian Military Buildup: What Sort of Threat to Persian Gulf Oil Supply?* by Lawrence Kumins and Kenneth Katzman. May 1, 1995.

[10]CRS Report 95-862 F, *Conventional Arms Transfers to Developing Nations, 1987-1994*, by Richard Grimmett. August 4, 1995.

Mounting concerns over Iran's weapons programs and its reputed involvement in acts of terrorism against the Arab-Israeli peace process prompted calls in Congress for tighter sanctions on Iran and on countries and companies that provided advanced technology to Iran or invested in Iran's economy. The Administration agreed that policy toward Iran needed to be hardened but preferred to act diplomatically and multilaterally rather than through further sanctions, especially secondary sanctions on countries or companies that dealt with Iran. However, in April 1995, the Administration concluded a review of policy toward Iran that found that continued U.S. trade with Iran was undermining U.S. efforts to persuade its allies and other countries to help isolate Iran. Japan and the European Union countries, in particular, had been critical of the United States for conducting high volumes of trade[11] with Iran even as it tried to isolate Iran. On April 30, 1995, the Administration announced a total trade and investment ban on Iran.

Although no major trading partners of Iran joined the ban outright, the Administration appeared to derive some benefits from imposing the new sanctions. At a May 10-11, 1995 Clinton-Yeltsin summit, the Administration strongly pressed Russia to abandon its nuclear reactor contract with Iran. It did not do so, but it agreed to ensure that the contract would be limited to prevent the transfer of any skills or technology that could help Iran develop a nuclear weapon. That summit also resulted in final agreement for Russia not to sign any new arms contracts with Iran, although existing contracts could be fulfilled. A similar agreement was later reached with Poland. In September 1995, the United States and 27 other countries reached agreement (formal agreement was reached in December 1995) on an export control regime to succeed COCOM (Coordinating Committee on Multilateral Export Controls) that would bar regime member states from exporting sophisticated weapons or dual use technology to Iran (and Iraq, Libya, and North Korea). In December 1995, amid reports that European companies were moving to invest in Iran's oil industry, the Administration backed a compromise version of legislation (S.1228) to mandate that the President impose at least one of several sanctions against foreign companies that invest in Iranian Petroleum resources.

---

[11]In 1994, the last full year during which U.S. trade with Iran was permitted, foreign affiliates of U.S. companies bought about $4.3 billion in Iranian oil for trade overseas (importation has been banned since 1987.) U.S. firms were therefore among Iran's largest oil customers.

Iraq Chronology[12]

NUCLEAR PROGRAM

06/21/93 ---   An IAEA report to the Security Council indicated that the agency had significant doubts about Iraq's nuclear material declarations. The IAEA indicated that Iraq had misrepresented the origins of some of its uranium, and that Iraq might have been processing a greater amount of its own uranium -- as opposed to foreign supplied uranium -- than Iraq had previously declared. (If that were the case, it would indicate that Iraq had violated its nuclear materials safeguard agreements to a greater degree than previously believed.)

11/07/93 ---   The head of an IAEA Iraq inspection team said Iraq had revealed the country or persons that helped it develop a centrifuge needed to enrich uranium. The team declined to publicly name those who assisted Iraq. (UNSCOM and the IAEA have refused to name Iraq's suppliers because they believe doing so will discourage further supplier cooperation with their efforts to uncover all aspects of Iraq's WMD programs.)

01/14/94 ---   An IAEA report to the Security Council said Iraq had identified an individual as its agent for the procurement of maraging steel used in its nuclear program. One hundred tons of the special steel was shipped to Iraq in two consignments from a northern European port. The report added that Iraq had obtained outside help, including detailed drawings of assemblies and components, to develop nuclear-related centrifuges. The drawings greatly accelerated the Iraqi program, according to the IAEA.

01/25/94 ---   Director of Central Intelligence James Woolsey testified before the Senate Intelligence committee that the U.S. intelligence community had helped foil a delivery to Iraq of a chemical used in nuclear materials processing and in nerve agents.

07/29/94 ---   The *Washington Times* reported that German investigators were trying to track down five Iraqis suspected of trying to purchase a shipment of Russian weapons-grade plutonium. 1.7 ounces of the plutonium, which was believed smuggled out of Russia, were intercepted by German police on May 10, 1994.

---

[12]The following chronology discusses revelations by UNSCOM, IAEA, and other sources, about the weapons capabilities and technology transfers to Iraq since 1993. Because Iraq is subject to systematic and rigorous UNSCOM inspections, each of the four major WMD caegories (ballistic missiles, nuclear, biological, and chemical) are differentiated. IAEA and UNSCOM reports to the Security Council may be obtained from UNSCOM headquarters in New York. Although Iraq's conventional forces are believed to be close to 50% of their pre-Persian Gulf war strength, there do not appear to have been any major shipments to Iraq of conventional weapons since U.N. sanctions against such shipments were imposed in 1991.

10/10/94 ---   In a report to the Security Council, the IAEA said it had resolved two procurement issues with Iraq: (1) the amount of natural uranium oxide Iraq had purchased from Brazil, and (2) the amount and origin of Maraging steel, used to produce nuclear related centrifuges. The latter was obtained from a United Kingdom-based intermediary.

10/22/94 ---   The IAEA reported to the Security Council that Iraq, contrary to previous declarations, had now admitted experimenting with laser isotope separation (LIS) as a means of enriching uranium. The IAEA report added that Iraq had not made substantial progress on this project, partly because several foreign equipment suppliers had refused to supply Iraq with critical technologies, most notably a copper vapor laser system.

12/--/94 --- *The Middle East*, a magazine of Middle Eastern affairs, reported that a subsidiary of Austria's state-owned Voest-Alpine group supplied 100 tons of maraging steel to Iraq prior to Iraq's 1990 invasion of Kuwait. Iraq apparently was to use the steel to make centrifuges for enriching uranium. Iraq reportedly purchased the steel through a middleman in the United Kingdom.

12/22/94 ---   The IAEA reported to the Security Council that, with the assistance of Brazilian authorities, it had verified information provided by Iraq on the amount of natural uranium oxide of Brazilian origin exported to Iraq.

04/11/95 ---   In a report to the Security Council, the IAEA said it was confident that the essential components of Iraq's clandestine nuclear program have been identified and destroyed or rendered harmless, and that the scope of Iraq's past nuclear program is well understood. The IAEA based this assessment on its inspections, on Iraqi documents, and on information from Iraq's suppliers and other U.N. member states.

07/24/95 ---   According to press reports, the IAEA said there was no evidence to support allegations by a defector that Iraq was covertly continuing to conduct theoretical computer-based programs on nuclear weapons designs.

08/30/95 ---   The *New York Times* reported that IAEA and outside experts disagree over the pre-war status of Iraq's nuclear program. IAEA experts said Iraq lacked both the fissile material and sufficient knowledge of nuclear weapons design to build a bomb by Iraq's target date of April 1991. One outside expert believed Iraq could have acquired nuclear weapons material by that time but could not have constructed a workable explosive device. Another outside expert believed that Iraq probably could have constructed a bomb once it had produced the necessary fissile material. (See also below).

09/21/95 ---   Defector Husayn Kamil al-Majid, Saddam's son-in-law and WMD organizer, told Cable News Network that, at the time of the Persian Gulf war, Iraqi scientists were trying to make small (300 kg - 500 kg) nuclear warheads that could be carried on missiles or combat aircraft. Such warheads would have required more sophisticated design information than that found in possession of Iraqi nuclear scientists.

10/06/95 ---   In a report to the Security Council, the IAEA said Iraqi officials had revealed that Iraq launched a rash program in September 1990 (one month after the invasion of Kuwait) to extract and further enrich the highly enriched uranium (HEU) contained in safeguarded research reactor fuel at Iraq's Tuwaitha nuclear site. Iraq was hoping to accelerate the availability of weapons-grade material for the fabrication of a nuclear device. (An August 26, 1995 *New York Times* report said there was no evidence of foreign complicity in the diversion plan). The success of the operation would have provided enough nuclear material for a bomb in a shorter time than would have been necessary under Iraq's covert program to enrich natural uranium. By January 1991, Iraq had built and tested equipment needed to carry out the nuclear material diversion. However, the material was never diverted because coalition air raids on Tuwaitha and other facilities made the project too difficult. The IAEA report said Iraq revealed that work on a nuclear explosive device at the Al Atheer and Tuwaitha facilities continued through mid-January 1991, when the air war began. Iraq's reported intention, had the war not intervened to derail the program, was to have a nuclear explosive device by April 1991.

10/19/95 ---   Reuters reported that UNSCOM and IAEA, based on information from unnamed sources, were looking into the possibility that Iraq had tried to develop a radiological weapon before the Gulf war. Such a weapon would involve scattering radioactive material but without causing a nuclear explosion. UNSCOM interprets relevant U.N. resolutions on Iraq as including radiological weapons in their discussions of nuclear weapons programs.

11/08/95 ---   According to the *Washington Post*, UNSCOM Chairman Rolf Ekeus said Iraq worked on a radiological weapon before the Persian Gulf war. He said that UNSCOM and IAEA would assess the significance of Iraq's past radiological weapons program.

12/20/95 ---   According to a Reuters report, the IAEA said that, as a result of its examination of Iraqi documents handed over since August 1995, previously undeclared nuclear materials might have been salvaged by Iraq after the Persian Gulf war and remain in Iraq. These materials would need to be located and destroyed or removed.

12/21/95 ---   Presenting the December 17, 1995 UNSCOM report, Ekeus told the Security Council that casings for radiological weapons were unaccounted for. He said that, in the late 1980s, three radiological bombs had been tested but that Iraq decided the radioactive material in the bombs did not travel far enough from the bomb craters to be a significant deterrent to enemy troops.

CHEMICAL WEAPONS

12/21/93 ---   UNSCOM reported to the Security Council that, during an inspection in July 1993, Iraq declared it had larger stocks than previously declared of a prototype chemical bomb.

01/25/94 ---   Director of Central Intelligence James Woolsey said the CIA had helped prevent a shipment of nerve agent to Iraq via Egypt.

04/22/94 ---   An UNSCOM report to the Security Council said that in October 1993 Iraq declared it had 13,221 tons of traceable imported precursor chemicals. In February 1994, it changed its declaration to 15,037 tons, and in March 1994, it amended its declaration again to 17,657 tons. It did not alter its declaration of produced agents, however (4,340.5 tons). UNSCOM noted, however, that Iraq had not provided documentary evidence to confirm any of these declarations.

10/26/94 ---   In a speech to the Washington Institute for Near East Policy, UNSCOM Chairman Rolf Ekeus said UNSCOM had obtained from Iraq over 800 letters of credit for past imports by Iraq. Of those, about 45 were determined to be imports for Iraq's chemical weapons program. He added that UNSCOM still lacked much information on Iraq's foreign suppliers.

11/04/95 ---   The *Washington Post* reported that Iraqi procurement records indicated that, prior to 1986, Iraq purchased most of its chemical weapons precursors from Western Europe and the United States. After 1986, India appeared to be the main supplier of those chemicals.

04/10/95 ---   In a report to the Security Council, UNSCOM said Iraq still had the capability to produce equipment used to manufacture chemical agents. However, Iraq is dependent on imports of corrosion-resistant metal alloys to do so. UNSCOM said it was unable to independently verify Iraqi claims that all the laboratory equipment it used in its chemical program was destroyed during the Gulf war.

06/19/95 ---   UNSCOM, in a report to the Security Council, said that it was confident it had a good overall picture of the extent of Iraq's past chemical weapons capabilities and that the essential elements of it had been destroyed.

10/11/95 ---   UNSCOM's report to the Security Council said that in August 1995 Iraq acknowledged a much larger and more advanced program than previously admitted for the production and storage of VX nerve agent. UNSCOM had not yet verified that all chemical agents and precursors have been destroyed. The report said that Iraq's declarations in the spring of 1995 regarding its VX stockpile had been clearly deceptive, and that Iraq had enough precursors to produce over 400 tons of VX agent. The report added that Iraq had admitted to three separate flight tests of chemical warheads on ballistic missile systems, and to having developed prototypes of sarin filled artillery shells, 122 mm rockets, and aerial bombs. It also admitted to having received significant foreign assistance in this program, including munitions designed to hold chemical agents, and technical support for indigenous production of VX.

12/17/95 ---   In a report to the Security Council, UNSCOM said Iraq had admitted to producing 1.8 tons of VX in 1988, and 1.5 additional tons in 1990. Previous Iraqi declarations had said it produced only 260 kilograms in 1988. The report said the Commission was still unable to confirm that stocks of VX, VX precursors, or related weapons do not remain in Iraq. The report added that UNSCOM monitors were continuing to find in Iraq non-declared equipment that could be used for chemical weapons production.

12/27/95 ---   Jordanian sources said they had seized "highly dangerous acids and chemicals" bound for Iraq. The chemical shipment, which violated U.N. sanctions on Iraq, was concealed in a consignment of drugs being exported to Iraq by a Jordanian firm. Medicines are exempt from the embargo against Iraq.

BIOLOGICAL WEAPONS

11/04/94 ---   According to the *Washington Post*, Iraq had been constructing a sophisticated pharmaceutical plant, containing foreign-made equipment, near the northern city of Nineveh. Iraq did not inform UNSCOM about the plant, which could have been used in a biological weapons program had UNSCOM not discovered it.

12/19/94 ---   According to Reuters, UNSCOM inspectors found in Iraq 55 pints of growth media for cholera and tuberculosis, not previously declared by Iraq. The find raised UNSCOM's suspicions about a wider biological program than previously believed.

02/16/95 ---   Columnist William Safire published an editorial in the *New York Times* asserting that Iraq was hiding biological agent production equipment (fermentors, mixing tanks) provided by the Italian company Olsa, and the Swiss company Chemak. The piece noted that an Iraqi facility in Daura, currently producing vaccines, could be rapidly converted to biological warfare agent production, if UNSCOM inspections ceased.

03/21/95 ---   The German Foreign Ministry said that, according to a briefing by UNSCOM Chairman Rolf Ekeus, Iraq might be using permitted imports of live vaccines to produce cultures and viruses which could be used for biological weapons.

04/10/95 ---   In its report to the Security Council, UNSCOM disputed Iraq's claim that its 1988 imports of complex growth media were used for hospital diagnostic purposes. According to UNSCOM, the quantities imported were too large

(39 tons) and of inappropriate size and packaging for hospital use. The report said UNSCOM had still not accounted for 17 of the 39 tons imported. Seventeen tons of growth media are sufficient to produce about one and a half tons of biological warfare agent. UNSCOM added that Iraq had still not provided satisfactory explanations for other biological-related imports, such as filling machines, a spray dryer, and various anthrax strains. Its biological construction activities also were cause for USNCOM concern, as the layouts and certain equipment in some biological facilities were inconsistent with civilian uses.

06/20/95 --- According to the *New York Times*, UNSCOM Chairman Rolf Ekeus told the Security council that the April 1995 assessment of Iraq's procurement of biological growth media was too low, and that Iraq had acquired components needed to make biological weapons. He did not say how much extra growth media was unaccounted for. Ekeus also reportedly said that Iraq had encountered a bottleneck in trying to build a weapon sophisticated enough to deliver biological agents.

07/01/95 --- Iraq made a brief oral presentation to UNSCOM Chairman Rolf Ekeus acknowledging that it had an offensive biological weapons program. Iraq denied that it had actually weaponized biological agents, and said it had destroyed all these agents by October 1990.

08/22/95 --- UNSCOM deputy Chairman Charles Duelfer said that Iraqi officials admitted to destroying their biological agent stockpiles after the Persian Gulf war, rather than in the fall of 1990, as Iraq had asserted previously.

09/04/95 --- UNSCOM Chairman Rolf Ekeus said Iraq had plenty of empty munitions as well as the components for biological weapons. They therefore retained the capability to produce new biological weapons. Ekeus said his Commission could prevent Iraq from restarting its biological weapons if given enough international support.

10/11/95 --- UNSCOM's report to the Security Council said that, on August 17, 1995, Iraq acknowledged that it had weaponized biological agents, had produced more agents, and had more biological sites (five, as opposed to previously declared one site) than admitted prior to the August 1995 defection of Husayn Kamil. Iraq had conducted tests of these agents on sheep, donkeys, monkeys, and dogs, in laboratories, inhalation chambers, and in the field. It had also been researching fungus-based mycotoxins, plant pathogens, ricin, bacteria that attack wheat crops, and viruses. According to the report, weaponization began in December 1990, four months after the invasion of Kuwait, as Iraq intensified its biological program. After experimenting unsuccessfully with self-propelled drone delivery vehicles, 100 bombs were filled with botulinum, 50 with anthrax, and 16 with aflatoxin. Twenty-five Scud-variant missiles were filled with those agents as well. These weapons were deployed in early January 1991 at four locations, but were not used during the Gulf war and, according to Iraq, ordered destroyed in May or June 1991. UNSCOM has not yet confirmed Iraq's declarations that all biological agents have been destroyed.

12/21/95 --- In briefing UNSCOM's December 17, 1995 report to the Security Council, Ekeus said Iraq was still failing to provide definite figures on amounts of biological weapons agents and munitions produced, weaponized, and destroyed, and that the Commission had no evidence that biological missile warheads had been destroyed. He said UNSCOM's "working proposition" was that some warheads must still remain in Iraq. The December 17 report said that UNSCOM had begun to identify what biological equipment, material, and facilities should be subject to the long term monitoring regime.

BALLISTIC MISSILES

01/27/93 --- According to the *Washington Post*, UNSCOM sources had disclosed that Iraq had concentrated virtually all its top rocket scientists and engineers at a large research facility (Ibn al-Haythim) outside Baghdad. UNSCOM said it would monitor the facility continuously to ensure that no work was conducted on prohibited missile systems (ballistic missiles of ranges greater than 150 km). The inspectors said that Iraq was developing at the facility 6 new types of short range ballistic missiles and cruise missiles. These programs are technically permitted under the relevant U.N. resolutions.

12/21/93 --- UNSCOM reported that, in November 1993, Iraq had launched some short range missiles during an army exercise. UNSCOM informed Iraq that it would require Iraq to inform it of such launches in the future.

12/30/93 --- The *Jerusalem Report* (a magazine of Israeli affairs) quoted a U.S. chemical weapons expert who served as an UNSCOM inspector as saying he helped supervise destruction of at least 16 Scud-type missiles modified to carry chemical weapons.

01/24/94 --- The German government announced that a German origin ship carrying a chemical used in solid rocket fuel had been intercepted on its way to Iraq. The ship was carrying cargo from China to the Middle East. Officials who searched the ship emphasized that there was no indication that Chinese authorities were responsible for or even aware of the shipment.

09/25/94 --- The *Washington Times* quoted the German newsmagazine *Der Spiegel* as saying a number of German companies might be helping Iraq work on a prohibited missile program. *Der Spiegel* quoted German customs officials as saying Iraqi, Iranian, and Libyan buyers were searching the German market for weapons of mass destruction technology.

12/15/94 --- In a report to the Security Council, UNSCOM said that, despite Iraqi misinformation, the Commission had firm evidence that Iraq possessed a high-precision instrumentation radar that was imported and used, in late 1990, to test missile systems now banned by Council resolutions. UNSCOM said it would destroy the radar system. (In its December 17, 1995 report to the Council, UNSCOM said Iraq admitted that the radar system was used for proscribed activities.)

03/11/95 ---   *Jane's Defence Weekly* reported that in April 1994 a team from Iraq's Military Industrialization Organization (MIO) traveled to Tunisia for secret meetings with executives from four French companies that previously exported to Iraq's military industries. The MIO team was believed to be seeking to purchase a large furnace, possibly for a missile plant. The report added that similar contacts are being reestablished with former Iraqi suppliers in Austria, Italy, and Russia.

04/10/95 ---   In a report to the Security Council, UNSCOM said Iraq had tried to develop a parachute recovery system for a Scud-variant missile warhead. A parachute system might be used to enable a missile to deliver biological warheads, which need to descend to the ground slowly in order to disperse their contents efficiently. Iraq approached at least three different foreign companies for the system but no systems were ever provided to Iraq. The report added that UNSCOM has information to suggest that Iraq experimented with UDH (unsymmetrical dimethyl hydrazine), a liquid fuel which can improve the performance of liquid-propellant rocket engines.

06/20/95 ---   UNSCOM said, in a report to the Security Council, that although uncertainties in its understanding of Iraq's missile programs remained, UNSCOM was sufficiently certain that Iraq's prohibited missile activities had been eliminated and its dual-purpose capabilities were being adequately monitored. The report added that responses to UNSCOM's requests for information from some former suppliers of Iraq would assist UNSCOM's efforts to close remaining gaps. The U.S. intelligence community maintains that Iraq might still be hiding 50 or more Scud-like missiles.

10/11/95 ---   In a report to the Security Council, UNSCOM said that Iraq had previously falsified the number of Scud-variant missiles it had destroyed unilaterally, in order to conceal its indigenous production of engines for Scud-type missiles. (It declared 89 missiles destroyed, but UNSCOM verified that only 83 were destroyed.) The engines were assembled from both imported and locally-produced parts, and were tested; three al-Husayn (Scud-variant) missiles were produced indigenously. Iraq also had presented to UNSCOM an incorrect accounting of missile warheads -- both imported and indigenously produced -- to hide its projects involving unconventional and separating warheads. The report added that UNSCOM had obtained information that Iraq had placed a number of orders, directly or through middlemen or front companies, for missile equipment and supplies. Iraq claimed the supplies were for permitted missile programs (less than 150 km range) but the import of such technology is nonetheless prohibited under U.N. sanctions. In an article on October 14, 1995, the *Washington Post* said the technology (accelerometers, gyroscopes, special metals and machine tools, and a furnace) was purchased from firms in Russia, Ukraine, France, and Germany. In addition, according to the

UNSCOM report, in August 1995 Iraq acknowledged, for the first time, work on advanced rocket engines, including those with increased thrust.

12/08/95 ---   Jordanian authorities announced that they had intercepted in Amman a shipment of 115 Russian-made missile guidance systems destined for Iraq. U.S. intelligence agencies reportedly aided the interception. The shipments suggested Iraq was clandestinely trying to develop ballistic missiles or prohibited ranges, in violation of U.N. resolutions. Russia denied providing the components and Iraq denied trying to import the parts.

12/21/95 ---   Briefing the Security Council and reporters on UNSCOM's December 17, 1995 report, Ekeus said Iraq had failed to account for dozens of Scud missile engines and other missile components. Ekeus showed the Council a missile guidance component that UNSCOM had retrieved from the Tigris Canal in Baghdad after Iraq apparently tried to dump the components in the water to avoid their discovery. The components were similar to those seized by Jordan earlier in the month (see above). According to the report, Iraq had indigenously produced 80 Scud-like missile engine subsystems, using some components procured after U.N. sanctions were imposed in 1991. Ten of these subsystems remain unaccounted for. Ekeus said that Iraq had recently admitted covertly trying to develop prohibited missiles and conducting a number of missile tests after sanctions were imposed.

OTHER WMD ISSUES

06/29/93 ---   A staff report by the Subcommittee on International Security, International Organizations, and Human Rights, of the House Foreign Affairs Committee said that Iraq had rebuilt many of the weapons plants damaged in the Persian Gulf war. Many of the facilities discussed in the report deal with conventional weapons production, not restricted by U.N. resolutions. The report discussed rebuilt WMD facilities, but stopped short of alleging that Iraq had actually restarted any of its banned WMD programs. The report added that Iraq was continuing to operate an extensive clandestine procurement network in Europe the Middle East, and possibly the United States. According to the report, the investigative arm of German customs is investigating more than 150 German and Iraqi-owned companies based on German territory for possible violations of U.N. sanctions. With the exception of the German subsidiary of Minolta, the report did not specify whether the named companies exported WMD related technology to Iraq; some of the companies cited apparently committed other breaches of the sanctions, or exported conventional weapons technology.

12/21/93 ---   UNSCOM reported that, for the first time, Iraq had submitted details on its foreign suppliers of critical WMD equipment and materials, including entities that provided technical advice. UNSCOM noted in its report that some of the imported items of concern to it and the IAEA did not require export licenses to be shipped or, where such licenses were required, Iraq had developed means to circumvent them. UNSCOM summarized routes of supply as follows: (1) direct from the manufacturer to Iraq, (2) via a middleman to Iraq, (3) via a third country, or (4) via a second company in the same country.

05/02/94 ---   In a *New York Times* editorial, William Safire named several companies that he said were identified to UNSCOM inspectors as suppliers of WMD technology to Iraq. According to the editorial, a French company, Imphy-Techpy, was among those that supplied Iraq maraging steel for its centrifuge programs. He reported that France's Robatel supplied plutonium extraction equipment, Calorstat helped Iraq with centifuge-making equipment, and the Société Nouvelle Exploitation advised Iraq on the handling of spent nuclear fuel. Two Swiss firms, Lasag and Alwo, allegedly supplied equipment for Iraq's centrifuges. He reported three Belgian companies (Trane, Belgonucleaire, and Sybetra), the Italina firm Snia Techint, the German firm Maschinefabrik J. Diffenbacher, and the British company Air Products, as suppliers of unspecified technology to Iraq. The report added that another Italian company, Nuovo Pignone, supplied gas-diffusing compressors to enrich uranium. In addition, according to the report, India's Transpek reportedly supplied precursor chemicals for chemical weapons. The companies named above are among many others that have been previously cited by press reports and books as WMD technology suppliers to Iraq. (In response to previous reports on supplier involvement in Iraq, some firms have denied involvement with Iraq and others have said they violated no laws, at the time, in exporting their technology to Iraq. Some, particularly German firms, have been investigated by their host governments to determine whether or not they broke any laws in their dealings with Iraq.)

09/26/94 ---   Director of Central Intelligence James Woolsey told the Washington Institute for Near East policy that Iraq was accelerating construction of deep underground shelters and tunnels to produce and store weapons of mass destruction. He added that Iraq has the largest pool of scientific and technical expertise in the Arab world -- over 7,000 nuclear scientists and engineers alone.

3/19/95 --- According to Reuters, Defense Secretary Perry showed satellite photos to Saudi defense officials showing that Iraq had rebuilt artillery production plants, chemical warfare facilities, and rocket engine plants, which were destroyed in the Persian Gulf war. Two days later, U.S. Ambassador to the United Nations Madeleine Albright showed U.S. senators aerial photos indicating that Iraq had rebuilt and expanded its Al Kindi missile research and development facility, and the main production building and chlorine plant at its Habbaniyah II chemical facility. Responding to the reports of the Perry tour of the Gulf and the Albright briefings, UNSCOM Chairman Ekeus said Iraq was using its rebuilt chemical facilities for legitimate purposes, including production of pesticides and chemicals for water purification.

09/21/95 ---   UNSCOM Chairman Rolf Ekeus said that Iraqi commanders in the Persian Gulf war had orders to launch chemical and biological weapons against enemy capitals and troops if Baghdad were hit by a nuclear weapon. He had previously said that Iraq had contemplated using these weapons, even absent a nuclear attack on Baghdad, but had been deterred by U.S. statements threatening retaliation.

Iran Chronology[13]

02/10/93 ---   According to the Jerusalem Israel Television Network, Iran recently took delivery from North Korea of some Scud-C surface-to-surface missiles (about 300 mile range), as well as a number of launchers.

02/17/93 ---   A U.S. naval intelligence official said Iran was negotiating with an unspecified source to purchase five minisubmarines, to augment the three Kilo class submarines it was purchasing from Russia.

04/08/93 ---   The *New York Times* reported that Iran was close to concluding a deal with North Korea to buy the Nodong 1 intermediate-range missile when it is ready for export. The Nodong I is believed to have a range of 600 miles, although an extended range version of the missile might be able to reach 800 miles, placing Israel within reach of western Iran.

05/11/93 ---   The *Washington Times* reported that Iran had taken delivery of eight supersonic, sea-skimming cruise missiles from Ukraine as part of a $1.5 billion barter arrangement between Iran, Russia, and Ukraine. The reported deal also included MiG-29 and other aircraft, more than 200 T-72 tanks, and S-300 air defense missile systems. (Ukraine subsequently said that its discussions with Iran were limited to military spare parts.)

08/0893 ---   Iran took delivery of its second Russian-made Kilo-class diesel submarine, out of an order for three of the subs. The first was delivered in November 1992, and each is said to cost about $450 million.

01/17/94 ---   *Defense News* reported that Iran was negotiating with China to purchase a rocket-propelled mine (the EM52) that is planted on the sea floor until it detects a target. The report added that Iran had purchased over 1,000 modern mines from Russia, including those that detect approaching ships with magnetic, acoustic, and pressure sensors. Four months later, *Jane's Defence Weekly* reported that Iran had bought an estimated 1,800 mines of various types from Russia in conjunction with its receipt of the first Kilo submarine in November 1992.

---

[13]In contrast with Iraq, Iran is not subject to any systematic international inspection regime, although IAEA officials, at Iran's invitation, have made visits to declared Iranian nuclear sites. It is therefore more difficult to obtain confirmed information about Iran's weapons and technology acquisitions, and suppliers, than in the case of Iraq. The chronology below is derived largely from press reports which, in some cases, quote U.S. or foreign intelligence agencies.

09/19/94 ---   According to U.S. Vice Admiral Douglas Katz, Iran recently received four or five Hegu class fast attack missile boats (FACM's) from China. The vessels are capable of being armed with C-801 and C-802 surface-to-surface missiles. Iran was said to want the more sophisticated C-802, but China was said to be offering the C-801.

09/2694 ---   Director of Central Intelligence James Woolsey said publicly that Iran had acquired MiG-29 and Su-24 combat aircraft, and T-72 tanks and two Kilo submarines from Russia. He added that Iran had turned to suppliers in "both East and West," using intermediaries, to purchase military technology clandestinely.

09/27/94 ---   On the eve of a U.S.-Russia summit at which Russian arms sales to Iran were to be discussed, a U.S. official told the *Washington Post* that Russia had sold Iran sophisticated aircraft missiles to go along with the combat aircraft Iran had bought.

12/14/94 ---   Reuters reported that Iran was trying to buy weapons technology in Germany for use in building Scud-like missiles. (Two months earlier, the International Institute for Strategic Studies said Iran had obtained additional Chinese-made CSS-8 surface-to-surface missiles, armed with conventional warheads, and according to the congressional testimony of Washington Institute analyst Michael Eisenstadt on November 9, 1995, Iran has 200 CSS-8's.)

01/08/95 ---   Russia and Iran signed a deal under which Russia would build up to four nuclear power reactors in Iran, including two at the Bushehr nuclear complex, several research reactors, and a nuclear water desalinization plant at the Bushehr site. Under the agreement, Russia's Ministry of Atomic Energy (MINATOM), would also provide a wide range of other nuclear services for Iran, including the training of Iranian nuclear engineers and technicians in Russia. If fully implemented, the deal could total as much as $8 billion, with the construction of the first reactor at Bushehr (begun in the 1970's by Siemens of Germany but not completed) worth about $800 million to $1 billion. The reactors are of the "light water" variety, which use low-enriched uranium fuel that lack explosive properties, and Russia has agreed to provide fuel for the reactors.

01/30/95 ---   The *Washington Times* reported that, according to German intelligence, Iran had secured the assistance of unnamed Indian companies in the construction of a chemical weapons complex. The report said the Indian firms had told authorities in Europe and elsewhere that they are building a pesticide factory outside Tehran.

03/02/95 ---   The Associated Press reported that Israel claimed Iran signed a contract with Argentina to buy fuel rods for reactors and was negotiating the purchase of heavy water, which is considered essential for a nuclear weapons program. The report did not make clear whether or not the United States or other authorities had succeeded in blocking the deal. (To date, there has been no corroboration of the report or confirmation of nuclear deals between Iran and Argentina.)

03/15/95 ---   The *New York Times* reported that Iran had developed a vast network in Europe, Russia, and Central Asian states to smuggle weapons parts and nuclear technology. Intelligence reports of Iranian technology buying efforts had prompted Secretary of State Christopher to testify before the House International Relations Committee on January 25, 1995 that Iran was engaged in a "crash program" to acquire nuclear weapons. He has not since deviated from that characterization. On the other hand, U.S. arms control officials have said that Iran is abiding by its obligations under the Nuclear Non-Proliferation Treaty (NPT) to which it is a party.

03/17/95 ---   Poland announced that it would honor any existing contracts to supply tanks to Iran. Poland did not reveal the details of its tank sale, however. (See below).

04/03/95 ---   The *New York Times* reported that the United States had provided intelligence to Russia about Iran's nuclear program, as part of an effort to dissuade Russia from providing nuclear technology to Iran. The intelligence reportedly showed that Iran was importing equipment needed to acquire nuclear weapons, that it had sought to enrich uranium from former Soviet republics such as Kazakhstan, and that it is using many of the same smuggling techniques and routes that Iraq and Pakistan used in their efforts to acquire nuclear technology.

04/13/95 ---   The *Los Angeles Times* reported that Iran was aggressively seeking new suppliers of conventional arms and technology. Iran reportedly has sought long-range artillery from South Africa, and tanks from Poland and Slovakia. U.S. officials reportedly said Iran's campaign to line up new arms deals had met with mixed success.

04/19/95 ---   At a press conference during his visit to India, Iran's President Ali Akbar Hashemi-Rafsanjani reportedly said, "So far, [Iran] has no plans to build atomic weapons...this type of weapon will have a devastating effect on humanity." A State Department spokesman said the Department had no indication that India has a nuclear relationship with Iran "along the lines of" that which existed between Russia and Iran or China and Iran.

04/28/95 ---   U.S. officials disclosed that, as part of its January 1995 nuclear deal with Iran, Russia had promised to provide Iran sophisticated gas centrifuge equipment that could be used to enrich uranium. U.S. officials strongly urged Russia to drop that provision of its nuclear deal with Iran and, at the May 10-11, 1995 Clinton-Yeltsin summit, Russia agreed not to provide the centrifuge. Russia apparently also agreed not to train Iranian nuclear scientists, an important U.S. concern. Despite U.S. efforts to dissuade it, Russia has gone ahead with a deal to provide Iran with three nuclear reactors and the training of Iranian scientists.

(According to press reports, as of November 1995, about 200 Russian technicians were at the Bushehr reactor site and relevant studies had been completed, paving the way for construction to begin.)

05/11/95 --- The two-day Clinton-Yeltsin summit ended with an agreement for Russia to end new conventional arms contracts with Iran, subject to final approval within the framework of the Gore-Chernomyrdin commission. Yeltsin also agreed to allow the commission to discuss Russia's nuclear deal with Iran to ensure that it does not provide Iran with any nuclear technology that could have military applications.

05/13/95 --- *Jane's Defence Weekly* reported that, according to the Central Intelligence Agency, North Korea had recently provided at least four transporter-erector-launchers for Scud missiles. According to the CIA, the transfer represented evidence of growing cooperation between Iran and North Korea on a broad range of ballistic missile issues.

04/14/95 --- Based on an interview with Iran's top civilian nuclear official, Reza Amrollahi, the *New York Times* reported that, within twenty years, Iran planned to obtain 20 percent of its energy from nuclear power. He acknowledged that doing so would entail the construction of about ten nuclear reactors. Amrollahi subsequently clarified his remarks by saying Iran had the capability to build ten nuclear plants, but it had no plans to do so.

05/18/95 --- The State Department announced that the United States had concluded an agreement with Poland under which that country would fulfill a contract with Iran for up to 100 T-72 tanks but not engage in any future conventional arms sales to the Islamic Republic. The Polish government had earlier confirmed that 34 of the tanks had already been delivered.
--- In the first of two articles, the *Washington Times* reported that China might have provided technical assistance to enable Iran to enrich uranium. The following day, the paper said European officials had broken up several attempts by Iran to acquire high-speed centrifuges needed to enrich uranium, but that Iran might have succeeded in acquiring some enriched uranium from Central Asian states.

05/19/95 --- A State Department spokesman said at a news conference that the United States was satisfied that none of its Group of Seven allies was engaged in any form of nuclear cooperation with Iran.

05/31/95 --- In a letter to the editor of the *Wall Street Journal*, France's Ambassador to the United States categorically denied the assertion of a May 4, 1995 editorial in that paper that France had sold Exocet missiles to Iran. The letter said that France had sued the magazine that had originally published that allegation.

06/22/95 --- The *New York Times* reported that a May 1995 CIA report to policymakers had concluded that China had recently delivered missile guidance systems and computerized machine tools to Iran. A subsequent report in *Jane's*

Defence Weekly said the shipments included rocket propellant ingredients as well. The CIA report said that the shipments could give Iran the ability to improve the accuracy of North Korean-supplied Scud missiles in Iran's inventory and enable it to produce missiles indigenously, with ranges and payload limits that exceed limits of the Missile Technology Control Regime (MTCR). Because China had not shipped entire missiles or complete missile systems to Iran, the Clinton Administration was divided over whether or not China had violated the MTCR and should therefore be subject to additional U.S. sanctions. (As of late November 1995, no U.S. determination of Chinese violation had been made.) Some experts contrasted the reported Chinese shipments with previous successful U.S. efforts to dissuade China from selling M-9 and M-11 missiles to Iran.

--- According to the Islamic Republic News Agency, Iran's President Ali Akbar Hashemi-Rafsanjani inaugurated the first section of a nuclear research center in East Azerbaijan province. The facility will enable Iran to experiment with preserving fresh fruit and vegetables by irradiation. The announcement said the next phase of the project would be devoted in part to the production of lasers for scientific applications. In January 1995, Rafsanjani opened a cyclotron accelerator at a nuclear medical center in Karaj.

07/06/95 -- The *Iran Brief*, a newsletter of Iranian affairs, reported that Chinese companies had been caught shipping chemical weapons precursors, production equipment, and protection gear to Iran, directly and through front companies. In March 1995, the State Department identified three companies in Hong Kong -- Asian Ways Limited, WorldCo Limited, and Mainway International -- allegedly engaged in this activity. A March 10, 1995 entry in the *Federal Register* (p. 13201) indicated that the United States had imposed sanctions against these companies for engaging in chemical weapons proliferation activities, but did not specify to which country the companies had exported.

07/14/95 -- A report by the U.S. Arms Control and Disarmament Agency said that Iran had weaponized a small quantity of biological agents. Weaponization was thought to be a critical bottleneck in Iran's biological weapons program.

07/21/95 --- The *Journal of Commerce* reported that the United States was investigating a July 14, 1995 arms agreement between Iran and Balarus. The relationship was reported to include consultations between Iran and Belarus on some "technological processes," possibly indicating nuclear technology. Belarus officials had said Iran was seeking from the former Soviet republic missile transport vehicles and optical equipment for its Soviet made aircraft. U.S. officials reportedly feared that Russia might use the Belarus-Iran pact to export goods to Iran in violation of U.S.-Russia understandings on Russian conventional sales to Iran and nuclear cooperation.

08/21/95 --- According to Reuters, South Africa's Foreign Minister said his country would cooperate with Iran on peaceful nuclear technology but would not help Iran develop nuclear arms.

08/24/95 ---   Russian Atomic Energy Minister Viktor Mikhailov said Russia had signed an agreement with Iran to supply nuclear fuel, for ten years, for the reactors it is building in southern Iran. The deal requires Iran to return spent reactor fuel to Russia. The used reactor fuel, in the form of plutonium-laden fuel rods, could provide the fissile material needed for Iran to develop a nuclear weapons capability.

08/26/95 ---   *Jane's Defence Weekly* reported that Iran claimed to have developed air-to-air refuelling systems for its Russian-made MiG-29 aircraft. The report said Iran had previously made "extravagant" claims for indigenous weapons production, but noted that Iran had operated Boeing 707 tankers during the Shah's regime.

09/00/95 ---   *Jane's Intelligence Review* reported that Iranian Navy commander Ali Shamkhani's October 1994 visit to India included talks on the possibility of India servicing Iran's two Russian-made Kilo class submarines. According to the report, Iran also asked India to help upgrade its military communications and to provide T-72 tanks, which India produces under Russian license.

09/05/95 ---   The head of construction for Russia's Atomic Energy Ministry said work had begun on the Bushehr reactor in Iran, the first of three reactors Russia will build in Iran under two contracts signed with the country in 1995.

09/14/95 ---   Assistant Secretary of State for South Asian Affairs Robin Raphel testified before the Senate Foreign Relations committee that the State Department was not aware of any Pakistani assistance to Iran's nuclear program or significant Indian contacts with Iran's military. Deputy Assistant Secretary of Defense Bruce Reidel said the Defense Department believed Iran sought Indian assistance in maintaining its Kilo class submarines, but could not confirm that India had agreed to do so. At the hearing, Senator Larry Pressler said that Iran and Pakistan had reportedly been cooperating on nuclear weapons research for a decade, and that they have been engaged in cooperative military efforts, including joint naval maneuvers.

09/25/95 ---   The *Washington Times* reprinted an article from the London Sunday Telegraph alleging that Chinese technicians had constructed a calutron system for enriching uranium at Iran's Karaj nuclear facility. The article did not provide corroborating evidence for its allegations, citing only "exclusive information acquired by the Sunday Telegraph." U.S. officials did not subsequently mention or corroborate the report.

09/27/95 ---   According to U.S. officials, Chinese Foreign Minister Qian Qichen told Secretary of State Warren Christopher that China would not pursue a tentative deal to sell Iran two 300-megawatt nuclear reactors. Some attributed the development to Iran's inability to pay for the reactors, its preference for pursuing its broader nuclear deal with Russia, or China's apparent inability to supply critical components for the reactors. Others believed China dropped the deal in order to improve relations with the United States. In meetings with Chinese officials in April 1995, U.S. officials had been unable to dissuade China from the deal but, in May 1995, Chinese officials had told reporters that the deal was in difficulty over siting, technical, and financial issues. After the U.S. announcement of the deal's cancellation, Chinese and Iranian statements indicated that the deal had been suspended, but was still under consideration. During the Bush Administration, according to press reports, China had provided Iran a small research reactor and an electromagnetic isotope separation machine that could be used to enrich small amounts of uranium.

10/14/95 ---   *Jane's Defence Weekly* reported on Iran's claim that it was relatively self-sufficient in military production. Iran also claimed to be exporting arms and ammunition to 14 countries, most likely Sudan, other African, and some Asian states. Iran was said by experts to be indigenously producing small arms, mortars, ammunition, artillery rockets, armored vehicles, small aircraft, and remotely piloted vehicles. Two days after the Jane's report, Iran's Supreme Leader Ali Khamene'i said that Iran's Revolutionary Guard was indigenously producing unspecified electronic warfare equipment.

11/03/95 ---   According to the *Middle East Economic Digest*, the Skoda Pilzen company of the Czech Republic said it was interested in selling nuclear technology to Iran despite having to abandon such plans after Czech government intervention in 1993. A company Vice President reportedly said October 20, 1995 that the company was not currently in talks with Iran, but there were no legal or other reasons to prevent sales to Iran.

11/06/95 ---   The *Iran Brief* newsletter quoted an October 19, 1995 article in *Paris Match* as saying that Iran had built a series of clandestine nuclear facilities, including two underground reactors, with North Korean help. The *Paris Match* article quoted Israeli intelligence sources as reporting that Iran had also constructed an underground uranium enrichment facility. The *Iran Brief* article did not offer any independent corroboration for the story, which was reported in *Paris Match* by Iranian journalist Fereydoun Sahebjam. Recent public testimony by U.S. intelligence officials have not mentioned these allegations or any other evidence of clandestine Iranian nuclear sites, although senior U.S. officials appear united in the view that Iran is trying to develop a nuclear weapons capability.

11/09/95 ---   Deputy Assistant Secretary of Defense Bruce Reidel testified before the House International Relations Committee that some Chinese firms had provided Iran infrastructure and chemical precursors for its chemical weapons program. He said the Chinese chemical industry was growing rapidly and that not all facets of that industry were under full scrutiny of the Chinese government. He testified that the United States had raised these reports with the government of China, with mixed success thus far. At the same hearing, Michael Eisenstadt, a senior fellow at the Washington Institute for Near East Policy, testified that falling revenues have forced Iran to reduce its military procurement by about 50% from earlier projections. For example, according to the testimony, Iran had only acquired about 200 of the 1000 tanks it had wanted, and about 100 of the 200-300 artillery pieces it had planned to buy.

11/11/95 --- *Jane's Defence Weekly* quoted Director of Central Intelligence John Deutch as saying that Iran continued to be a customer for Scud B and Scud C missiles, and would like to purchase North Korea's medium range Nodong 1 missile when it is ready for export. Deutch reportedly has said that North Korea would probably deploy the Nodong 1 by the end of 1996.

11/18/95 --- The *Washington Post,* quoting U.S. defense sources, said that Iranian budget constraints had made Iran postpone planned purchases of Russian SA-10 anti-aircraft missiles, logistics vehicles, and hundreds of armored personnel carriers. A planned purchase of North Korean NoDong medium-range ballistic missiles also had been cancelled or postponed, although China and North Korea are providing Iran with missile guidance equipment and shorter range Scud type missiles. The report added that Iran had not scaled back its chemical and biological weapons programs, however. The purchase of a third Russian-made Kilo class submarine also was on hold because of Iran's unhappiness with its performance in the warm waters of the Gulf.

--- *Jane's Defence Weekly* reported that Iran had integrated into its air force 24 Su-24 and 4 MiG-29 aircraft flown there by Iraq at the start of the Persian Gulf war. Iran's Foreign Minister was quoted as saying that, even after U.N. sanctions against Iraq are lifted, Iran would only return 22 of the 115 military and civilian aircraft flown to Iran.

11/28/95 --- The Associated Press reported that a Russian submission to the United Nations Register of Conventional Arms showed that Russia had shipped 94 unspecified types of missiles or missile launchers to Iran within the past year.

12/09/95 --- *Jane's Defence Weekly* reported that Iran claimed to have fired a domestically build anti-ship cruise missile during naval exercises in the Gulf. The Jane's report added that Iran was "known to have" 50-60 Chinese IIY-2 Silkworm anti-ship missiles, 60-100 C-801 missiles for its Chinese patrol boats, and a quantity of Sunburn cruise missiles supplied by Ukraine in 1992.

12/21/95 --- According to Reuters, Iran's Revolutionary Guard tested seized Iraqi tanks rebuilt and upgraded by Iranian experts. Iran said it had improved the tanks' engine power, transmission, and firepower.

12/25/95 --- The deputy Commander-in-Chief of Iran's Revolutionary Guard Rahim Safavi said the Guard had made "great progress" in manufacturing ballistic missiles with a range of at least 500 km, as well as surface-to-air missiles capable of hitting targets within a range of 200 km.

01/02/96 --- According to Reuters, on a visit to an Iranian atomic energy research center, President Rafsanjani said that research into nuclear fusion and other alternative energies would go forward despite U.S. efforts to isolate Iran.

JERUSALEM[*]

Clyde R. Mark

Historical and Religious Background

Jerusalem may be one of the most ancient of cities, either built as a citadel protecting an east-west trade route across the mountains between the Mediterranean coast and the Jordan River Valley, or founded as a religious center. The name may be derived from Semitic languages and means "city of peace" of "founded by Salim," a Semitic god. Jerusalem was a secondary military, political, or trade outpost on the fringe of successive Syrian, Egyptian, Babylonian, Persian, Roman, Byzantine, Arab, and Ottoman empires during their reigns of glory. It was the capital of the independent Hebrew state founded by King David, c. 1000 B.C., lasting until the Babylonian conquest in 586 B.C. The Arabs conquered the city and its environs in 638 A.D., and, except for the Crusader hiatus (1091 - 1187), held it until the coming of the Ottomans in the 16th century. Britain assumed control over Jerusalem after defeating the Ottoman Turks in World War I, and administered the League of Nations Mandate for Palestine from Jerusalem. The Mandate ended and the Arab-Israeli war began in May 1948, which resulted in Jerusalem being divided between Israel and Jordan. In 1967, Israel conquered the eastern, Arab part of the city, which included the Old City with many important religious sites, and annexed it.

Jerusalem is important to Jews because it was the site of Abraham's near sacrifice of his son, and the site of the first Temple built by Solomon (c. 952 B.C.) and the second Temple built after the Babylonian captivity (c. 515 B.C.). Jerusalem is important to Christians because of its connection to the old testament prophets, and because Jerusalem was the site of events in the life and death of Jesus Christ. Jerusalem is important to Muslims because of the old testament prophets, the life of Jesus Christ, the early focus for Muslim prayer, and the prophet Muhammad's departure from Jerusalem on his journey to heaven. Each of the faiths holds dear sacred sites in Jerusalem; among the more important are the Tomb of the Holy Sepulchre for Christians, the Western Wall for Jews, and the Dome of the Rock and al-Aqsa mosques for Muslims.

---

[*]Excerpted from *CRS Report 94-755 F.*

Arabs and Israelis accuse each other of destroying or defacing religious shrines and denying religious pilgrims access to holy sites. Israelis point to Arab destruction of several important synagogues in the Jewish Quarter of the Old City between 1947 and 1967, the scattering of tombstones on the Mount of Olives Jewish cemetery, and the use by Jordanian soldiers of Jewish grave markers in barracks paving. Arabs point to Israeli destruction of the Mamilya cemetery in west Jerusalem and the shrine at Ain Kerem during the 1948-1967 period, and the obliteration of Waqf (religious charitable foundation) property in the Mughrabi Quarter of Jerusalem after Israel seized the Old City in 1967. Israel claims that Jordan denied Israeli citizens the right to visit religious shrines under Jordanian control, and Jordan claims that Israel denied Jordanian citizens access to religious shrines in the Israeli area. Both Israel and Jordan claim that Jews, Christians, or Muslims from countries not at war with Israel or the Arabs could visit religious sites.

THE UNITED NATIONS AND THE CORPUS SEPARATUM

United Nations General Assembly (U.N.G.A.) Resolution 181 of Nov. 27, 1947, recommended that Palestine be divided into an Arab state, a Jewish state, and a separate international zone (the "corpus separatum") for the city of Jerusalem.[1] The United Nations viewed the corpus separatum for Jerusalem as a way to avoid conflicts between Arab and Jew over their political claims to Jerusalem, and among the three monotheist religions, Judaism, Christianity, and Islam, over their attachments to religious sites, and as a way to protect the holy sites and access to them for all people. The U.N. Trusteeship Council drafted a Statute for Jerusalem, to govern the corpus separatum, in April 1948. U.N.G.A. Resolution 194 of December 1948 and U.N.G.A. Resolution 303 of December 1949 reaffirmed the U.N. recommendation for the corpus separatum.

But, as a result of the 1948-1949 war, Israeli troops controlled the western part of Jerusalem, which Israel declared to be the capital of Israel. Jordanian troops controlled the eastern part of Jerusalem, which Jordan annexed, along with the rest of the West Bank territory, in 1950. The Conciliation Commission, established by U.N.G.A. Resolution 194 of 1948, proposed in September 1949 that an Arab-Israeli joint council administer the city and that the U.N. appoint a Commissioner to administer the holy places. In submitting the proposal, the Conciliation Commission ignored the corpus separatum and recognized the reality that Jerusalem was divided between Israel and Jordan. In April 1950, two years after presenting its draft, the U.N. Trusteeship Council approved the Statute for Jerusalem called for in U.N.G.A. Resolution 181. The General Assembly never voted on the Statute or on the Conciliation Commission proposal.

---

[1]For the text of U.N. Resolutions 181, an for other U.N. documents mentioned below (Resolutions 194 and 303, the Trusteeship Council Statute for Jerusalem, and the Conciliation Commission proposal for Jerusalem), see: Moore, John Norton. ed. The Arab-Israeli Conflict. volume III: documents. Princeton, Princeton University Press, 1974.

The Current Status of Jerusalem

Technically, the international community remains committed to the corpus separatum (see above), but many, perhaps most, nations accept the fact that the Palestinians, Israel, and/or Jordan may have political stakes in the city, that it is unlikely that Jerusalem will become an international city as envisioned in the corpus separatum, and that a workable international solution may emerge from Arab-Israeli peace negotiations. Many observers believe that Jerusalem will be the most difficult issue in the peace talks.

On Sept. 13, 1993, Israel and the Palestine Liberation Organization signed an accord that provided for Israeli withdrawal from the Gaza Strip and the area around Jericho, the transfer of authority over the two areas to a to-be-elected Palestinian Authority, the transfer of authority from Israel to the Palestinian Authority over West Bank/Gaza education, health, taxation, welfare, and culture, and negotiations on further transfers of authority and further Israeli withdrawals. The Israel-PLO agreement said in Article V, part 3 that negotiations for permanent status of the occupied territories, scheduled to begin not later than the beginning of the third year after Israel's withdrawal from Gaza and Jericho, may include the status of Jerusalem. (Israel withdrew from Gaza and Jericho in May 1994, which means that negotiations over Jerusalem probably will begin about June 1996.) Including Jerusalem among the issues to be negotiated appeared to be a major Israeli concession; prior to the September 1993 agreement, Israeli governments had maintained that Jerusalem was Israel's capital and that its status was non-negotiable.

No other country recognizes Israeli sovereignty over the city, or recognizes Jerusalem as the capital of Israel, although as many as 16 nations maintained embassies in Israeli west Jerusalem prior to the 1967 war. At present, only Costa Rica and El Salvador have embassies in Jerusalem, although Bolivia, Paraguay, the Dominican Republic, and Guatemala reportedly will move their embassies to the Jerusalem area in exchange for Israel retaining embassies in their countries.[2] Most nations have not recognized Israel's unilateral actions to alter the city, such as expanding the city's boundaries or building Jewish settlements in east Jerusalem, and most nations maintain that Israeli settlements are illegal under the fourth Geneva Convention that prohibits an occupying power from transferring its population into occupied territories.[3] The 1978 Camp David accords did not mention Jerusalem, although Egypt and Israel exchanged letters concerning the holy city: the Israeli

---

[2]Kampeas, Ron. Three Embassies to Move to Jerusalem Area, Associated Press, Aug. 15, 1994.

[3]One measure of opposition to Israel's changes to Jerusalem or Israel's contention that the Geneva Conventions do not apply to east Jerusalem are votes in the Untied Nations. For example, the vote on General Assembly Resolution 2253 (ES-V) on July 4, 1967, calling Israel's measures to change the city invalid, was 99-0-20 (the U.S. abstained). In another example, the vote on Resolution 31/106, part A, on Dec. 16, 1976, which called Israel's measures to change the city invalid, was 129-3-4 (the U.S. voted No), and the vote on pat B, which stated that the Geneva Conventions applied to east Jerusalem, was 134-0-2 (the U.S. voted Yes). The vote on Resolution 1/162, part C, on Dec. 4, 1986, which condemned Israel's actions on Jerusalem, was 141-3-11 (the U.S. abstained). Votes on any of the several other Security Council and General Assembly resolutions on Jerusalem show a similar pattern, that a significant number of nations disagree with Israel's position on Jerusalem.

letter said Jerusalem was the undivided capital of Israel; and the Egyptian letter said the city was part of the occupied West Bank from which Israel must withdraw.[4]

On July 18, 1994, the Israel cabinet approved a draft bill, presented to and passed by the Knesset, that prohibits any official Palestinian entity meetings or offices in Israel, which includes east Jerusalem according to Israeli law. The Palestinians have held or scheduled formal and informal meetings at Orient House, an Arab center in east Jerusalem.[5]

Israeli Policy Toward Jerusalem

In response to the 1937 British Peel Commission proposal to partition Palestine, the Jews proposed their own partition plan that included a divided Jerusalem, with western Jerusalem and Mount Scopus in the Jewish state and the rest of the city, including the Old City and the Western Wall, in the British Mandata territory. The Jewish Agency proposed a similar division in 1946, leaving the Western Wall and the Old City out of Israeli Jerusalem and in the Arab state.[6] Shortly after the 1948-1949 war began, Israel declared that Israel was sovereign in any territory under its control, which had the practical effect of including the western half of Jerusalem, then occupied by Israeli troops, in the state of Israel. Israel began moving its government offices from Tel Aviv to Jerusalem on Dec. 26, 1949, and declared Jerusalem to be the capital of Israel on Jan. 23, 1950. On May 26, 1950, Israel accepted functional internationalization of the holy places. At the time, Israel and Jordan were locked in a controversy over access to holy places, each accusing the other of denying access to its citizens despite U.N. Resolutions and the Jordan-Israel Armistice Agreement of 1949 that stated that the holy places were to be open.[7]

On June 27, following the Israeli conquest of the Jordanian, or eastern, half of the city in the June 1967 war, the Israeli Knesset passed three laws; to amend the Municipal Corporation Ordnance to expand Israeli Jerusalem city boundaries to include eastern Jerusalem, to amend the Law and Administration Ordnance to extend Israeli law and jurisdiction to east Jerusalem, and to protect the city's holy places. Israel maintains that the holy places are open to pilgrims of all faiths. Between June 1967 and September 1993, Israel maintained that undivided Jerusalem was the permanent capital of Israel and that the status of Jerusalem was not negotiable. The

---

[4]See letters on Jerusalem in: U.S. Congress. House of Representatives. Committee on Foreign affairs. Subcommittee on Europe and the Middle East. The Search for Peace in the Middle East: Documents and Statements, 1967-1979. Committee Print, Report Prepared for the Subcommittee, 96th Congress, 1st session. Washington, U.S. Gov't. Print. Off., 1979. p. 27.

[5]To cite one example, Palestinian negotiator Nabil Shaath toured Jerusalem and prayed at the al-Aqsa Mosque in August 1994. Murphy, Caryle. A Palestinian's Visit Highlights Rival Claims to Jerusalem. Washington Post, Aug. 13, 1994: A13.

[6]Bovis, H. Eugene. The Jerusalem Question, 1917-1968. Stanford, California, Hoover Institution Press, 1971. 175 p. See p. 28-29 for the Jewish Agency 1937 plan and p. 40 for the 1946 plan.

[7]Article VIII of the Armistice Agreement of April 3, 1949; see: Moore, Arab-Israeli Conflict.

September 13, 1993 accord with the PLO (see above) stated that the future status of Jerusalem may be an issue in the negotiations tentatively scheduled to begin in 3 years.

Arab and Muslim Policy Toward Jerusalem

Arabs and Muslims in general opposed the 1947 U.N. Partition Plan for Palestine, and the corpus separatum for Jerusalem, as they had opposed previous partition plans. Arabs favored a single, secular, Arab-dominated state, with Jerusalem as its capital. The Arabs maintained that Jerusalem's holy sites were protected and open during the centuries of Arab rule, and would remain open and protected in an Arab Palestine state. Jordan annexed the West Bank, including east Jerusalem, in April 1950, and announced in 1960 that Jerusalem would become Jordan's second capital, although the Jordanians never followed through on the proposal. The Arab League rejected Israel's and Jordan's annexation of Jerusalem, and maintains either that the city should be redivided along the lines of 1948-1967, or that its future should be the subject of negotiations. In 1975, the 44-member Organization of the Islamic conference formed a Jerusalem Committee chaired by King Hassan of Morocco, and called for the "liberation" of Jerusalem from Israeli control and the restoration of Jerusalem to Arab rule.

Between 1950 and 1967, Jordan exercised sovereignty over east Jerusalem and was the protector of holy sites, a role it continued to perform to a limited degree with Israeli sufferance after Israel occupied east Jerusalem in June 1967. In part because of its role as protector of the cities of Mecca and Medina and their Islamic holy sites, Saudi Arabia manifests a special interest in the Islamic holy sites in Jerusalem. The Saudi-Jordanian rivalry over protection of Jerusalem continues, as witnessed in the Saudi dissatisfaction with Jordan's restoration of the Dome of the Rock mosque, completed in 1994.

Palestinian Arabs claim that east Jerusalem will be the capital of the Palestinian state they hope will be created by the current peace talks. The Palestinians and Jordan may be in conflict over Jerusalem's future status. The July 25, 1994 Jordan-Israel declaration stated, in article B-3, that "Israel respects the present special role of the Hashimite Kingdom of Jordan in Muslim Holy shrines in Jerusalem." The "special role" was not defined. Arafat and other PLO members rejected the implication that Jerusalem's future rested with Jordan and Israel rather than with the PLO and Israel, and called for immediate Israel-Palestinian negotiations on Jerusalem rather than wait until 1996 as called for in the Sept. 13, 1993 PLO-Israel agreement. Arafat and other Palestinian leaders appealed to other Arab governments for support in opposing the Jordanian "special role" in Jerusalem, but the outcome of the Jordan-PLO rivalry to represent Arab interests in Jerusalem is not predictable.

Another conflict may develop between the Palestinians and the Organization of the Islamic Conference (OIL). Twenty years ago, the OIL formed a Jerusalem Committee, chaired by King Hassan of Morocco, to represent Islamic interests in Jerusalem. Some have speculated that one possible reason for Morocco agreeing to exchange diplomatic liaison offices with Israel in September 1994 was to ensure that the Moroccan King would be able to represent Muslim interests and to participate in Jerusalem negotiations.

U.S. Policy Toward Jerusalem

The United States voted for U.N.G.A. Resolution 181 in November 1947, which included the corpus separatum for Jerusalem. In March 1948, at the same time that the Trusteeship Council finished the Statute for Jerusalem that would have created the corpus separatum, the United States proposed that all of Palestine be placed under a U.N. Trusteeship as a way to avoid war. Some observers viewed the U.S. proposal as a policy shift away from the corpus separatum. If the United States shifted policy in March 1948, it shifted back in December 1948, when it voted for Resolution 194 which reconfirmed the U.N. intention to create the corpus separatum. In September 1949, the United States, as a member of the Conciliation Commission with Turkey and France, proposed that a joint Arab-Israeli council be named to administer the city and that a U.N. Commissioner be named to administer the holy places. The change in U.S. policy acknowledged that Israel and Jordan had taken military and political control over their respective halves of the city, and endorsed functional internationalization, which meant internationalizing just the holy places and not the whole city. The new U.S. policy of acknowledging the Jordanian and Israeli claims to the city was confirmed in December 1949, when the United States voted against U.N.G.A. Resolution 303 because the resolution reaffirmed the corpus separatum, which the United States said was unenforceable.

From 1949 until June 1967, the United States continued to support the "principle of an international regime for Jerusalem," but favored the approach of the Conciliation Commission in acknowledging the Jordanian and Israeli presence in Jerusalem.[8] The United States criticized Israel's moving its capital to Jerusalem in 1949, criticized Jordan's 1960 announcement that it would make Jerusalem its second capital, and criticized Israel's unilateral action of June 27, 1967, annexing the eastern or Jordanian half of Jerusalem.[9] Since 1967, the United States has called for a negotiated resolution of Jerusalem's status. In December 1969, Secretary of State William Rogers added another element to U.S. policy on Jerusalem when he said that Jerusalem should remain a unified city[10], a point repeated by subsequent Administrations.

Some observers perceived a change in U.S. policy toward Jerusalem when the United States abstained on a separate vote on a paragraph of U.N. General Assembly

---

[8]Statement by Ambassador John Ross before the U.N. General Assembly Ad Hoc Committee, Dec. 12, 1950.

[9]See statements in Appendix on U.S. protest to Israel in 1952 and Jordan in 1960, and President Johnson's 1967 statement. Ambassador Arthur Goldberg voiced U.S. opposition to Israel's unilateral action before the U.N. General Assembly on July 3 1967 and July 14, 1967.

[10]Speech before the Galaxy Conference, Dec. 9, 1969. See also statement by U.S. Ambassador George Bush to the U.N. Security Council, Sept. 25, 1971.

Resolution 904 on Mar. 18, 1994.[11] U.S. Ambassador to the United Nations Madeleine Albright said the United States abstained because Jerusalem was listed as part of the occupied territory, and that the United States would continue to oppose including Jerusalem as part of the occupied territories.[12] Previously the United States considered east Jerusalem part of the occupied territory and had voted for resolutions in which east Jerusalem was included in the occupied territory.[13] The Ambassador did not explain the apparent change in the United States perception of Jerusalem.

U.S. Congressional Interest in Jerusalem

Congress maintains an active interest in Jerusalem because the city's future is an important focus of concern for Jews, Christians, and Muslims, and because Jerusalem will be an important component in resolving the Arab-Israeli dispute. In general, Congress has agreed with Israel's viewpoints that Jerusalem is Israel's indivisible capital, that Israel will ensure Christian and Muslim rights at the holy places, and that the U.S. embassy in Israel should be located in Jerusalem, not Tel Aviv. Successive U.S. Administrations have agreed that Jerusalem should remain unified, but have adhered to a policy that the United States should not move the embassy or recognize Israeli or any other claims to the city until and unless the Arabs and Israelis agree through negotiations on the future status of Jerusalem. U.S. Administrations have maintained that moving the U.S. Embassy from Tel Aviv to Jerusalem would demonstrate a preference for the position taken by one of the parties to the dispute, Israel, and would be a signal to the other parties, the Arabs, that the United States would accept only the solution that satisfied Israel. Under those circumstances, Administration officials contend that the United States would have difficulty playing the role of "honest broker" and that the Arabs would have little reason to pursue negotiations.

In 1984, Congress considered H.R. 4877 and S. 2031, which would have required the President to move the U.S. Embassy from Tel Aviv to Jerusalem. Neither bill reached the floor for a vote. Also in 1984, the House Foreign Affairs Committee considered H.Con.Res. 352, which stated the sense of the Congress that the U.S. embassy should be moved from Tel Aviv to Jerusalem, but the bill died in Committee.

In 1985, the Senate attached an amendment to the Diplomatic Security Act that a new U.S. embassy in Israel could be built only in Jerusalem, but Senate-House conferees could not agree on the language, and a compromise banned construction of

---

[11]U.N. Security Council Resolution 904, passed on Mar. 18, 1994, condemned the Jewish gunman attack on Muslim worshippers at Hebron on Feb. 24, 1994. The United States also abstained on another paragraph in the same resolution that referred to "occupied Palestinian territory" because the United States believed the phrase implied sovereignty. See the January 1992 statements of Ambassador Thomas Pickering and State Department Spokesperson Margaret Tutwiler, and the March 1994 statement by Ambassador Maeleine Albright in the Appendices.

[12]An excerpt of Ambassador Albright's statement is included in the Appendices.

[13]For example, see the statements by Ambassador Charles Yost on July 1, 1969, and Ambassador Thomas Pickering on Jan. 6, 1992, included in the Appendices.

a new embassy anywhere in Israel, Jerusalem, or the occupied territories.[14] The State Department Appropriation bill of 1988, in Section 305, stated that any funds authorized, appropriate, or obligated for constructing an embassy to represent the United States in Israel must provide for two buildings, either of which could be used as an embassy.[15] One building was to be in Tel Aviv and the other in Jerusalem, and the President would select one of the two buildings to be the U.S. embassy to Israel. No funds have been appropriated and construction on the two buildings has yet to begin. In January 1989, the United States signed a 99-year lease with the Government of Israel at $1 per year for a 14-acre site in southwest Jerusalem.[16]

On Mar. 22, 1990, the Senate passed S. Con. Res. 106 (voice vote), and on April 24, 1990, the House passed H. Con. Res. 290 (378 -34), both of which stated the sense of the Congress that Jerusalem is Israel's undivided capital and that Israel protects all religious rights.

Two bills, S.Con.Res. 113 and H.Con.Res. 316, introduced in May 1992, congratulated Israel on the 25th anniversary of the reunification of Jerusalem, and stated that the city should remain undivided with all religious rights protected. Opponents of the bills argued that passage would imply a change in U.S. policy that would undermine the U.S. role in the peace process. Supporters of the bills maintained that passage would express Congressional will and demonstrate Congress's authority to advocate, or to direct, foreign policy. The Senate passed S.Con.Res. 113 on June 10, 1992 by voice vote and the House passed S.Con.Res. 113 on June 18, 1992 by voice vote.

In the 103rd congress, Members introduced bills to congratulate Israel on the anniversary of Jerusalem's reunification (H.Con.Res. 101, 225, and 239), and to call for the United States to move the embassy from Tel Aviv to Jerusalem (H.Con.Res. 281). None of these bills passed. Section 703 of P.L. 103-325 expresses the sense of Congress that the United States should veto any U.N. resolutions that refer to Jerusalem as occupied territory. Section 599I of P.L. 103-306 denies funds for U.S. officials meeting with members of the Palestine Authority in Jerusalem.[17]

Early in the 104th Congress, Members circulated a letter for signature directed at the Secretary of State stating that they believed Jerusalem to be the undivided capital of Israel and that the Secretary should begin planning to move the embassy from Tel Aviv to Jerusalem by May 1999.

---

[14]Section 414 of the Omnibus Diplomatic Security and Antiterrorism Act of 1986, signed into law Aug. 27, 1986, P.L. 99-399 (H.R. 4141), 100 Stat 868, 22 USC 4862. The prohibition against building an embassy in Israel, Jerusalem, or the West Bank was repeated in Section 130 of the Foreign Relations Authorization Act, 1988-1089, P.O. 100-204 (101 Stat.1344) of Dec. 22, 1987.

[15]he Departments of Commerce, Justice, and State, the Judiciary and Related Agencies appropriations Act, 1989, P. 100-459 (102 Stat. 2209), 1 October 1988.

[16]See Evans and Novak, Another Time Bomb in Jerusalem, Washington Post, Feb. 2, 1995.

[17]P.L. 103-306, H.R. 4426, signed into law Aug. 24, 1994, is the foreign assistance appropriations bill. P.L. 103-25, H.R. 3474, signed into law on Sept. 23, 1994, is the Community Development Banking and Financial Institutions Act of 1993.

Appendix 1. Jerusalem Statistics

JERUSALEM STATISTICS			
	Area Sq. Mi.	Population Arabs	Jews
Corpus Separatum (1947)	98.5	106,000	100,000
Mandate City (1947)	7.86	65,000	100,000
Divided City (1966) Israel Jordanian	14.67 2 to 3	2,680 70,000	193,000 0
Current (1992)	about 40	144,000	393,000

MAP 1. "CORPUS SEPARATUM"

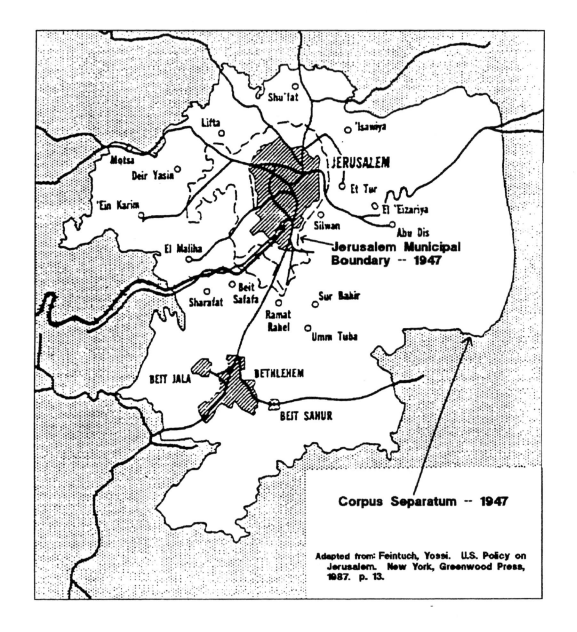

Corpus Separatum -- 1947

Adapted from: Feintuch, Yossi. U.S. Policy on
Jerusalem. New York, Greenwood Press,
1987. p. 13.

MAP 2. JERUSALEM UNDER ISRAELI OCCUPATION

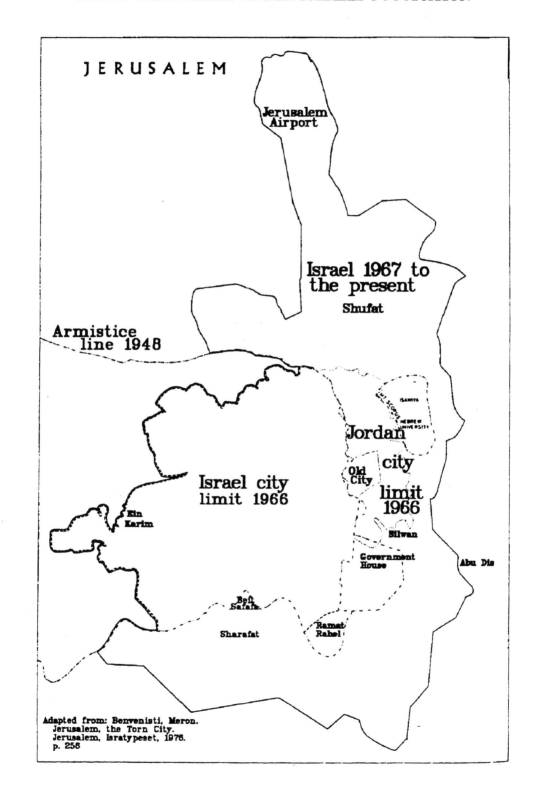

JERUSALEM

Jerusalem
Airport

Israel 1967 to
the present

Shufat

Armistice
line 1948

ISAWIYA

HEBREW
UNIVERSITY

Jordan

city

Old
City

Israel city
limit 1966

limit
1966

Ein
Karim

Silwan

Government
House

Abu Dis

Beit
Safafa

Ramat
Rahel

Sharafat

Adapted from: Benvenisti, Meron.
Jerusalem, the Torn City.
Jerusalem, Isratypeset, 1976.
p. 256

Syrian-U.S. Relations[*]

Alfred B. Prados

Background and Analysis

U.S.-Syrian relations, frequently strained by longstanding disagreements over regional and international policy, have warmed somewhat as a result of several developments: the collapse of the Soviet Union, Syria's participation in the allied coalition against Iraq in 1990-91, and Syrian agreement to participate in Arab-Israeli peace talks. This thaw in bilateral relations has led some Members of Congress to inquire whether or not the Administration has made any private commitment to Syria, such as an undertaking to relax economic sanctions, in return for Syrian support on regional issues. Several legislative proposals have sought to condition relaxation of aid and trade restrictions on further changes in Syrian policy. The Administration, though not inclined to lift sanctions on Syria at this time, believes it is in U.S. interests to encourage Syria to play a positive role in postwar Persian Gulf security arrangements and in the Arab-Israeli peace process. The issue for U.S. policy makers is the degree to which the United States should work for better relations with Syria in an effort to enlist Syrian cooperation on regional issues.

Syrian Politics and External Relations

Syria achieved independence after World War II, following four centuries of Ottoman Turkish domination and over two decades of semi-colonial administration by France. Under a succession of weak, unstable governments Syria moved generally to the left until 1970, when the then Minister of Defense and Air Force Commander, Lt. General Hafiz al-Asad, assumed power in a bloodless coup. President Asad, who was elected to his fourth term in 1992 by Syria's mainly consultative parliament, exercises ultimate authority through his personal prestige and through his control of the ruling Arab Socialist Resurrection (Ba'th) Party, the military establishment, and the intelligence apparatus which form the triple pillars of the regime. President Asad also has strong support among the members of his Alawite religious sect, which comprises approximately 12% of the population but is disproportionately represented in the country's political and military institutions. Currently 64 years old, an exceptionally hard worker, and reportedly suffering from some health problems, President Asad does not have a clearly designated successor; commentators variously suggest that he might be followed by one of several relatives or a collective leadership.

For much of its existence, Syria has faced economic difficulties and problems in its foreign relations. The economy, long based on agriculture and commerce, is dominated by an inefficient public sector, excessive central planning, and administrative controls. The regime has begun to promote the private sector through deregulation and various incentives. Also, revenue sources have increased somewhat with the advent of oil production (580,000 barrels per day) and renewed aid from leading Arab oil producers. Syria's relations with its neighbors have been marred by border problems (with Turkey and Israel), disputes over water sharing (with Turkey and Iraq), and political differences (sometimes with Jordan and especially with Iraq, which is governed by a rival wing of the Ba'th Party). Syria maintains a dominant influence over Lebanon through its troop presence in that country, and aroused widespread opposition among other Arab states by its support of Iran during the Iran-Iraq war of the 1980s. Subsequently, however, Syrian relations with Egypt and the Arabian Peninsula states markedly improved, especially after Syria joined the allied coalition against Iraq during the Gulf crisis. Syria continues to maintain a strategic relationship with Iran, although Iranian officials reportedly are concerned over Syria's participation in the Arab-Israeli peace process (which Iran opposes) and Syria's endorsement of territorial claims by the United Arab Emirates to three Persian Gulf islands occupied by Iran. A scheduled visit to Syria by Iranian Vice President Hassan Habibi in January 1996 was postponed for several weeks, apparently over the Gulf islands issue, but the disagreement seems to have been largely healed.

SYRIAN-U.S. RELATIONS AND BILATERAL ISSUES

U.S.-Syrian relations have been frequently strained, mainly because of Syria's long-standing confrontation with Israel and its position for many years as a major recipient of Soviet military aid and political support. Syria broke relations with the Untied States during the June 1967 Arab-Israeli War, but the two countries reestablished ties in 1974 during an intensive Middle East peacemaking endeavor by then U.S. Secretary of State Henry Kissinger. Soviet-Syrian ties remained strong, however, and by 1979 U.S.-Syrian relations had deteriorated once more as the countries disagreed over numerous regional issues. A slow improvement in U.S.-Syrian relations began in the late 1980s, with the gradual disintegration and ultimate collapse of the Soviet Union, Syria's long-standing superpower ally, and closer collaboration between Syria and pro-Western Arab states, particularly following the Iraqi invasion of Kuwait.

Arab-Israeli Peace Negotiations

The Golan Heights Territory. During the June 1967 Arab-Israeli War, Israel occupied a 450-square mile portion of southwestern Syria known as the Golan Heights. (Syria recovered a tiny segment of this territory including the abandoned town of Qunaytra as part of a U.S.-brokered disengagement agreement following the October 1973 war.) On December 14, 1981, the Israeli Knesset voted 63-21 to extend Israeli law to the Golan Heights, thereby effectively annexing this territory. (No other country has recognized the Israeli de facto annexation.) An estimated 117,500 Arabs (100,000 Syrians and 17,500 Palestinians) fled from Golan after its occupation by Israel in 1967. The remaining population consists of approximately 15,000-18,000 Arabs, mostly belonging to the Druze minority, and some 12,000-16,000 Jews (including 1,000 Soviet immigrants) who have settled there since 1967.

Syria believes that Israel is bound to return this territory under the provisions of United Nations Security Council Resolution 242, which calls for withdrawal of Israeli forces from territories occupied in the June 1967 war. Israel's ruling Labor Party believes that the withdrawal clause in Resolution 242 means withdrawal from some, but not necessarily all Arab territories occupied in 1967, while the opposition Likud Party takes the position that Israel has complied with Resolution 242 by returning the Sinai Peninsula to Egypt. Israeli leaders of both parties have long regarded the Golan Heights territory as being of vital strategic importance because of its commanding terrain. On July 26, 1995, the Israeli Knesset narrowly defeated a motion that would have required that either a 70-member majority of the 120-member Knesset or a popular referendum approve any Israeli withdrawal from the Golan Heights. This provision, if it had passed, would have made an Israeli withdrawal virtually impossible. An additional complication involves disposition of several small enclaves that were part of the pre-1948 Palestine mandate territory but came under Syrian control between 1948 and 1967; Israel, Syria, and the Palestinians all advance claims to these areas.

Issues and Positions. In October, 1991, President Asad agreed to attend the peace talks inaugurated in Madrid under U.S. and Soviet sponsorship. Since then, Syrian representatives have attended intermittent bilateral talks with Israeli counterparts. Syria has refused so far to participate in the other phase of U.S.-Russian sponsored negotiations -- the multilateral talks on regional issues -- until there is tangible progress on territorial issues. In general, Syria favors a comprehensive Arab--Israeli settlement and opposes separate peace arrangements like those reached with Israel by the Palestinians in 1993 and by Jordan in 1994.

Syria and Israel remain deadlocked over two basic issues: Syria's demand for unconditional Israel withdrawal from the Golan territory, as well as southern Lebanon; and Israel's insistence on a prior Syrian commitment to establish full diplomatic and economic relations before any withdrawal takes place. In a meeting with President Clinton on October 28, 1994, President Asad states Syria's position as follows: "I also reaffirmed to President Clinton Syria's readiness to commit itself to the objective requirements of peace, emanating from the principle of full withdrawal for full peace, through the establishment of peaceful, normal relations with Israel in return for Israel's full withdrawal from the Golan to the line of June 4, 1967, and from southern Lebanon." Israeli leaders seek a more detailed explanation of Syria's concept of full peace.

Ancillary issues include the timing of any Israeli withdrawal that might take place; security guarantees for Israel; the size of demilitarized or limited armament zones on each side of the border; and sharing of water resources. Israeli officials have raised the possibility of a very limited pull-back in the Golan territory for a three-year period as a test, which if successful could be followed by further unspecified withdrawals. Syrian officials have indicated that complete withdrawal should take place in no more than 12 to 18 months. Israel has proposed that it retain observation posts on the Golan Heights; Syria rejected this proposal as an infringement of its sovereignty, but reportedly suggested aerial reconnaissance or observation posts manned by international forces. Israel wants a wider demilitarized zone on the Syrian side of a future border between the two countries, in view of Syria's greater strategic depth. Syria initially demanded that such zones be "symmetrical" (i.e., equal in width), but reportedly has suggested subsequently that the width of zones on the Syrian and Israel sides could be at a ratio of 10:6 (for example, a 10-kilometer demilitarized zone on the Syrian side, and a 6-kilometer zone on the Israeli side). On February 13, 1996, Israeli Prime Minister suggested that Syria could obtain needed water from the Euphrates and that Israel would retain all Jordan River water sources under its present control; Syria, already embroiled in a dispute with Turkey over Euphrates water sharing, is likely to insist on a significant share of the Jordan River waters.

Recent negotiations. Meetings between the Syrian and Israeli Armed Forces Chiefs of Staff under U.S. auspices in December 1994 and June 1995 addressed some of these security and technical issues but did not result in any agreements. After a six-month hiatus, a new series of U.S.-sponsored talks between Syrian and Israeli representatives were held at the Wye Plantation Conference Center in Maryland during the periods December 27, 1995-January 5, 1996; January 24-February 1, 1996; and February 28-March 4, 1996. Israel suspended its participation on March 4 after a series of bombings by the militant Palestinian organization, Hamas, that killed an estimated 58 people in three Israeli cities, as explained below.

Both diplomatic and military experts from the two countries attended the Maryland talks, which drew mixed reactions from the participants. On January 10, President Asad, according to his spokesman, said the Maryland talks were conducted in "a better atmosphere than before." On February 1, however, Syria's press complained over "Israel's commitment to impossible and provocative demands regarding the security arrangements" (presumably referring to proposals for an Israeli presence at early warning stations on Golan). The Syrian press further complained on February 6 that Israeli Prime Minister Yitzhak Peres' plans to hold elections in May would complicate bilateral negotiations. Although President Asad agreed to continue the talks after a meeting with Secretary of State Christopher, observers speculated that negotiators would be able to do little more than tread water until the Israeli elections were over. On March 1, a State Department spokesman told reporters that the third round of talks then under way had been "detailed, practical, and constructive" so far. These talks reportedly covered a range of issues including security, economic development, and water rights.

Effect of Bombings in Israel. Despite the first two bombings (February 25), Israel agreed to go forward with the third round of talks with Syria starting on February 28; moreover, in a rare gesture, the official Syrian press obliquely condemned the random killing of Israelis (The Syria Times observed that "Although the incidents are condemned, these bombings and acts of violence ... must be a lesson ... that real peace is the only way to end tension and violence.") Israel subsequently suspended talks to enable its team to attend the funerals of victims of the third bombing (March 3), and after the fourth bombing (March 4) Israel announced that it was suspending its participation indefinitely. Israel has asked the United States to convey to Syria that it will not tolerate the continuation of these attacks. Although Syrian newspapers spoke of Syria's continued commitment to the peace process, there has been no statement of condemnation from Syrian officials or media since the two latest attacks, and the Syrian press dismissed a call by the Israeli Foreign Minister to close down offices of militant Palestinian organizations. One paper opined that "It is strange that Israel drops tons of bombs on innocent civilians in south Lebanon ... without anyone reacting to her."

On March 12, Syrian Foreign Minister Faruk al-Shar'a informed the U.S. Ambassador that Syria would not attend the "Summit of Peace Builders" conference, which was held the following day at Sharm al-Shaykh, Egypt, at the invitation of President Clinton and Egyptian President Husni Mubarak. Al-Shar'a said a preparatory meeting and an agreement on an agenda should have preceded the conference; he added that the conference as structured under the Clinton-Mubarak invitation would "serve the positions and interests of Israel at the expense of the interests and rights of Arabs;" and he affirmed Syria's commitment to work for "a just and comprehensive peace." President Clinton described Syria's failure to attend the conference as "a missed opportunity," but agreed with Israeli Prime Minister Peres that Syrian-Israeli negotiations should continue. According to the press, some U.S. and Israeli officials think these negotiations are likely to remain on hold until after the Israeli elections on late May. On March 14, the Israeli Foreign Minister said the time was not right to resume talks with Syria, and demanded that Syria condemn attacks against Israel. Syria's government press rejected this condition, and rejoined other countries should not dictate Syrian policy to Syrians. On April 9, Israeli Prime Minister Peres said he had received an indirect message from President Asad that the latter would be agreeable to a summit conference sometime in the future; however, an official Syrian spokesman said there had been no change in Syria's position, namely, that any such meeting would be linked to the termination of Israel's occupation of Arab territory.

Syria's Proposal. On March 9, Syrian Foreign Minister al-Shar'a, in letters to his U.S. and Russian counterparts, said the peace process was in crisis and called for reconvening the original Madrid peace conference to revive it. (The plenary conference held at Madrid on October 30, 1991, was designed as a one-day inaugural meeting to usher in the Arab-Israeli peace talks; it was followed by the bilateral and multilateral talks that have continued since that time.) Al-Shar'a reiterated this proposal to the U.S. Ambassador in Syria on March 12, as an alternative to the Sharm al-Shaykh conference. Russian President Boris Yeltsin and Saudi Arabian Foreign Minister Saudi al-Faysal, both attendees at the Sharm al-Shaykh conference, supported Syria's proposal. Meanwhile, on April 9, Syria also expressed deep concern over a military cooperation accord between Israel and Turkey reportedly reached in February.

Israel's Campaign in Lebanon. The escalation of tension between Israel and militant Hizballah forces in Lebanon in mid-April dealt another setback to Syrian-Israeli peacemaking. In early April, Hizballah forces based in southern Lebanon began firing rockets at Israeli forces in Israel's self-proclaimed security zone in southern Lebanon and in some cases at northern Israel as well. In retaliation, Israel launched a series of air and artillery strikes in an operation code named "Grapes of Wrath" between April 11 and 27, against Hizballah targets in Lebanon. Syria strongly condemned the Israeli operation. On April 21, Syrian official media demanded that Israel pay compensation for losses inflicted by its artillery and air strikes against Lebanon; and on May 7 and again on May 9, Syrian media called on the United Nations to try as war criminals those Israeli leaders responsible for artillery strikes on April 18 that killed 102 Lebanese civilians sheltering in a U.N. base in southern Lebanon. Syrian media also criticized the United States for compromising its role as an honest broker in the Arab-Israeli peace process, for opposing condemnation of Israel in the United Nations, and for allegedly seeking to prevent publication of a U.N. report that suggested that Israeli artillery strikes against the U.N. base may have been deliberate.

After intensive diplomacy by U.S. Secretary of State Christopher, Syria agreed to the terms of a cease-fire, which became effective on April 27, under which (2) Israeli forces and forces cooperating with them will not fire on civilian targets in Lebanon, (2) armed groups in Lebanon will not fire on targets in Israel, (3) a committee consisting of the United States, France, Syria, Lebanon, and Israel will be established to monitor compliance with the agreement. Syria continues to disagree with the Untied States and Israel over the mandate of the committee, insisting that the committee should be purely military in nature and not a substitute for broader bilateral talks. U.S. officials have criticized Syria for permitting resupply of Hizballah, and an unidentified State Department official reportedly said on May 14 that the United States plans to complain to Syria over new arms shipments reaching Hizballah via Syria from Iran.

Monitoring an Agreement on the Golan. U.S. and Israel officials have begun to raise the subject of security arrangements and the possibility of an international monitoring or peacekeeping force in the event of an agreement on full or partial Israeli withdrawal from the Golan territory. On October 4, 1994, Assistant Secretary of State for Near East Affairs Robert M. Pelletreau, replying to a question from a member of the House Foreign Affairs Committee, said the U.S. Government has received no specific request from either side for U.S. troops to help monitor a settlement, but would be prepared to consider such a request "in accordance with our constitutional processes" (i.e., appropriate consultation with Congress) if it received one. Secretary Pelletreau reiterated this position in response to congressional hearings on April 6, 1995, adding that "There is ample time for very complete consultations with Congress on the question of any kind of a U.S. presence on the Golan" after the parties have decided what type of international force they might request. On January 9, 1995, Secretary of Defense William Perry noted that U.S.

participants in such a force "would not be security forces... [They] would be strictly monitors to monitor the peace process and if the parties ask us to do that, we're certainly prepared to consider that request" after consulting with Congress. A year later, on January 8, 1996, following the first round of Maryland talks, Secretary Perry reiterated this position, saying that "If the peace agreement between Israel and Syria is reached ... and if that calls for a peace monitoring force in the Golan Heights, and if both Israel and Syria request the U.S. to participate in that, we are prepared to do that."

On January 9, 1995, the Speaker of the U.S. House of Representatives voiced reservations over stationing U.S. troops on Golan, saying that he was "not closing the door" but that the United States would need to examine such a proposal and consider worst case scenarios. In a January 11, 1995 press interview, the Chairman of the Senate Foreign Relations Committee expressed the view that if Syria and Israel "cannot make a deal without a payoff, or troops, or both, from the United States, I would not favor a deal and there should not be one." Supporters of a U.S. role believe U.S. participation would be an important factor in obtaining a Syrian-Israeli agreement on Golan; they point out that a U.S. contingent to Golan would overextend U.S. forces, expose U.S. troops to undue risk, undermine U.S. commitments to Israel, and embroil the United States directly in the event of a future outbreak of hostilities.

Arms Proliferation

For many years the Soviet Union was Syria's main source of military hardware, enabling Syria to acquire arms inventories comparable to those of Israel. Soviet deliveries began to taper off after 1985, as former President Gorbachev began to retrench on Middle East commitments. Syrian arms purchase agreements from the former Soviet Union dropped from $5.2 billion in the four-year period 1986-1989 to $0.5 billion for the four-year period 1990-1993. Moreover, financial subsidies to Syria from Arab Gulf states declined as the Soviet role diminished. Since 1990, however, Syria apparently has applied some funds it received from wealthy Arab donors for its role in the allied coalition to additional arms purchases, reportedly including up to 300 T72 tanks from Czechoslovakia, additional combat aircraft from the former Soviet Union, missile sub-systems and technology from China, and SCUD surface-to-surface missiles from North Korea. Russia reportedly was still maintaining 2,400 military advisors in Syria in mid-1993 [*Congressional Record*, June 15, 1993, p. H3589]. In May 1994, Russia reportedly wrote off $10 billion of Syrian military debt inherited from the former Soviet Union and agreed to sell an estimated $500 million worth of defensive equipment to Syria.

U.S. officials are concerned that Syrian acquisition of additional weapons including improved missiles will cause further regional tensions, increase potential threats to Israel, and undermine arms control efforts. The Administration has urged suppliers to refrain from delivering destabilizing weapons to the region. Syria resents what it regards as U.S. interference in its attempts to resupply its armed forces. Also, Syria, like Egypt, has taken the position that it will refuse to support indefinite extension of the Nuclear Non-Proliferation Treaty (NPT) until Israel signs the treaty, and Syria has criticized the Arab League for not passing a binding resolution requiring all member states to adopt the same position. Syria has approached Argentina about the purchase of a nuclear reactor for medical research, but the Argentine Foreign Minister stated on July 23, 1995 that such a sale would not occur unless Syria and Israel reached a peace agreement.

Terrorist Activity

Allegations of Syrian involvement with terrorist groups have been a longstanding point of contention between Washington and Damascus. Some observers believe Syria was involved in the 1983 bombing of the U.S. Marine barracks by Shi'ite Muslim militants in Lebanon, although others have blamed Iran, which had closer ties with the group responsible for this atrocity. Syrian intelligence was implicated in an abortive attempt to place a bomb on an El Al airliner in London in 1986, after which the United States withdrew its ambassador to Syria for a year. Initial reports indicated that the destruction of the Pan American Flight 103 over Lockerbie, Scotland in December 1988 was the work of a Palestinian group headquartered in Damascus and responsible to Syria; subsequent international police investigations have led the international community to charge Libya with responsibility [see below], but some observers continue to believe there was a Syrian or Iranian connection. Turkey has long complained that Syria supports the separatist Kurdish Labor party (PKK), which the U.S. State Department lists as a terrorist organization. On November 21, 1995, Syrian Vice President Abd al-Halim Khaddam denied that Syria supports the PKK, but Turkish leaders remain unconvinced, and on January 8, 1996, Turkish Foreign Ministry Officials asked for U.S. pressure on Syria to end its support for the PKK.

Since 1979, Syria has appeared regularly on a list of countries which the State Department identifies as supportive of international terrorism (see below). According to the State Department's April 1995 report on terrorism, "There is no evidence that Syrian officials have been directly involved in planning or executing terrorist attacks since 1986 ... However, Syria continues to provide safehaven and support for several groups that engage in international terrorism ..." The report mentions several radical Palestinian or pro-Iranian groups (including the Islamic fundamentalist Hamas organization) and the Japanese Red Army. Syria maintains that it is prepared to expel Palestinian and other groups if provided with direct evidence of their involvement in terrorist activity. On the other hand, Syria acknowledges its support for Palestinians pursuing armed struggle in Israeli occupied territories and for Shi'ite Muslim militias resisting the Israeli military presence in southern Lebanon; Syria claims that such operations constitute legitimate resistance activity, as distinguished from terrorism.

Syrian officials have pressed to have Syria removed from the State Department's list of countries providing support to international terrorism; the April 1995 State Department report acknowledges some steps by Syria to restrain terrorist groups but has not yet dropped Syria from the terrorism list. President Asad said he and President Clinton "did not discuss terrorism as a separate title" in their October 1994 meeting, but President Clinton quoted Asad as voicing opposition to the killing of innocent civilians wherever it occurs. In August 1995, according to press reports, Secretary of State Christopher warned Syria that threats against U.S. citizens emanating from groups based in Damascus are unacceptable.

NARCOTICS TRAFFIC

Syria is not known to be a drug producing country or a site for international money laundering; however, it is a transit country for the drug trade and a suspected site for refining small amounts of narcotics. Much of this traffic originates in Lebanon's Bekaa (Biqa') Valley, an area generally under Syrian occupation, and Syrian officials are widely reported to have profited from facilitating the sale and transit of Lebanese-produced hashish and heroin destined for Europe and the United States. These and other substances (morphine base, opium, psychotropic substances) also enter Syria via Turkey and Southwest Asia en route to other markets in the Middle East, including the Persian Gulf states. Since 1987, Syria has been cited in an annual Presidential Determination as a country that has not made sufficient efforts to curb production or transit of narcotics in areas under its control (see below).

Syria is a party to the 1961 narcotics convention to its amending 1972 protocol, and to the 1971 convention on psychotropic substances, and has ratified the 1988 U.N. Convention on narcotics. Syrian officials have stated their willingness to expand cooperation with other governments and international organizations in the war against drugs. Law No. 2, which took effect in July 1993, prescribes the death penalty for cultivating or dealing in narcotics, and President Asad reportedly has ordered security forces to crack down on drug smugglers, regardless of family connections, and relatives of the President have been arrested.

In a February 1995 report, the Administration noted some progress by Syria in 1994 in attempting to counter narcotics traffic: increased cooperation with Lebanese authorities to eradicate opium poppy and cannabis cultivation in the largely Syrian-controlled Biqa (Bekaa) Valley in Lebanon; increased seizures of cocaine, heroin, and hashish; and more arrests of drug traffickers in Syria and Lebanon. On the other hand, the Administration stated that the overall flow of narcotics did not diminish in 1994; neither Syrian nor Lebanese authorities moved successfully against cocaine and heroin laboratories; and no corruption charges were brought against any Syrian governmental or military officials in 1994, despite continuing reports of complicity by Syrian officials in drug traffic. According to a March 1, 1996 Presidential Determination (see below), Syria has not taken adequate steps to control narcotics traffic.

SYRIA'S ROLE IN LEBANON

Syrian Army units moved into large parts of northeastern and central Lebanon shortly after civil strike began in that country in 1975. A Syrian force of approximately 35,000-40,000 has remained there since 1976, ostensibly under an

Arab League peace-keeping mandate. At an Arab League sponsored meeting at Taif, Saudi Arabia in October 1989, the Lebanese Parliament agreed on a revised formula for power sharing within the Lebanese Government; it also adopted a plan for reestablishment of central authority and phased Syrian redeployment to the eastern Bekaa Valley, after which the two countries would agree on the ultimate status of Syrian forces in eastern Lebanon.

An impasse subsequently developed over the timing of Syrian force withdrawals and Lebanese parliamentary elections. Under the Taif Agreement, Syrian forces were scheduled for redeployment to the eastern Bekaa Valley and possible further withdrawals for two years after implementation of the Agreement, which most observers counted from September 1990. Syrian officials and pro-Syrian Lebanese have countered that not all conditions of the Taif Agreement were met at that time; that the Lebanese Armed Forces are not yet capable of maintaining internal security; and that Syrian forces should remain in Lebanon as long as Israel maintains its security zone in southern Lebanon. U.S. Administration spokesmen have criticized reported irregularities in the September 1992 elections, and both Administration representatives and Members of Congress have expressed the view that Syrian forces should redeploy pursuant to the Taif Agreement. As noted above, the Untied States has also criticized Syrian toleration of the presence of militant Shi'ite Muslim Hizballah by Iran.

Syria's Human Rights Record

Syria has been under a state of emergency tantamount to martial law since 1963, except for a brief interval in 1973-1974. in its annual 1994 report to Congress on human rights practices (published in February 1995), the State Department has commented: "Serious abuses include the widespread use of torture; arbitrary arrest and detention without trial; continued imprisonment after prisoners have served their sentences; unfair trials in state security cases; the denial of freedoms of speech, press and association; abuses committed under the state of emergency, and suppression of workers' rights." Particularly serious human rights violations took place in the northern cities of Aleppo and Hama in 1980 and 1982, respectively, when the Government suppressed uprisings by the fundamentalist Muslim Brotherhood and other opposition groups with much violence. Estimates of the number killed in Hama by government forces range from 3,000 (from Syrian Government sources) to 20,000 (from some independent sources). Syrian officials have pointed out, however, that by acting quickly to suppress Muslim extremists in the early 1980s, the Syrian regime has spared the country from the outbreaks of Islamic fundamentalist violence that have currently marred domestic tranquility in Egypt, Algeria, and other North African countries.

Syria denies that it holds political prisoners, and claims that persons are detained only for criminal or security offenses; however, some sources believe at least 7,000 such prisoners were held as of early 1991, including over 2,000 in detention facilities in Lebanon.Since then, the government has announced three amnesties resulting in the release of a total of 4,018 prisoners and detainees (December 1991 -- 2,864;

March 1992 -- 600: December 1992 -- 554) accused of offenses against state security. Small groups were reportedly released in 1993, and another 300 in 1994. On November 29, 1995, Amnesty International welcomed the release by Syria of "hundreds" of political prisoners in an amnesty marking the 25th anniversary of President Asad's assumption of power November 16, 1970); according to a January 7, 1996 news report, those released included 1,200 members and supporters of the banned Muslim Brotherhood. It is believed, however, that some individuals have continued to be arrested for security offenses.

Syria supports freedom of religion and women's rights to a greater degree than do many Middle East governments. In accordance with the largely secular philosophy of the ruling Ba'th Party, the country's Christian community and tiny Jewish minority (see below) have been free to practice their religion without interference; some Christians have held high-level positions in the government and armed forces. (Official toleration does not extend to two sects that are considered subversive: Jehovah's Witnesses and Seventh Day Adventists.) Syrian law specified equal rights for women; Government policies stipulate equal pay for similar work; the Government discourages conservative religiously based restrictions on women; and women serve in governmental and diplomatic posts, including two cabinet ministers.

TREATMENT OF JEWISH MINORITY

On April 27, 1992, President Asad issued an order lifting travel restrictions and real estate controls on the Syrian Jewish community, and the government intermittently began permitting Syrian Jews to travel abroad freely. On February 24, 1994, Syria's Deputy Chief Rabbi announced that the Syrian Government had issued exit visas to all the estimated 1,000 Jews remaining in Syria; he added that three or four Syrian Jewish families had returned to Syria after facing financial and language problems abroad. According to the State Department human rights report published in February 1995, the Syrian Government "completed issuance of travel permits to all Jews wishing them." By October 1994, Israeli officials estimated that 3,670 Jews had left Syria since April 1992, about one third of whom had secretly moved to Israel. In the same month, a Syrian Jewish businessman said approximately 400 Jews remained in Syria of their own accord, since all of them had exit visas. Some Syrian Jews hesitate to leave their relatively prosperous lives in Syria, especially since the liberal decrees of April 1992, for a more uncertain economic future abroad, and some have remained because of age, health, or reluctance to move. Others want to join relatives and friends who have already departed, and fear a return to earlier repression if Asad should pass from the scene.

U.S. Aid And Sanctions

Since 1950, the United States has provided a total of $627.5 million in aid to Syria: $34.0 million in development assistance, $438.0 million in economic support, $155.4 million in food assistance, and $61 thousand in military training assistance. Most of this aid was provided during a brief warming trend in bilateral relations between 1974 and 1979. Significant projects funded under U.S. aid included water supply, irrigation, rural roads and electrification, and health and agricultural research. No aid has been provided to Syria since 1981, when the last aid programs were closed out. At present, a variety of legislative provisions and executive directives prohibit U.S. aid to Syria and restrict bilateral trade relations.

Sanctions Applicable to Syria

The *International Security Assistance and Arms Export Control Act of 1976* [P.L. 94-329]. Section 303 of this act [90 Stat. 753-754] required termination of foreign assistance to countries that aid or abet international terrorism. This provision was incorporated into the Foreign Assistance Act of 1961 as Section 620A [22 USC 2371]. (Syria was not affected by this ban until 1979, as explained below.) Most recently, this prohibition has been restated in Section 529 of the Foreign Operations, Export Financing, and Related Programs Appropriations Act for FY 1995 (P.L. 103-306).

The *Export Administration Act of 1979* [P.L. 96-72]. Section 6(i) of this act [93 Stat. 515] required the Secretary of Commerce and the Secretary of State to notify Congress before licensing export of goods or technology values at more than $7 million to countries determined to have supported acts of international terrorism (Amendments adopted in 1985 and 1986 re-lettered Section 6(i) as 6(j) and lowered the threshold for notification from $7 million to $1 million.)

A by-product of these two laws was the so-called "terrorism list." This list is prepared annually by the State Department in accordance with Section 6(j) of the Export Administration Act. The list identifies those countries that repeatedly have provided support for acts of international terrorism. Syria has appeared on this list ever since it was first prepared in 1979; it appears most recently in the State Department's annual publication *Patterns of Global Terrorism: 1994*, published in April 1995. Syria's inclusion on this list in 1979 triggered the above-mentioned aid sanctions under P.L. 94-329 and trade restrictions under P.L. 96-72.

Omnibus Diplomatic Security and Antiterrorism Act of 1986 [P.L. 99-399]. Section 509(a) of this act [100 Stat. 853] amended Section 40 of the Arms Export Control Act to prohibit export of items on the munitions list to countries determined to be supportive of international terrorism, thus banning any U.S. military equipment sales to Syria. (This ban was reaffirmed by the Anti-Terrorism and Arms Export Amendments Act of 1989 -- see below.)

Omnibus Budget Reconciliation Act of 1986 [P.L. 99-509]. Section 8041(a) of this act [100 Stat. 1962] amended the Internal Revenue Code of 1954 to deny foreign tax credits on income or war profits from countries identified by the Secretary of State as supporting international terrorism. [26 USC 901}.

Anti-Drug Abuse Act of 1986 [P.L. 99-570]. Section 2005 of this act [100 Stat. 3207] required a Presidential certification citing those drug-producing or drug transit countries that have cooperated with the Untied States or taken adequate steps on their own to control narcotics production, trafficking, or money laundering. (This requirement was incorporated as Section 481 of the Foreign Assistance Act of 1961 -- 22 USC 2291. These provisions were modified by the International Narcotics Control Act of 1992 -- P.L. 102-583 -- and incorporated as Section 490 of the Foreign Assistance Act of 1961.]

The Anti-Drug Abuse Act created another list, the "narcotics list." This list groups narcotics-producing or narcotics transit countries into three categories: (1) those countries certified as having cooperated fully in controlling drug production or trafficking; (2) countries that have failed to meet that standard but are exempt from accompanying U.S. Sanctions because of vital U.S. interests; and (3) countries that have failed to meet that standard and are not exempt from U.S. sanctions. Annual Presidential Determinations (PDs) since 1987 have listed Syria in the third category, most recently, PD 96-13 of March 1, 1996. Though moot in the case of Syria because of other prohibitions already in effect, countries not certified are subject to both mandatory sanctions (generally involving suspension of aid) and discretionary sanctions (involving trade restrictions). (See also U.S. Congress, Senate, Committee on Foreign Relations, International Narcotics Control and Foreign Assistance Certification: Requirements, Procedures, Timetables, and Guidance, Senate Print 100-83, 100th Cong., 2d Sess., Washington, U.S. Government Printing Office, 1988.)

The *Anti-Terrorism and Arms Export Control Amendments Act of 1989* [P.L. 101-222]. Section 4 amended Section 6(j) of the Export Administration Act to impose a congressional notification and licensing requirement for export of goods or technology, irrespective of dollar value, to countries on the terrorism list, if such exports could contribute to their military capability or enhance their ability to support terrorism.

Section 4 also prescribed conditions for removal of a country from the terrorism list: prior notification by the President to the Speaker of the House of Representatives and the chairmen of two specified committees of the Senate. In conjunction with the requisite notification, the President must certify that the country has met several conditions that clearly indicate it is no longer involved in supporting terrorist activity. (In some cases, certification must be provided 45 days in advance of removal of a country from the terrorist list.)

The *Anti-Economic Discrimination Act of 1994* [Part C, P.L. 103-236, the Foreign Relations Authorization Act, FY1994-1995]. Section 564(a) bans the sale or lease of U.S. defense articles and services to any country that questions U.S. firms about their compliance with the Arab boycott of Israel. Section 564(b) contains provisions for a Presidential Waiver. In PD 95-20 of May 1, 1995, President Clinton exempted 21 countries from the application of this law, but did not include Syria among the countries thus exempted. Again, this provision is moot in Syria's case because of other prohibitions already in effect.

Specific Sanctions Against Syria

In addition to the general sanctions listed above, specific provisions in foreign assistance appropriations enacted since 1981 have barred Syria by name from receiving U.S. aid. The latest ban appears in *H.R. 1868, the Foreign Operations, Export Financing, and Related Programs Appropriations Act, 1996* (P.L. 104-107, February 12, 1996). Section 507 bars the obligation or expenditure of funds appropriated under this act for any direct assistance or reparations to eight specified countries, including Syria. Section 523 also prohibits indirect assistance or reparations to seven specified countries including Syria; however, it provides for a Presidential waiver, which has been exercised in previous years on grounds that withholding funds to multilateral development banks and other international organizations and programs under this limitation would be contrary to the national interest (the most recent waiver of this provision was issued by PD 96-19 of March 19, 1996). Section 527 directs U.S. representatives to vote against aid to countries identified as supporting international terrorism by international financial institutions; this provision does not allow for a Presidential waiver. Section 527A bans bilateral aid to countries identified as supporting international terrorism. Section 307 of the *Foreign Assistance Act of 1961, as amended by Section 431 of the Foreign Relations Authorization Act for FY1994-1995* (P.L. 103-236, April 30, 1994) requires the United States to withhold a proportionate share of contributions to international organizations for programs that benefit eight specified countries or entities, including Syria.

Drawing on appropriate legislation, the Administration has imposed detailed trade restrictions on exports to Syria. Under Section 6(j) of the Export Administration Act of 1979, trade controls were instituted after Syria was designated as a country supporting international terrorism in 1979, and further controls were imposed after Syrian intelligence was implicated in an abortive airline bombing in 1986. At present, the Department of Commerce lists 33 categories of exports requiring a validated license for shipment to Syria; these include aircraft, vessels, most vehicles, parts, machine tools, computer equipment, and other high technology goods. (Routine exports like foodstuffs are exempt from these controls.) Moreover, Commerce Department guidelines specify that applications for licenses will generally be denied except for medical equipment, items under pre-1986 contracts, and U.S.-origin goods largely incorporated into foreign products. According to Department of Commerce, during FY1994, export licenses valued at $31 million were approved for Syria, consisting mainly of parts for U.S.-manufactured aircraft previously sold, computer equipment, and oil well perforators. Re-export licenses valued at $45.3 million were also approved for Syria during FY1994, much of this amount representing a one-time transfer of three aging U.S.-made Boeing 727 airliners from Kuwait to Syria. Licenses for export or re-export of goods valued at $0.6 million to Syria were denied during FY 1994.

Permitted Activities

Syria continues to be eligible for small programs not funded by the Foreign Operations, Export Financing, and Related Programs Appropriations Act. For example, small groups of Syrian government and professional representatives have visited the United States on orientation tours under the International Visitor Program, which is administered by the U.S. Information Agency (USIA) and funded under Department of State appropriations. In each of fiscal years 1991 through 1994, 14 Syrians participated (or were scheduled to participate) in the International Visitor Program at approximate annual costs of $105,000 (FY1991), $113,681 (FY1992), $115,948 (FY1993), and $115,948 (FY1994); 16 were scheduled in FY1995 at an estimated cost of $123,930; and 17 are scheduled in FY1996 at an estimated cost of $122,873.

Recent Congressional Action

With the improvement in U.S.-Syrian relations since mid-1990, some Members of Congress have expressed periodic concerns that the Administration may have made undisclosed commitments to Syria in return for its support of the allied coalition during the Gulf war and its subsequent agreement to attend peace talks with Israel. In response to a query from a member of the House Foreign Affairs Committee on October 4, 1994, about the possibility of removing Syria from the terrorism list, Assistant Secretary Pelletreau said this would not be done as long as Syria provides safehaven and support to terrorist organizations; however he added that "It is our hope that over time, as progress in the peace process continues, that Syrian policies toward these organizations will also change, and that this would give way to an eventual removal of Syria from the terrorism list." In a January 11, 1995 press interview, the Chairman of the Senate Foreign Relations Committee implicated Syria in the 1983 U.S. Marine barracks bombing and the 1988 Pam Am 103 bombing and stated that "the Syrian government has American blood on its hands." In a March 24 interview he stated that "apparently, they [the Syrians] were involved also in the attack on Pam Am 103, that killed 270 innocent people" and added that he is "unalterably opposed" to any U.S. aid to Syria in connection with a Syrian-Israeli peace accord.

Several legislative proposals introduced in the 104th Congress would prohibit aid to Russia if it provided material that could be used to develop mass destruction weapons or advanced conventional weapons to countries on the terrorism list (H.R. 519); would prohibit arms sales to 12 named countries (including Syria) unless the President certifies that a state of war does not exist between them and Israel (H.R. 1189); and criticize Syria for granting safehaven and support to the Palestinian fundamentalist group Hamas (S.Res. 67). In addition, the National Security Revitalization Act (H.R. 7) contains a finding that the Untied States and its allies face a ballistic missile threat from five names countries, including Syria.

ALTERNATIVES AND IMPLICATIONS

Debate continues within the U.S. Administration and Congress over the lengths to which the United States should go in seeking to enlist Syrian support for U.S. endeavors in the Middle East. According to one theory, normal bilateral relations should be contingent upon improvements in Syria's human rights record, a clear renunciation of terrorism and narcotics trafficking, and reversal of other policies deemed inimical to U.S. interests. Advocates of this view are particularly concerned over any possibility that the Administration has made promises to ease sanctions (for example, removing Syria from the terrorism or narcotics list) to obtain Syrian cooperation in regional affairs. They tend to discourage bilateral contacts such as visits by Syrian officials, which they see as a potential vehicle for trapping the Administration into premature concessions. They favor continued legislation to ensure that relaxation of sanctions can occur only with congressional approval.

Those who support this first approach see little prospect for a long-term relationship with the Syrian regime, which they consider basically antithetical to U.S. interests and values. They see Syria's alignment with the coalition and agreement to attend peace talks as tactical moves that offered Syria an end to regional isolation, a free hand in Lebanon, and access to financial support from the Gulf states. They point to Syria's previous lack of flexibility on Arab-Israeli issues, periodic bellicose pronouncements from Damascus, and ongoing rearmament programs as indications that Syria will remain a threat to regional stability. They warn that efforts to bring about a closer relationship with President Asad risk repeating the earlier disastrous policy of courting Saddam Husayn.

According to a second theory, quiet diplomacy aimed at encouraging Syria to play a constructive and responsible role in regional affairs could yield benefits. Proponents of this approach do not advocate the immediate termination of sanctions (such as removing Syria from the "black" lists) without further action on Syria's part; however, they support wider contacts between diplomatic and security officials of the two countries to discuss sensitive issues, seek common ground, and identify possible areas of cooperation. They favor a series of small, reciprocal steps that could lead to a warmer relationship over time. Rather than legislative sanctions, they generally prefer an arrangement under which the Administration has the flexibility to apply or ease sanctions in accordance with the current state of bilateral relations.

PALESTINE LIBERATION ORGANIZATION COVENANT[*]

Clyde R. Mark

PLO Commitment to Change the Covenant

The thirty-three article Palestine National Covenant was adopted on July 7, 1968, by the Palestine National Council, the PLO "parliament in exile." Following Arafat's December 1988 renunciation of terrorism, acceptance of U.N. Resolutions 242 and 338, and recognition of Israel, the PLO Chairman was pressed to eliminate from the Covenant references to the struggle with Israel. In May 1989, Yasir Arafat told a Paris audience that the Covenant was "caduque," a French word meaning obsolete or null and void. The next day, Arafat used the English word "superseded" to describe the Covenant. Arafat was criticized by some Palestinians for assuming that he alone could declare the Covenant null.[1]

PLO Chairman Yasir Arafat states in his September 9, 1993 letter to Israeli Prime Minister Yitzhak Rabin, that:

The PLO affirms that those articles of the Palestinian Covenant which deny Israel's right to exist, and the provisions of the Covenant which are inconsistent with the commitments of this letter are now inoperative and no longer valid. Consequently, the PLO undertakes to submit to the Palestinian National Council for formal approval the necessary changes in regard to the Palestinian Covenant.

The PLO-Israel Interim Agreement of September 28, 1995, also popularly called the Taba Agreement or Oslo II, stated in Chapter 5, Article XXXI, that:

The PLO undertakes that, within two months of the date of the inauguration of the Council, the Palestinian National Council will convene and formally approve the

---

[*]Excerpted from *CRS Report 96-324 F.*

[1]The "caduque" statement was reported by Radio Monte Carlo, May 2, 1989, reprinted in Foreign Broadcast Information Service (FBIS), Near East and South Asia, daily report, May 3, 1989. For reactions from radical groups that opposed Arafat's concessions, see FBIS, May 4 and 5, 1989.

necessary changes in regard to the Palestinian Covenant, as undertaken in the letters signed by the Chairman of the PLO and addressed to the Prime Minister of Israel, dated September 9, 1993 and May 4, 1994.

(The "Council" mentioned in the Taba Agreement is the 88-member Palestinian Assembly elected on January 20, 1996. The Assembly met for the first time on March 7, 1996, so the two month deadline was scheduled to expire on May 7, 1996. The "May 4, 1994" letter refers to the Israeli-PLO agreement for the Israeli withdrawal from Gaza and Jericho signed on that date.)

IMPLEMENTING THE CHANGES

In February 1996, Arafat told reporters that he did not have the authority to change the Covenant on his own, that only the PNC could make amendments. The statement appeared to contradict his 1989 statement in which he implied that he had the authority to declare that the Covenant was "caduque" or the implied authority to speak for the PLO in September 1993, when he said the Covenant was "inoperative."

The press reported that the PLO had set conditions for amending the Covenant, that the Palestinians would not consider changing the Covenant unless Israel recognized the Palestinian's right to a state, released the Palestinian prisoners held in Israeli jails as promised in the Taba Agreement, canceled indictments on PFLP, DFLP, and other Palestinian radicals and allowed them to return to the occupied territories,[2] and made concessions on Jerusalem. The PNC acted on the Covenant before Israel satisfied any of these reported conditions.

According to Article 33, the Palestine Liberation Organization Covenant can be amended by a majority vote of two-thirds of the members of the Palestine National Council (PNC). There are 669 members of the PNC; two-thirds of whom, or 446, constitute the quorum necessary to amend the Covenant. On 24 April 1996, 572 PNC members were present at Gaza for the vote on amending the Covenant, and voted 504 in favor, 54 opposed, with 14 abstentions, to pass a resolution that may or may not have amended the Covenant, depending upon one's interpretation of the resolution.

Salim al-Zaanun, PNC Speaker, announced that the PNC legal committee would have six months to redraft the Covenant, but it is not clear if the legal committee will recommend amendments to the present Covenant, or will draft a new Covenant to replace the 1968 version.

---

[2]Israel approved a PLO request to allow PNC members to enter the occupied territories; Israeli approval was needed because PNC members en route to Palestinian-held areas had to pass through Israeli-held territory and Israeli check points, including the Egyptian border -with Gaza. Israel still controls about 70% of the West Bank and 30% of Gaza. The Popular Front for the Liberation of Palestine (PFLP), the Democratic Front for the Liberation of Palestine (DFLP), the PFLP-General Command, and others headquartered in Damascus reject the peace process and did not attend the PNC session in April 1996.

Did the 24 April 1996 PNC Resolution Fulfill the PLO Commitment?

Yasir Arafat sent a letter to Israeli Prime Minister Peres stating that the PLO met its commitment to change the Covenant. Attached to the letter were two "official" copies, one in Arabic and one in English, of the resolution passed by the PNC,[3] including the following two operative clauses:

The Palestinian National Council ... decides:

1. The Palestine National Charter is hereby amended by canceling the articles that are contrary to the letters exchanged between the P.L.O. and the Government of Israel 9-10 September 1993.

2. Assigns its legal committee with the task of redrafting the Palestinian National Charter in order to present it to the first session of the Palestinian central council.

One could infer from reading the operative paragraphs that the amendment process was completed, the offending articles or phrases had been deleted, and that the PLO legal committee was engaged in redrafting the Covenant. Apparently, this is the interpretation accepted by the Israeli and U.S. Governments. Israeli Prime Minister Peres told a Washington meeting on April 28, 1996, that the PNC "... has voted to abolish those articles of the Covenant that call for the destruction of Israel ..." President Clinton told the same audience that the PNC "... finally did change the PLO Charter and deleted the hateful clause calling for the destruction of Israel."[4] Prime Minister Peres and President Clinton issued a joint communique at the end of their Washington meetings that said the two welcomed the decision by the Palestinian National Council to cancel all the provisions of the Palestinian National Covenant which deny Israel's right to exist or are otherwise inconsistent with the September 1993 exchange of letters between Prime Minister Rabin and Chairman Arafat.[5]

Israeli Foreign Minister Ehud Baraq said on May 3, 1996, that "the Charter has been repealed."[6]

But, there is another interpretation of the PNC actions. Binyamin Netanyahu, Likud Party leader and candidate for Prime Minister, said:

---

[3]See FBIS, NES, May 6, 1996, p. 4, or [gopher://israel-info.gov.il:70/OR225636-229608-/new/pprocess1].

[4]Israel Government Press Office, released April 29, 1996; reprinted in FBIS, April 30, 1996, p. 29. USNewswire, April 28, 1996. The Prime Minister and President were speaking to the policy conference of the American Israel Public Affairs Committee.

[5]Israel Government press office, May 1, 1996; reprinted in FBIS, May 2, 1996, p. 15.

[6]Baraq interview in Davar Rishon, May 3, 1996, reprinted in FBIS, May 6, 1996, p. 39.

the PNC gave a committee power of attorney to amend in the future clauses it decides contravene the Oslo accords.

Netanyahu added that Likud demanded the abrogation of 22 clauses in the Covenant and that none of the relevant clauses had been repealed by the PNC vote.[7] Some may dismiss Natanyahu's complaint as politically motivated, an attempt to distinguish himself from Peres in the Prime Minister's race.

Other people may have concluded, as did Netanyahu and the Likud, that the Covenant had not been amended, after reading a different, unofficial translation of the Arafat-to-Peres letter and the April 24, 1996 resolution. According to this alternate translation, the PNC decided "to amend" the Covenant, and said it "will entrust" the PLO Legal Committee with redrafting the Covenant and submitting the revised version to the PLO Central Council.[8] In this alternative translation, "to amend" and "will entrust" clearly imply that the PNC did not amend the Covenant, and that the actual act of amending the Covenant will take place in the future.

Deciding if the Covenant has or has not been amended may depend upon one's perspective. One person, eager to see the peace process succeed, may minimize details in each step to maintain the momentum toward the overall goal of peace. According to this view the PNC signaled its good intentions by voting to amend the Covenant, and the peace process may carry on. But, another person may believe that the whole peace process is at risk unless each detail in turn is complete and acceptable before preceding with the next step. Under this alternate interpretation, the PNC vote was a gesture, but the gesture must be followed with concrete action before proceeding to the next step.

COVENANT CHANGES

If it was the intention of the PNC to amend the present Covenant, it is not clear which articles or passages were changed. If it was the intention of the PNC to amend the Covenant in the future, it is not clear which articles the PNC intends to change. Earlier, both PLO and Israeli representatives stated that changes probably would be negotiated.[9] As far as is known, such negotiations have not been held.

Israel has not offered an official list of which Covenant articles were or must be changed, or the nature of the changes expected.[10] An Israeli embassy official said the Israeli Government did not have a list of articles or phrases that it expected the PLO

---

[7]Interview broadcast over Qol Israel radio, April 25, 1996; reprinted in FBIS, April 25, 1996, p. 28-29.

[8]Broadcast over Jericho Voice of Palestine radio on April 24, 1996; reprinted in FBIS, April 25, 1996, p. 2.

[9]Telephone conversation with Palestinian and Israeli representative on February 6, 1996.

[10]The Israeli focus on the Covenant is not new. See the monograph: Harkabi, Yehoshofat. The Position of the Palestinians in the Israel-Arab Conflict and Their National Covenant (198), n.p., 1970. 35 p. Harkabi followed his first work with: The Palestinian Covenant and its Meaning, London, Vallentine, Mitchell, 1979. 159 p.

to amend.[11]   The Israeli Foreign Ministry is circulating a copy of the Covenant with nine articles highlighted, implying that the PLO must change the highlighted nine.[12] The list of nine articles may represent an official Israeli government position on the Covenant passages to be altered, or it may represent an unofficial guide to inform readers. Earlier, the February 28, 1996 Jerusalem Post reported that Israeli "officials" said 30 of the 33 articles must be "eliminated." Another report said "at least half" the 33 articles must be altered.[13]

A State Department official said that the Covenant had been changed, but that there was no list of which articles or phrases had been amended or of the nature of the changes.[14]

Some people may be confused by reports, in the press or elsewhere, that the PNC must delete passages calling for the destruction of Israel, but then discover that the phrase "destruction of Israel" does not appear in the Covenant. Although the phrase does not appear, one may infer from reading passages in the Covenant that the destruction of Israel is intended. For example, Article 15 speaks of the Palestinian national duty to "repel the Zionist and imperialist aggression" and adds that the liberation of Palestine "aims at the elimination of Zionism in Palestine." Article 22 states that the "liberation of Palestine will destroy the Zionist and imperialist presence."

Similarly, it is not clear what the PLO legal committee will do during the six months following the April 24, 1996 PNC vote. The legal committee is charged with redrafting the Covenant, but redrafting may mean drafting a new Covenant to replace the 1968 version or it could mean altering the 1968 Covenant by removing or rephrasing articles that may be construed as denying Israel's right to exist.

United States Position on Changing the Covenant

The United States supported the Israeli position that the Covenant had to be amended, and the present Administration agrees with the Israeli Government that the Covenant has been amended. But not all agree with the Administration position. The Chairman of the Senate Foreign Relations Committee wrote to Secretary of State Warren Christopher seeking clarification to determine if the April 24, 1996 resolution amended the Covenant and which articles had been changed by the resolution.[15]

---

[11]Telephone conversation with the Israeli embassy, February 6, 1996.

[12]See Appendix. The Israeli Foreign Ministry printed version of the Palestinian Covenant can be found at http://www.israel.org/peace/plocov.html

[13]Kershner, Isabel, The People of the Covenant, The Jerusalem Report, Vol. VI, no. 24, April 4, 1996, p. 33.

[14]Telephone conversation, May 8, 1996.

[15]Carter, Tom, Helms Hits at Palestinian Aid Cutoff, Washington Times, May 10, 1996, p. 1. Also see US Senator Jesse Helms Questions PLO Charter Change, Reuters, May 8, 1996.

The Middle East Peace Facilitation Act (MEPFA) of 1995 (P.O. 104-107, February 12, 1996) has several sections dealing with changes in the Covenant.

(1) The Findings, Sect. 602(9), state that the PLO must submit to the PNC for amendment those Covenant articles that call for Israel's destruction.

(2) Section 603 states that it is the sense of the Congress that the PLO must demonstrate its denunciation of terrorism by submitting to the PNC changes to delete passages in the Covenant that call for the destruction of Israel.

(3) Section 604(b)(2) of the MEPFA of 1995, states that the President must certify to the Congress that the PLO has submitted to the PNC changes in the Covenant to remove calls for the destruction of Israel (as listed in Sec. 604(b)(4)(A)(vi)).

(4) Section 604(b)(5)(A) states that the Presidential justification called for in Section 604(b)(1) must include a description of the manner in which the PLO complied with its commitments, including the commitment to change the Covenant as listed in Section 604(b)(4)(A)(vi).

(5) Section 604(c)(1) states that the United States will furnish no assistance unless the President determines and certifies to Congress that the Palestinian Assembly, elected on January 20, 1996, has disavowed and nullified the PLO Covenant if the PNC has not changed the Covenant within two months of the Assembly having "assumed responsibility."[16]

United States officials have said U.S. financial assistance to the Palestinians would stop unless the Covenant was amended.

Appendix 1 – The PLO Covenant

Note: The following copy of the PLO Covenant is reprinted from the Israeli Ministry of Foreign Affairs version of the Palestinian Covenant. The Israeli version may be found at: [http://www.israel.org/peace/plocov.html].

---

[16]The Middle East Peace Facilitation Act first appeared in 1993, as Section 3(b)(4)(A) of P.L. 103-125, October 28, 1993, and was repeated in 1994 as Part E, Title V of P.L. 103-236, April 30, 1994. Prior to MEPFA, the PLO Commitments Compliance Act of 1989, P.L. 101-246, Section 803(b)(2)(E) called for the PLO to amend the Covenant to remove provisions that undermined Israel's legitimacy or called for Israel's destruction.

THE PALESTINIAN NATIONAL CHARTER:
RESOLUTIONS OF THE PALESTINE NATIONAL COUNCIL

July 1-17, 1968

The following is the complete and unabridged text of the Palestinian National Covenant, as published officially in English by the PLO*.

In his letter of September 9, 1993 to Prime Minister Rabin, Yasser Arafat stated that those articles which deny Israel's right to exist or are inconsistent with the PLO's new commitments to Israel following their mutual recognition, are no longer valid. The necessary changes are to be approved by the Palestinian National Council. The key articles in questions are **highlighted**.

Text of the Charter:

Article 1: Palestine is the homeland of the Arab Palestinian people; it is an indivisible part of the Arab homeland, and the Palestinian people are an integral part of the Arab nation.

Article 2: Palestine, with the boundaries it had during the British Mandate, is an indivisible territorial unit.

Article 3: The Palestinian Arab people possess the legal right to their homeland and have the right to determine their destiny after achieving the liberation of their country in accordance with their wishes and entirely of their own accord and will.

Article 4: The Palestinian identity is a genuine, essential, and inherent characteristic; it is transmitted from parents to children. The Zionist occupation and the dispersal of the Palestinian Arab people, through the disasters which befell them, do not make them lose their Palestinian identity and their membership in the Palestinian community, nor do they negate them.

Article 5: The Palestinians are those Arab nationals who, until 1947, normally resided in Palestine regardless of whether they were evicted from it or have stayed there. Anyone born, after that date, of a Palestinian father - whether inside Palestine or outside it - is also a Palestinian.

Article 6: The Jews who had normally resided in Palestine until the beginning of the Zionist invasion will be considered Palestinians.

Article 7: That there is a Palestinian community and that it has material, spiritual, and historical connection with Palestine are indisputable facts. It is a national duty to bring up individual Palestinians in an Arab revolutionary manner. All means of information and education must be adopted in order to acquaint the Palestinian with his country in the most profound manner, both spiritual and material, that is possible. He must be prepared for the armed struggle and ready to sacrifice his wealth and life in order to win back his homeland and bring about its liberation.

Article 8: The phase in their history, through which the Palestinian people are now living, is that of national (watani) struggle for the liberation of Palestine. Thus the conflicts among the Palestinian national forces are secondary, and should be ended for the sake of the basic conflict that exists between the forces of Zionism and of imperialism on the one hand, and the Palestinian Arab people on the other. On this basis the Palestinian masses, regardless of whether they are residing in the national homeland or in diaspora (mahajir) constitute - both their organizations and the individuals - one national front working for the retrieval of Palestine and its liberation through armed struggle.

Article 9: Armed struggle is the only way to liberate Palestine. This it is the overall strategy, not merely a tactical phase. The Palestinian Arab people assert their absolute determination and firm resolution to continue their armed struggle and to work for an armed popular revolution for the liberation of their country and their return to it. They also assert their right to normal life in Palestine and to exercise their right to self-determination and sovereignty over it.

Article 10: Commando action constitutes the nucleus of the Palestinian popular liberation war. This requires its escalation, comprehensiveness, and the mobilization of all the Palestinian popular and educational efforts and their organization and involvement in the armed Palestinian revolution. It also requires the achieving of unity for the national (watani) struggle among the different groupings of the Palestinian people, and between the Palestinian people and the Arab masses, so as to secure the continuation of the revolution, its escalation, and victory.

Article 11: The Palestinians will have three mottoes: national (wataniyya) unity, national (qawmiyya) mobilization, and liberation.

Article 12: The Palestinian people believe in Arab unity. In order to contribute their share toward the attainment of that objective, however, they must, at the present stage of their struggle, safeguard their Palestinian identity and develop their consciousness of that identity, and oppose any plan that may dissolve or impair it.

Article 13: Arab unity and the liberation of Palestine are two complementary objectives, the attainment of either of which facilitates the attainment of the other. Thus, Arab unity leads to the liberation of Palestine, the liberation of Palestine leads to Arab unity; and work toward the realization of one objective proceeds side by side with work toward the realization of the other.

Article 14: The destiny of the Arab nation, and indeed Arab existence itself, depend upon the destiny of the Palestine cause. From this interdependence springs the Arab nation's pursuit of, and striving for, the liberation of Palestine. The people of Palestine play the role of the vanguard in the realization of this sacred (qawmi) goal.

Article 15: The liberation of Palestine, from an Arab viewpoint, is a national (qawmi) duty and it attempts to repel the Zionist and imperialist aggression against the Arab homeland, and aims at the elimination of Zionism in Palestine. Absolute responsibility for this falls upon the Arab nation - peoples and governments - with the Arab people of Palestine in the vanguard. Accordingly, the Arab nation must mobilize all its military, human, moral, and spiritual capabilities to participate actively with the Palestinian people in the liberation of Palestine. It must, particularly in the phase of the armed Palestinian revolution, offer and furnish the Palestinian people with all possible help, and material and human support, and make available to them the means and opportunities that will enable them to continue to carry out their leading role in the armed revolution, until they liberate their homeland.

Article 16: The liberation of Palestine, from a spiritual point of view, will provide the Holy Land with an atmosphere of safety and tranquility, which in turn will safeguard the country's religious sanctuaries and guarantee freedom of worship and of visit to all, without discrimination of race, color, language, or religion. Accordingly, the people of Palestine look to all spiritual forces in the world for support.

Article 17: The liberation of Palestine, from a human point of view, will restore to the Palestinian individual his dignity, pride, and freedom. Accordingly the Palestinian Arab people look forward to the support of all those who believe in the dignity of man and his freedom in the world.

Article 18: The liberation of Palestine, from an international point of view, is a defensive action necessitated by the demands of self-defense. Accordingly the Palestinian people, desirous as they are of the friendship of all people, look to freedom-loving, and peace-loving states for support in order to restore their legitimate rights in Palestine, to re-establish peace and security in the country, and to enable its people to exercise national sovereignty and freedom.

Article 19: The partition of Palestine in 1947 and the establishment of the state of Israel are entirely illegal, regardless of the passage of time, because they were contrary to the will of the Palestinian people and to their natural right in their homeland, and inconsistent with the principles embodied in the Charter of the United Nations, particularly the right to self-determination.

Article 20: The Balfour Declaration, the Mandate for Palestine, and everything that has been based upon them, are deemed null and void. Claims of historical or religious ties of Jews with Palestine are incompatible with the facts of history and the true conception of what constitutes statehood. Judaism, being a religion, is not an independent nationality. Nor do Jews constitute a single nation with an identity of its own; they are citizens of the states to which they belong.

Article 21: The Arab Palestinian people, expressing themselves by the armed Palestinian revolution, reject all solutions which are substitutes for the total liberation of Palestine and reject all proposals aiming at the liquidation of the Palestinian problem, or its internationalization.

Article 22: Zionism is a political movement organically associated with international imperialism and antagonistic to all action for liberation and to progressive movements in the world. It is racist and fanatic in its nature, aggressive, expansionist, and colonial in its aims, and fascist in its methods. Israel is the instrument of the Zionist movement, and geographical base for world imperialism placed strategically in the midst of the Arab homeland to combat the hopes of the Arab nation for liberation, unity, and progress. Israel is a constant source of threat vis-a-vis peace in the Middle East and the whole world. Since the liberation of Palestine will destroy the Zionist and imperialist presence and will contribute to the establishment of peace in the Middle East, the Palestinian people look for the support of all the progressive and peaceful forces and urge them all, irrespective of their affiliations and beliefs, to offer the Palestinian people all aid and support in their just struggle for the liberation of their homeland.

Article 23: The demand of security and peace, as well as the demand of right and justice, require all states to consider Zionism an illegitimate movement, to outlaw its existence, and to ban its operations, in order that friendly relations among peoples may be preserved, and the loyalty of citizens to their respective homelands safeguarded.

Article 24: The Palestinian people believe in the principles of justice, freedom, sovereignty, self-determination, human dignity, and in the right of all peoples to exercise them.

Article 25: For the realization of the goals of this Charter and its principles, the Palestine Liberation Organization will perform its role in the liberation of Palestine in accordance with the Constitution of this Organization.

Article 26: The Palestine Liberation Organization, representative of the Palestinian revolutionary forces, is responsible for the Palestinian Arab people's movement in its struggle - to retrieve its homeland, liberate and return to it and exercise the right to self-determination in it - in all military, political, and financial fields and also for whatever may be required by the Palestine case on the inter-Arab and international levels.

Article 27: The Palestine Liberation Organization shall cooperate with all Arab states, each according to its potentialities; and will adopt a neutral policy among them in the light of the requirements of the war of liberation; and on this basis it shall not interfere in the internal affairs of any Arab state.

Article 28: The Palestinian Arab people assert the genuineness and independence of their national (wataniyya) revolution and reject all forms of intervention, trusteeship, and subordination.

Article 29: The Palestinian people possess the fundamental and genuine legal right to liberate and retrieve their homeland. The Palestinian people determine their attitude toward all states and forces on the basis of the stands they adopt vis-a-vis to the Palestinian revolution to fulfill the aims of the Palestinian people.

Article 30: Fighters and carriers of arms in the war of liberation are the nucleus of the popular army which will be the protective force for the gains of the Palestinian Arab people.

Article 31: The Organization shall have a flag, an oath of allegiance, and an anthem. All this shall be decided upon in accordance with a special regulation.

Article 32: Regulations, which shall be known as the Constitution of the Palestinian Liberation Organization, shall be annexed to this Charter. It will lay down the manner in which the Organization, and its organs and institutions, shall be constituted; the respective competence of each; and the requirements of its obligation under the Charter.

Article 33: This Charter shall not be amended save by [vote of] a majority of two-thirds of the total membership of the National Congress of the Palestine Liberation Organization [taken] at a special session convened for that purpose.
*English rendition as published in Basic Political Documents of the Armed Palestinian Resistance Movement; Leila S. .Kadi (ed.), Palestine Research Centre, Beirut, December 1969. p. 137-141.
Appendix   2 -- The PNC Resolution

Note: The following copy of the Arafat letter to Peres and the attached PNC Resolution passes on April 24, 1996, were taken from [gopher://israel-info.gov.il: 70/OR225636-229608-/new/pprocess1].

Information Division, Israel Foreign Ministry - Jerusalem
Mail all Queries to ask@israel-info.gov.il
URL: http://www.israel-mfa.gov.il
gopher://israel-info.gov.il

THE AMENDMENT OF THE PALESTINIAN COVENANT

LETTER FROM PALESTINIAN AUTHORITY PRESIDENT YASSER ARAFAT

TO PRIME MINISTER SHIMON PERES

May 4, 1996

Mr. Shimon Peres
Prime Minister of Israel

Dear Mr. Peres,

I convey my best wishes to your excellency, and I would like to convey to you the recent historic resolution adopted by the Palestinian National Council at its 21st session held in Gaza city.

As part of our commitment to the peace process, and in adhering to the mutual recognition between the Palestinian Liberation Organization and the Government of Israel, the P.N.C. was held in Gaza city between 22-25 of April 1996, and in an extraordinary session decided that the Palestine National Charter is hereby amended by cancelling the provisions that are contrary to the letters exchanged between the P.L.O. and the government of Israel on 9/10 Sept. 1993.

Please find enclosed copies of the official Arabic and English texts of the P.N.C.s resolutions.

We remain committed to the peace process.

Gaza: 4/5/1996

Yasser Arafat
Chairman of the Executive Committee of
Palestine Liberation Organization
President of the Palestinian National Authority

OFFICIAL TRANSLATION

The Palestinian National Council, at its 21st session held in the city of Gaza,

Emanating from the declaration of independence and the political statement adopted at its 19th session held in Algiers on Nov. 15, 1988, which affirmed the resolution of conflicts by peaceful means and accepted the two states solution,

And based on the introduction of the Declaration of Principles signed in Washington, D.C. on 13 September 1993, which included the agreement of both sides to put an end to decades of confrontation and conflict and to live in peaceful coexistence, mutual dignity and security, while recognizing their mutual legitimate and political right,

And reaffirming their desire to achieve a just, lasting and comprehensive peace settlement and historic reconciliation through the agreed political process,

And based on international legitimacy represented by the United Nations Resolutions relevant to the Palestinian question, including those relating to Jerusalem, Refugees and Settlements, and the other issues of the permanent status and the implementation of Security Council Resolutions 242 and 338,

And affirming the adherence of the Palestine Liberation Organization to its commitments deriving from the D.O.P. (Oslo 1), the provisional Cairo Agreement, the letter of mutual recognition signed on 9 and 10 September 1993, the Israeli-Palestinian Interim Agreement on the West Bank and the Gaza Strip (Oslo 2) signed in Washington D.C. on 28 September 1995, and reconfirm the resolution of the central Council of the P.L.O. adopted in October 1993, which approved the Oslo Agreement and all its annexes,

And based on the principles which constituted the foundation of the Madrid Peace Conference and the Washington negotiations, decides:

1. The Palestinian National Charter is hereby amended by canceling the articles that are contrary to the letters exchanged between the P.L.O. and the Government of Israel 9-10 September 1993.

2. Assigns its legal committee with the task of redrafting the Palestinian National Charter in order to present it to the first session of the Palestinian central council.

Iran: U.S. Containment Policy[*]

Kenneth Katzman

Introduction

The United States and Iran were allies when the Shah ruled Iran prior to 1979, but animosity between the United States and Iran has dissipated little in the nearly fifteen years since Iranian radicals took over the U.S. Embassy in Tehran and held 52 Americans there hostage for 444 days. At a February 24, 1994 Middle East Policy Council symposium on Capitol Hill, the National Security Council's senior director for Middle East affairs, Martin Indyk, articulated five areas in which Iran continues to challenge U.S. interests: (2) Iran's efforts to acquire nuclear weapons and other weapons of mass destruction; (2) its acquisition of potentially destabilizing conventional arms; (3) its promotion of terrorism and assassination worldwide; (4) its attempts to undermine the Arab-Israeli peace process, primarily by supporting groups that use violence to try to derail that process; and (5) its efforts to subvert U.S. allies in the region. The Administration and Congress are also highly concerned about Iran's human rights abuses and its continuation of a death sentence against British author Salman Rushdie.[1]

On the other hand, some experts within and outside the Administration believe the potential threat from Iran is waning.[2] They see Iran weighted down by factional infighting, outstanding debts to Western creditors, and falling oil prices that have slowed its military modernization programs. Some of its reported weapons agreements are believed to be on hold because Iran does not have the hard currency to pay for the orders.

---

[*]Excerpted from *CRS Report 94-652 F.*

[1]The late Ayatollah Khomeini issued a religious proclamation in February 1989 calling for Rushdie's death for writing the novel "The Satanic Verses," which Khomeini and his aides believed blasphemed Islam. For further information on Iranian activities of concern to the United States, see U.S. Library of Congress Congressional Research Service. Iran: Current Developments and U.S. Policy. Issue Brief 93033, updated regularly, by Kenneth Katzman. 15 p.

[2]For a further discussion of this view, see Sciolino, Elaine. Iran's Difficulties Lead Some in U.S. to Doubt Threat. New York Times, July 5, 1994. P. 1. See also the comments by an unnamed senior Administration official. Foreign Correspondents Association Background Briefing. Reuters, July 7, 1994.

For its part, Iran defends its international behavior as an answer to U.S. hostility toward it and Islam. Iran portrays its military procurement and foreign policies as essentially defensive -- to guard the revolution against encirclement by Iran's enemies, including Israel and Saudi Arabia, which are supported by the United States. Iran explains its aid to groups opposed to the Arab-Israeli peace process as an effort to prevent the purported "sellout" of Muslim lands represented by Israel's continued existence.

The seemingly irreconcilable differences between the United States and Iran have led the Clinton Administration, even more than the Reagan or Bush Administrations, to try to contain Iran. The Reagan Administration sought out Iranian "moderates" to promote a strategic opening to Iran. That policy led to the disastrous 1985-86 arms dealings and hostage exchanges that developed into the Iran-Contra Affair. President Bush, in his January 1989 inaugural address, seemed to reach out to Iran when he said that "goodwill begets goodwill" -- that Iranian help in gaining release of American hostages in Lebanon might earn some U.S. reciprocation. By contrast, Secretary of State Christopher, who as Deputy Secretary of State negotiated the 1981 hostage crisis settlement with Iran, has consistently characterized Iran as an "outlaw state" that should be contained and isolated. The Secretary of State condemned Iran following bombings in July 1994 of Israeli and Jewish installations in Argentina and London.[3] During a visit to the Persian Gulf region in May 1994, Assistant Secretary of State for Near East Affairs Robert Pelletreau said that U.S. policy toward Iran is to seek all effective means to contain Iran and press it to change its policies. The Clinton Administration has placed the containment of Iran within a broader policy framework that seeks to keep both Iraq and Iran weak. On May 19, 1993, at a speech in Washington, NSC staffer Indyk unveiled the Administration's policy as one of "dual containment" of Iran and Iraq.[4]

Evolution of a New Policy

BALANCING THE TWO GULF POWERS

The Administration has presented dual containment as a sharp departure from previous U.S. Gulf policies that have relied on balancing Iran and Iraq by alternately tilting toward one or the other. The "balancing" policy began more than two decades ago after Britain, in 1971, militarily withdrew from the Gulf and the United states assumed responsibility for defending Western interests there. During 1971-79, the United States sought to strengthen Iran, then led by the Shah, and Saudi Arabia as "twin pillars" -- or policemen -- of U.S. policy in the Gulf. The effort to strengthen the Shah was partly a response to the 1968 coup in Iraq which brought the leftwing

---

[3]Testimony of Secretary of State Christopher before the House Foreign Affairs Committee. Federal News Service, July 28, 1994.

[4]Text of Martin Indyk's speech can be found in the proceedings of the Soref Symposium, Challenges to U.S. Interests in the Middle East: Obstacles and Opportunities, May 18-19, 1993. Washington, Washington Institute for Near East Policy. pp. 1-8.

Ba'th (Arabic for renaissance) Party to power.[5] The Ba'thist regime had turned to the Soviet Union for arms and political support, signing a treaty of friendship with the Soviets in April 1972. President Nixon's then National Security Adviser Henry Kissinger visited Tehran a month after the treaty was signed to discuss U.S. and Iranian assistance to the Kurds of Iraq, as a means of placing pressure on the regime in Baghdad.[6] The policy appeared to show some success when Iraq and Iran reached a comprehensive understanding in their 1975 Algiers Accords, in which both states agreed to share control of the Shatt al-Arab waterway and to refrain from interfering in each others' affairs. Iraq also put some political distance between itself and the Soviet Union and curtailed efforts to subvert the Persian Gulf monarchies.

A major blow to U.S. policy came in February 1979, when the Shah was overthrown by the Iranian Islamic revolution, led by Ayatollah Ruhollah Khomeini. The downfall of the U.S. ally in the Gulf led to a subsequent tilt toward Iraq, despite U.S. pledges to remain neutral in the Iran-Iraq war, which began when Iraq invaded Iran in September 1980.[7] The Reagan Administration opened export credits to Iraq in 1982 when it removed that Arab state from the list of state sponsors of terrorism; formal U.S.-Iraqi relations were resumed in 1984. The United States also undertook diplomatic efforts to persuade individual governments not to sell arms to Iran in the ongoing war.[8]

THE DUAL CONTAINMENT POLICY AND CRITICISMS

Citing the ineffectiveness of trying to contain Iraq or Iran by tilting toward one or the other, Clinton Administration officials explain the new dual containment policy as an effort to keep both regimes weak.[9] Both countries are considered hostile to U.S. interests. Administration officials contend that the new policy does not ignore balance of power considerations, but, rather, seeks to maintain that balance at a low level of Iranian and Iraqi capability. The Administration maintains that the

---

[5]Saddam Husayn was a high ranking Ba'thist and played a key role in the 1968 coup, emerging almost immediately as the second power in the regime. He did not formally assume the presidency of Iraq until July 1979 when he persuaded President Ahmad al-Bakr to retire.

[6]Helms, Christine. Iraq: Eastern Flank of the Arab World. Washington, Brookings Institution, 1974. p. 146.

[7]Analysts give several explanations for Iraq's decision to invade Iran. (1) Iraq wanted to regain control of the Shatt al-Arab waterway between the two nations; (2) Iraq sought to assume the "policeman of the Gulf" role played by the Shah until his downfall; and (3) Iran was weak and disorganized after its Islamic revolution and the Iraqi leadership felt its invasion could trigger an overturning of the Islamic revolution. Iraq hoped thereby to blunt the revolution's effects on Iraq's own Shiite population, much of which looks to Iran for inspiration.

[8]This diplomatic effort was known as "Operation Staunch." Staunch lost must of its credibility after the November 1986 revelations of secret U.S. arms sales to Iran as part of what became known as the Iran-Contra Affair.

[9]The rationale for the dual containment policy is discussed in Lake, Anthony. Confronting Backlash States. Foreign Affairs, Volume 73, No. 2, March/April 1994. pp. 45-55; and Symposium on Dual Containment: U.S. Policy Toward Iran and Iraq, in Middle East Policy, Volume III, No. 1, 1994. pp. 1-26.

past practice of tilting toward one or the other has created power imbalances and resulting instability in the Gulf, and that changed conditions in the Gulf have created a favorable climate for the dual containment policy. In particular, the collapse of the Soviet Union deprives Iran and Iraq of an alternate superpower that they can play off against the United States. Furthermore, the offensive capabilities of both states have been weakened by the Iran-Iraq war, which diminished Iran's force, and Desert Storm, which destroyed about 50% of Iraq's military capability and placed its surviving weapons of mass destruction programs under a tight U.N. inspection regime.

Administration officials add that dual containment does not mean that U.S. policy toward Iran will be exactly the same as it is toward Iraq. Iraq is contained by international implementation of very strict U.N. sanctions[10] and, for this reason, the policy community generally identifies dual containment with policy toward Iran rather than toward Iraq. Iran is not subject to any U.N. or sweeping international sanctions, nor is there pressure in the United Nations to impose such sanctions on Iran. Therefore, to contain Iran, the United States has acted outside the U.N. framework, and often unilaterally.

Clinton Administration policymakers further believe that U.S. Iran policy is showing some signs of success. They contend that Iran is weaker and more isolated than it was when Clinton took office. A senior administration official told journalists on July 7, 1994, that the United States "do[es] not see a change in the intentions or motivations of the Iranian government, but their capabilities at the moment to create problems have been reduced."[11] This and other officials have noted that deliveries of major military systems from Iran's biggest arms suppliers have slowed, largely because of Iran's inability to pay in hard currency. However, some of Iran's difficulties may be due to the fall in oil prices during late 1993 and early 1994 rather than the dual containment policy.

Some observers have criticized the dual containment policy as unrealistic and unworkable. According to Council on Foreign Relations fellow Gregory Gause, "the major logical flaw in dual containment is the contention that Iran and Iraq can be contained simultaneously."[12] According to this analysis, the weakness of either country invites destabilizing intervention by the other, and economic sanctions on either country are difficult to enforce without the cooperation of the other. Further, Gause argues, an important potential strategic consequence of dual containment is that, in classifying both countries as outcasts, the policy could bring Iran and Iraq closer together in an anti-U.S. alliance. Some supporting evidence for that judgment is provided by the growing political dialogue between the two historic adversaries.

---

[10]At the present time, these U.N. sanctions include intrusive inspections, dismantling, and monitoring of its weapons of mass destruction programs and facilities; a comprehensive U.N. ban on imports of goods (other than food and medicine); and a prohibition on the export of oil or other products.

[11]Comments by a senior administration official. Foreign Correspondents association, covered by Reuters, July 7, 1994.

[12]Gause rebutted the arguments for dual containment in an article that immediately followed National Security Adviser Anthony Lake's piece on that issued in the March/April issue of Foreign Affairs magazine. Gause, Gregory. The Illogic of Dual Containment, I=in Foreign Affairs. Volume 73, No. 2, March/April 1994. p. 60.

After several exchanges in 1992 and 1993 at the deputy Foreign Minister level, their Foreign Ministers met at the margins of a Non-Aligned Movement Conference in Egypt on June 1, 1994.

In recommending policy alternatives, Gause and other critics of dual containment envision a dialogue with Iran and other regional parties, taking into account Iran's legitimate interests. In advocating a dialogue, these analysts contend that the threat to U.S. interests posed by Iran is not as great as the Clinton Administration has portrayed it, and should not preclude talking to Iran. Gause, for example, distinguishes his proposal for a dialogue from a tilt toward Iran by arguing against selling arms to Iran or relaxing enforcement of nuclear nonproliferation policies toward Iran. In the region, several of the Gulf Cooperation Council (GCC) monarchies have not abandoned the former strategy of balancing, according to U.S. diplomats. The GCC states believe that their attempts at playing off Iran and Iraq during the 1980s kept the Iran-Iraq war relatively contained. Three of the GCC states, Qatar, Bahrain, and Oman believe that there currently is a power imbalance in the Gulf in favor of Iran and they have called for a relaxation of sanctions against Iraq, ostensibly on humanitarian grounds. In particular, Iran's assertion of control over the Persian Gulf island of Abu Musa, over which it has shared control with the United Arab Emirates under a 1971 agreement, has made the GCC states fearful of potential unchecked Iranian aggression.

Some critics of the policy also believe that there were differences within the Administration -- particularly between the National Security Council and the State Department -- about the dual containment policy. Some State Department officials, perhaps sensitive to criticism of the concept, appear to have interpreted dual containment differently than did the NSC's Lake and Indyk. Questioned about U.S. Persian Gulf policy at a July 23, 1993 hearing -- two months after NSC staff member Indyk unveiled the dual containment policy -- then assistant Secretary of State for Near Eastern Affairs Edward Djerejian passed up several opportunities to characterize U.S. Gulf policy as dual containment.[13] He indicated that the United States sought to move away from the past policy of balancing and wanted to change Iran's objectionable behavior, but he made clear that the United States does not seek to overturn the Iranian government[14] and would welcome a dialogue with an authoritative representative of Iran. These comments have been built upon in recent speeches and testimony that the United states is not against Islam or Islamic fundamentalism, but only the violent efforts to impose that ideology. Lake and Indyk also have integrated these more conciliatory nuances into their pronouncements, and have gone one step further, stating that the United States is not seeking to prevent

---

[13]U.S. Congress. House of Representatives. Subcommittee on Europe and the Middle East. Committee on Foreign Affairs. Developments in the Middle East: July 1993. Hearing, 103rd Congress, 1st session. Washington, G.P.O., July 27, 1993.

[14]The United States is obliged by Point I of the January 19, 1981 Algiers Accords "not to intervene, directly or indirectly, politically or militarily, in Iran's internal affairs." Some might consider past U.S. policies, including covert support for pro-Shah groups in the 1980s, and even the 1985-86 arms sales that sought to strengthen reputed "Iranian moderates," as U.S. violations of the clause. See text of the Algiers Accords, formally titled the "Declaration of the Government of the Democratic and Popular Republic of Algeria," in state Department Bulletin, February 1981. pp. 1-5.

all military equipment (non-American) from reaching Iran.[15] Directly addressing the speculation of NSC-State Department differences on dual containment, Indyk, in his February 24, 1994 presentation to the Middle East Policy council, indicated that his talk and his previous comments had been coordinated with the State Department and represented official Administration policy.

Implementing Containment of Iran

Even with the refinements to the original dual containment concept (as presented by Indyk in May 1993), Clinton Administration policy toward Iran appears less receptive to improving relations with Iran -- and more focussed on containment measures -- than have been preceding Administrations.[16] Implementation of the policy is multifaceted, relying on a combination of economic sanctions, strategic alliances, military posture, and multilateral diplomatic initiatives. Congress, possibly responding to the American public's equation of Iran with the holding of American diplomats hostage and subsequent acts of terrorism, has consistently supported a hard line toward the Islamic Republic. Over the past few years, Members have promoted legislation to tighten U.S. sanctions on Iran or to sanction other countries that help Iran, and congressional action against Iran has generally enjoyed bipartisan support.

It should be noted that, although U.S. relations with Iran are severely strained, there is not a sense of crisis. The most important issue that could provoke such a crisis would be a rapid acceleration or advance in Iran's nuclear program. Spectacular acts of Iranian-sponsored terrorism or military/subversive actions against U.S. allies or military forces in the Gulf would probably also focus immediate attention on Iran within the Administration. (Iran's involvement in the July 1994 bombings of Israeli and Jewish installations in Argentina and London, if established and sustained as a campaign, might qualify as crisis-provoking.) Iran's nuclear research program is a source of major U.S. concern, but Administration officials and the International Atomic Energy Agency (IAEA) have said that, for now, Iran is meeting its obligations under the 1968 Nuclear Non-Proliferation Treaty, to which Iran is a party.[17] Iran has granted IAEA inspectors access to its nuclear facilities and the inspectors, in February 1992 and again in November 1993, have said there is no evidence that Iran is developing nuclear weapons.[18] Some in the U.S. intelligence

---

[15]Lake, Anthony. Confronting Backlash States.

[16]The United States and Iran do not have a formal, political dialogue, but representatives from the United States and Iran meet under the auspices of the U.S.-Iran Claims Tribunal at the Hague. The tribunal is a process, set up by the January 19, 1981 Algiers Accords that resolved the hostage crisis, which arbitrates outstanding Iranian and American commercial disputes.

[17]Testimony of the Assistant Secretary of State for International Security, Lynn Davis, before the Subcommittee on East Asian Affairs of the Senate Foreign Relations Committee. Federal News Service, March 3, 1994.

[18]These assessments were based on IAEA visits, not full fledged inspections. Inspections generally involved the systematic taking of samples and the performance of tests to account for the host country's nuclear material. Reports about the IAEA visits to Iran suggest that only some of the standard IAEA procedures were performed, and only at some of the sites visited.

community disagree with this assessment, noting that Iran could quickly apply its peaceful nuclear research to a militarily useful program.

U.S. measures to contain Iran are addressed in greater detail in the sections below.

U.S. ECONOMIC SANCTIONS

The main purpose of U.S. sanctions against Iran is to deprive that country of the revenue and technology it needs to build up its strategic capabilities. The sanctions are also intended to send a political message that the United States wants Iran isolated, with the hope that other governments will also refuse to deal with Iran or sell it arms and technology. A wide range of economic sanctions on Iran have been in place for most of the time since the November 4, 1979 seizure of the American hostages.[19] The Algiers Accords that ended the hostage crisis required the United States to lift all previous sanctions. President Carter implemented these commitments in a series of executive orders in January 1991.[20] However, subsequent Iranian actions against the United States prompted Congress and/or the President to reimpose or add sanctions against Iran, to the point where Iran currently is subject to some of the strictest U.S. sanctions of any country in the world.[21]

---

[19]In the wake of the U.S. Embassy seizure, President Carter imposed a series of sanctions against Iran. These sanctions included: (1) the halting of U.S. military spare parts shipments to Iran, November 8, 1979 (authority cited: Arms Export Control Act, as amended, P.O. 90-629); (2) a ban on imports of Iranian crude oil and unfinished oil or finished products made from Iranian crude oil, November 12, 1979 (authority cited: Trade Expansion Act of 1962, P.O. 87-794); and (3) a declaration of a state of emergency against Iran, the blocking of all Iranian government property in the United States, and the freezing of Iranian deposits in U.S. banks and subsidiaries of U.S. banks, November 14, 1979 (authority cited: The International Emergency Economic Powers Act, P.L. 95-223 and National Emergencies Act, P.L. 94-412). On April 7, 1980, the President broke diplomatic relations with Iran and, in Executive Order 12205, imposed a ban on all U.S. exports, credits, performance of contracts, and most types of payments to Iran (authority cited: The International Emergency Economic Powers Act, and the National Emergencies Act, P.L. 94-412). Using the same authorities, on April 17, 1980 (one week before the failed hostage rescue mission), in Executive Order 12211, he banned all financial transactions with Iran and imposed an embargo on imports of Iranian goods. The same executive order also restricted the use of U.S. passports for travel to Iran, restricted travel by U.S. citizens and permanent residents to Iran, and revoked certain licenses for transactions with Iran Air, the National Iranian Oil Company, and the National Iranian Gas Company. The text of the executive orders cited in this section are contained in U.S. Congress. House and Senate,. Committee on Foreign Affairs and Committee on Foreign Relations. Legislation on Foreign Relations Through 1992. Joint Committee Print. Washington, G.P.O., June 1993. pp. 1059-1087.

[20]Out of a total of approximately $10 billion in Iranian assets in the United States, approximately $3.9 billion was transferred to Iran when the hostages were released. $3.7 billion was used to pay off principal and interest on U.S. loans to Iran. About $1.4 billion was retained in an escrow account to cover any other funds owed U.S. banks. Another $1 billion was used as an initial deposit in the Security Account, an escrow account used to pay judgments against Iran by U.S. claimants, as an initial deposit. The Security Account is discussed further below.

[21]For a further discussion of U.S. sanctions, see the sections on Iran in U.S. Library of Congress. Congressional Research Service. Economic Sanctions Imposed by the United States Against Specific Countries: 1979 Through 1992. CRS Report 92-631, by Erin Day. Revised August 10, 1992. 654 p.

PROHIBITIONS ON FOREIGN AID AND CREDITS

The prohibition on foreign aid and credits to Iran is primarily a result of Iran's designation as a state sponsor of terrorism. Based largely on evidence of Iran's involvement in the October 1983 bombing of the U.S. Marine barracks in Lebanon, Secretary of State George Shultz so designated Iran on January 19, 1984, acting under the authority of the Export Administration Act of 1979 (P.L. 96-72). Assistance and credits to states on the terrorism list are prohibited by Section 620 of the Foreign Assistance Act of 1961 (FAA), as amended. The terrorism list designation also triggers a requirement that U.S. Executive Directors of international financial institutions vote against any loan or program for a country on the terrorism list.

The following legislative and executive action reinforce these restrictions:

Iran's designation on February 28, 1987 as a country that had failed to curb -- or help the United States curb -- drug trafficking through its territory also mandates aid cuts and requires U.S. votes against multilateral loans to Iran. However, this sanction is currently moot because of Iran's place on the "terrorism list."

Certain voluntary sanctions under this provision would discriminate against Iranian exports to the United States, but those sanctions were rendered moot by a ban on Iranian imports imposed in October 1987 (see below).

Every year since FY 1988, Congress has reiterated the U.S. direct aid cutoff by including Iran in a provision (Section 507) of the Foreign Assistance Appropriations that prohibits direct aid to specified countries. Since FY 1990, the legislation has prohibited Export-Import bank credits, guarantees, and insurance.

Since 1985, Section 307 of the Foreign Assistance Act (FAA) bars U.S. contributions to international organizations and programs that might benefit Iran. No presidential waiver is provided for.

Since FY 1989, Iran has been named in a separate provision of the foreign assistance appropriations that bars indirect aid (U.S. contributions to multilateral development banks or international organizations that loan to or work in Iran) to named countries. Cutting off U.S. contributions represents a far stronger sanction than earlier legislation (Section 307 of the FAA) barring U.S. aid to specific programs for Iran or requiring votes against multilateral loans. On January 2, 1990 and in subsequent years, President Bush waived the ban on indirect aid (a waiver was provided for in the legislation) on the grounds that withholding U.S. contributions to multilateral development banks and international organizations -- even if they benefit Iran or other U.S. adversaries -- was contrary to the national interest. President Clinton also has continued to exercise that waiver.

Congressional opposition to multilateral loans to Iran, especially strong in the Senate Banking Committee and Foreign Operations Subcommittee of the House Appropriations Committee, prompted further tightening of sanctions in the FY 1994 Foreign Assistance Appropriations (P.L. 103-87). That law restated that U.S. officials must vote to oppose multilateral lending to Iran. Title I of that law cut U.S. funding to the World Bank by the amount the Bank had agreed in 1993 to lend Iran ($463 million) and added a new provision that the U.S. share of a portion of the

Bank's capital increase would be withheld if the Bank made any further loans to Iran. President Clinton has not yet chosen to exercise a national interest waiver allowed by that provision, and the World Bank reportedly is holding off on new loans to Iran, possibly because of the U.S. opposition.

Export Controls

A strict system of export controls is a cornerstone of the U.S. effort to prevent Iran from developing weapons of mass destruction or building up its conventional capabilities. With the temporary exception of the U.S. covert arms sales to Iran in 1985-86, the United States has adhered to an embargo on all exports of weapons or military spare parts since the November 1979 seizure of the American hostages.[22] U.S. neutrality in the Iran-Iraq war, which began in September 1980, gave the United States an additional rationale not to sell arms to Iran. Iran's placement on the terrorism list mandated a prohibition on the export to Iran of items on the U.S. Munitions Control List.[23]

In addition, successive Administrations and Congress have both sought to ensure that dual use items -- items primarily designed for civilian use, but also able to create or enhance the capabilities of military equipment -- do not reach Iran, while balancing the needs of American businesses to compete abroad. Iran's placement on the terrorism list in January 1984 restricted its access to U.S. dual use items. Under Section 6 of the Export Administration Act (EAA) of 1979 (P.L. 96-72), applications to export "controlled" items (See Appendix A) to terrorism list countries are generally denied if the item was destined for a military end-user. Exports to non-military end users -- or for non military end uses -- are to be considered on a case-by-case basis. These controls were tightened by administrative regulations and executive orders during 1984-89[24] and by Title XVI of the FY 1993 National Defense Authorization Act (P.L. 102-484), entitled the Iran-Iraq Arms Non-Proliferation

---

[22]Weapons and spare parts prohibited to be transferred to Iran are contained in the Munitions Control List. Section 38 of the Arms Export Control Act, as amended (P.L. 90-629) authorizes the President to control the import and export of defense articles and services.

[23]Section 40 of the Arms Export Control Act provides that no such items may be exported to any country designated a sponsor of terrorism.

[24]On March 30, 1984, in response to allegations of chemical weapons use in the Iran-Iraq war, the Commerce Department embargoed export to Iran (and Iraq) of five chemicals that had primarily agricultural applications but could be used to make chemical weapons. Three more chemicals were added to that prohibited list in October 1984. On September 28, 1994, the President placed stricter controls on exports of aircraft, helicopters, related parts, and avionics. On July 31, 1987, foreign policy controls on exports of chemicals to Iran (as well as Iraq and Syria) were expanded. On September 23, 1987, in response to Iranian naval actions (mining and small boat attacks) against U.S.-reflagged tankers in the Persian Gulf, President Reagan determined that the export or reexport to Iran of any SCUBA equipment posed a threat to U.S. interests and would not be allowed. On October 29, 1987, President Reagan banned export to Iran of an additional fourteen types of militarily useful goods, including inboard and outboard motors, mobile communications equipment, electrical generators, and hydrofoil vessels. On December 20, 1989, tighter controls were placed on the export of ten additional chemicals to Iran (as well as Iraq, Syria, and Libya).

Act. That Act required denial of all applications to export dual use items to Iran (and Iraq), with certain exceptions to protect contract sanctity rights, and imposed penalties on violators. The provision allows the President to waive these restrictions 15 days after reporting to the House and Senate Armed Services and Foreign Affairs/Relations committees that such a waiver is in the national interest, and the rationale for that determination.

The provision, introduced by Senator McCain, drew support from a major debate in Congress during 1992 over whether or not U.S. export laws had been too lax to prevent substantial transfers of U.S. technology to Iraq prior to the Persian Gulf war. Although some charge that U.S. dual use items continue to be exported to Iran,[25] the Commerce Department reports that since that Act took effect on October 23, 1992, it has issued no export licenses for sales to Iran that contradict that law; the few export licenses that were approved were covered by contract sanctity laws. The export of non-controlled items does not require an export license or any official review. Such items include foodstuffs, general industrial products, construction materials, electric power equipment, medical equipment, and unsophisticated data processing equipment.

Currently, Congress is considering a comprehensive rewrite of the Export Administration Act (EAA) of 1979, which expired in 1990 and has been continued by executive order or short term continuing legislation, such as P.L. 103-10, which extended the EAA until June 30, 1994. Versions in both the House (H.R. 3937) and the Senate (S.1902) tighten previous EAA restrictions on dual use exports to terrorism list countries. The bills prohibit U.S. exports to those countries of any items controlled by such non-proliferation regimes as the Missile Technology Control Regime, the Australia Group, or the Nuclear Suppliers Group.

IMPORT BAN

President Reagan prohibited the import of Iranian-origin goods into the United States on October 29, 1987, in retaliation for Iranian attacks (minings, small boat assaults) on U.S.-flagged Kuwaiti tankers in the Persian Gulf.[26] The goal of the move was to persuade Iran to end its attacks by depriving Iran of a large customer for its oil, and thereby forcing Iran to lower its oil prices and receive less revenue. However, the Administration tried to accommodate the needs of U.S. customers for Iranian goods, particularly U.S. oil companies. The import ban exempted Iranian publications; goods that were exported from Iran prior to October 29, 1987; and petroleum products that were refined from Iranian crude oil in a third country. American oil companies were not prohibited from buying Iranian oil and selling it outside the United States. U.S. oil companies currently buy about $3.5 billion per year worth of Iranian oil over the past few years (about one quarter of Iran's oil sales). Exxon reportedly buys about 300,000 barrels per day, and other U.S. buyers, including

---

[25]Timmerman, Kenneth. Caveat Venditor. New York Times, October 25, 1993. p. A19.

[26]Congress specifically authorized the President to ban imports from terrorist countries in Section 505 of the FY 1986 foreign aid authorization (P.L. 99-83).

Coastal, Philbro, Bay Oil, Texaco, Cargil, Caltex, Chevron, and Mobil, purchase between 50,000 and 100,000 barrels per day from Iran.[27]

An additional exemption to the ban came about as a result of U.S.-Iran negotiations at the Claims Tribunal. To address Iran's difficulties in maintaining the required $500 million in the U.S.-Iran Claims Tribunal security account, the two countries agreed that U.S. oil companies could import Iranian crude oil on a case-by-case basis if the proceeds were deposited in the security account or if the imported oil was accepted as settlement in a claims tribunal decision in favor of an American claimant.

"Frozen Assets"/Blocked Property

Iran has tried to link release of its "frozen assets" to improved relations with the United States. Iran claims that the United States retains Iranian assets in contravention of its obligations under the Algiers Accords. The United States maintains that Iranian claims are being arbitrated at the U.S.-Iran Claims Tribunal and, in this sense, there really are no frozen Iranian assets in the United States (with the possible exception of some blocked diplomatic property). Iran is required to maintain a Security Account -- an escrow account held against possible judgments against Iranian claimants -- in conjunction with the U.S.-Iran Claims Tribunal. (Iran is required at all times to keep $500 million in that account, which is managed by the tribunal.) However, as of November 1993, Iran has let the balance fall below $500 million about 50 times since the tribunal began, and the balance stood at $212 million as of March 31, 1994.[28] On June 7, 1994, Iranian President Rafsanjani said the United States had pledged to release Iran's frozen assets in exchange for Iran's help during 1991 in gaining the release of remaining U.S. hostages from Lebanon. In response to a question by House Foreign Affairs committee Chairman Lee Hamilton at a June 14, 1994 hearing, Assistant Secretary of State for the Near East Robert Pelletreau denied that the United States had ever pledged to release Iranian assets as part of a hostage deal.[29] The assets and accounts at issue are the following:

---

[27]MacKinnon, Colin. As U.S.-Iran Trade Soars, A Clinton Administration Crackdown? Washington Report on Middle East Affairs, July/August 1993. p. 41.

[28]U.S. Congress. House. Committee on Foreign Affairs. Developments Concerning the National Emergency With Respect to Iran. House Document 103-256. Presidential Report, 103rd Congress, 2nd Session. Washington, G.P.O., May 17, 1994.

[29]U.S. Congress. House. Committee on Foreign Affairs. Subcommittee on Europe and the Middle East. Testimony of Assistant Secretary of State Robert Pelletreau. June 14, 1994.

Diplomatic Property

To preserve some leverage over Tehran, a small amount of Iranian assets were not released in conjunction with the Algiers Accords. The U.S. Government retains control of approximately $22 million worth of Iranian diplomatic property (its Embassy in Washington, D.C. and several consulates), and bank operating accounts associated with that property. The United States acknowledges that this property belongs to Iran, but asserts that the property has been confiscated in reciprocity for Iran's seizure of the U.S. Embassy in Tehran. The United States opposed arbitration of Iran's claim to the property at the U.S.-Iran Claims Tribunal. Iran has threatened to take the case to the International Court of Justice.

Undelivered Military Equipment

A separate case is that of military equipment, paid for by the Shah, that the United States did not deliver to revolutionary Iran. The equipment includes several types of weapons and spare parts, including combat helicopters and parts, sold to Iran under 1,100 different contracts in the Foreign Military Sales (FMS) program. Since the 1979 seizure of the hostages, all deliveries of military equipment to Iran have been prohibited, and the equipment has sat in U.S. warehouses since the revolution. Iran asserts the value of the equipment to be about $11 billion. The United States acknowledges that it will have to compensate Iran for the equipment, but asserts that the value is far below the Iranian figure. Common U.S. estimates are about $1 -3 billion. The issue is being arbitrated in the U.S.-Iran Claims Tribunal as Case B/1.

Letters of Credit

Iran also claims that it should receive the balances of letters of credit issued by U.S. banks to guarantee the performance of U.S. contractors and suppliers of the Iranian government prior to the revolution. Such performance guarantees were generally issued as so-called standby letters of credit. The U.S. position is that Iran is not entitled to any such monies unless the Claims Tribunal issues a judgment in favor of Iran in a particular case against a U.S. contractor or supplier. U.S. officials say the potential value of the disputed letters of credit is very small compared to the issue of undelivered military equipment.

MULTILATERAL COOPERATION IN SANCTIONS ENFORCEMENT

Because there is no U.N. sanctions regime for Iran as there is for Iraq and no similar U.N. regime is under active consideration), the effectiveness of U.S. sanctions depends on cooperation from U.S. allies in Europe, Japan, and other countries. Differences in approaches to Iran have caused occasional strains between the United

States and its allies and undoubtedly weakened the effectiveness of U.S. sanctions in moderating Iranian behavior. In general, the allies of the United States believe that trade and contact with Iran, rather than isolation, will succeed in moderating Iran's international behavior by giving Iran a stake in the international community. They contend that improvements in the Iranian economy help the pragmatic President Rafsanjani in his competition with Iranian radicals who are the chief proponents of an anti-Western foreign policy. U.S. allies have also tried to resist U.S. pressure by pointing out that the United States, on the strength of its exports to Iran, is now one of Iran's largest trading partners.[30] On the other hand, U.S. allies may be using these arguments to cover a more hard-headed calculation of the economic benefits of dealing with Iran and its nearly 60 million people. European countries and Japan also have about $20 billion in outstanding loan exposure to Iran (almost exclusively import credits) and they want to ensure that Iran is able to service this debt.

The Clinton Administration has tried to find commonalities with its allies on Iran policy. At a June 1993 meeting with the foreign minister of the European Union (EU) and Canada, Secretary of State Christopher won agreement to form a U.S.-E.U.-Canadian working group on Iran, and talks began on July 9, 1993 in Brussels. The United States began a parallel effort with Japan. The Administration's objectives in these working groups has been to persuade U.S. allies not to export arms or dual use items to Iran, not to reschedule any credits they have issued to Iran or to issue any new credits, and not to support loans to Iran by international or multilateral banks. The United States has sought to persuade Japan to suspend its planned $1.4 billion development loan program for Iran, of which $350 million has already been disbursed. The Administration says it is not seeking to persuade its allies to cut off trade with Iran, but it does not want them to conduct normal relations with Iran unless or until Iran modifies its unacceptable behavior.[31] Diplomats who have participated in recent working group sessions say they are more a forum for exchanging ideas on how to change Iranian behavior than a formal effort to synchronize the policies of participating governments.

The U.S. attempt to forge a collective allied policy toward Iran has had mixed success. Over U.S. objections, U.S. allies voted with others in early 1993 to authorize $463 million in World Bank loans to Iran for power, irrigation, and health projects. However, because of U.S. pressure the World Bank has apparently decided not to go forward with any further loans to Iran ($400 million in loans had been under consideration). Two consecutive G-7 (industrialized nations) summits (in Tokyo in 1993 and Naples in 1994) have criticized Iran's international behavior, though somewhat more mildly than the United States would have liked. Iran's difficulties in servicing its debts, as well as the U.S. contention that Iran is a bad credit risk as well as an outlaw state, have led allied countries to stop providing new credits to Iran. However, over U.S. objections, the allies have rescheduled about $10 billion in

---

[30]The United States conducted $748 million in trade with Iran in 1992, and $616 million in 1993, according to the Commerce Department.

[31]U.S. Congress. House. Committee on Foreign Affairs. Subcommittee on Europe and the Middle East. Developments in the Middle East: July 1993. Hearing, 103rd Congress, 1st Session. Washington, G.P.O., July 27, 1993. p. 8.

existing Iranian debt since early 1994, reaching bilateral agreements with Iran rather than adhering to Paris Club rules that specify multilateral rescheduling with International Monetary Fund involvement. From the allies' perspective, refusing to reschedule the debt was likely to result in Iran's refusal to make any debt service payments.

The United States has not won agreement from all its allies to curtail dual use exports to Iran, although the allies did agree to study whether or not Iran is diverting dual use items to military rather than civilian uses. Germany, in particular, has balked at instituting a policy of denial for dual use exports to Iran, though it claims that all shipments to military end users are denied. Japan also has been reluctant to adopt the U.S. position on exports to Iran, arguing that U.S. export restrictions on Iran are so broad as to preclude exports to Iran of some types of harmless civilian equipment.

Russia

The United States has sought to change Russian policy toward Iran. Russian has become Iran's largest arms supplier since the Persian Gulf war, and the Clinton Administration has tried to dissuade Russia from future arms sales to Iran. The Administration is especially concerned about sales of destabilizing equipment, such as submarines, advanced aircraft, and tanks. President Clinton has raised the issue of arms sales with President Yeltsin at their summits in April 1993 and January 1994. Russia did not, at these meetings, promise the United States that it would end arms sales to Iran.[32]

In late 1993, Congress registered its strong concerns about Russian arms sales to Iran. Section 573 of the FY 1994 Foreign Operations Appropriations Act (P.L. 103-87) bans aid to countries that "export lethal military equipment to terrorist state [states on the terrorism list]." The President is authorized to waive the ban if he decides it is in the national interest to do so. Section 573 applies only to arms contracts entered into after the Foreign Operations Appropriations Act took effect on October 1, 1993. Delivery of a third Kilo-class submarine (two of the three sold to Iran have already been delivered) would therefore not disqualify Russia from receiving U.S. aid. The Administration has not determined that Russia is in violation of Section 573, and it intends to address concerns about Russia's arms sales policy in a report to Congress called for by the House Appropriations Committee. The new law strengthened a provision in the previous year's foreign aid appropriations (Section 599B) requiring the President to report to Congress that the Administration has entered discussions with Russia to reduce that country's major arms exports to Iran. It also strengthens provisions of the Iran-Iraq Arms Non-Proliferation Act (see above) that mandates a one year suspension of aid to countries that transfer advanced conventional weapons to Iran (or Iraq).

Both the Administration and Congress have felt that Russia's position on arms sales to Iran was threatening the multilateral effort to replace the COCOM

---

[32]Russia has held up delivery of the third and last Kilo class submarine sold to Iran, although the holdup reportedly is due more to Iran's financial difficulties than to U.S. pressure.

(Coordinating Committee on Multilateral Export Controls) export control regime. The COCOM regime was established by the United States and its allies during the Cold War to prohibit the transfer of sensitive technologies or weapons to Communist countries. The COCOM states agreed to end the COCOM regime as of March 31, 1994 and to "work together toward a new, more broadly based arrangement designed to enhance transparency and restraint in sales of conventional weapons and transfers of sophisticated technologies to countries whose behavior is cause for serious concern and also to regions of potential instability."[33] In other words, the new regime is to focus primarily on limiting proliferation as well as arms sales and technology to terrorist states. The White House statement specifically mentioned the U.S. hope that Russia would become a founding member of the new regime.

U.S. prodding may have made some headway with Russia. On July 10, 1994, appearing at a joint news conference with President Clinton at the Naples G-7 summit, President Yeltsin said Russia was "moving in the direction" of limiting trade with terrorist states, and that Russia would join a COCOM replacement regime "on an equal footing."[34]

The Administration and Congress have also been concerned about reports of potential Ukrainian sales to Iran of tanks and other equipment, and the Administration has warned Ukraine not to become an arms supplier of Iran. Ukraine denies it is discussing sales of major military equipment to Iran but claims that is has discussed with Iran only the sale of military spare parts.

Promoting Regional Peace

The Clinton Administration sees the establishment of a comprehensive Arab-Israeli peace as another tool in its arsenal for blunting Iranian adventurism, although U.S. administrations have long been committed to Arab-Israeli peacemaking regardless of its effects on Iran. A comprehensive peace, in the Administrations' view, will weaken radical Islamic groups in the region including those that are supported by Iran. Supporting this position, Administration officials note that Iran has harshly criticized the peace process but has done little to materially affect it. The Administration hopes that peace between Israel and Syria, which it is helping broker, will break up the tacit alliance between Syria and Iran that has existed since 1982. Syria currently tolerates the presence in Lebanon of Iran's Revolutionary Guard, which funnels arms to and helps train the radical Islamic organization Hizballah. Iran reportedly resupplies Hizballah through the Damascus airport, with tacit Syrian approval. A peace between Israel and Lebanon would presumably result in a withdrawal of Hizballah from southern Lebanon. Moreover, the Administration believes that solidifying the September 13, 1993 Israel-PLO agreement on Palestinian autonomy will deprive radical Islamic Palestinian groups such as Hamas and Palestinian Islamic Jihad of support among Palestinians in the West Bank and

---

[33]Statement by White House Press Secretary Dee Dee Myers, March 30, 1994; in State Department Dispatch. Volume 5, No. 15, April 11, 1994, p. 205.

[34]Yeltsin Willing to Limit Trade With Terrorist States. Reuter, July 10, 1994.

Gaza Strip. Both groups derive some financial support from Iran and from private sources in the Persian Gulf states.

The Administration's position is not without some potential risks. For example, the Syrian armed presence in Lebanon acts as something of a brake on Hizballah. Syria's 35,000 troops are deployed primarily in Hizballah's main power base in the Bekaa Valley and, when clashes threatened to interfere with the peace process, Syria has often worked to curb escalating violence between Hizballah and Israel in southern Lebanon. A peace agreement between Israel and Syria and Lebanon that provides for a Syrian withdrawal from Lebanon might possibly leave Hizballah with a freer rein in Lebanon than it now has. If Hizballah is redeployed from southern Lebanon as part of an Israel-Lebanon agreement, Hizballah could possibly turn its full attention to promoting Islamic revolution within Lebanon. In addition, some contend that Iran will step up its activities to derail a comprehensive peace settlement as peace comes closer to realization.

U.S. Military Measures

The posture statement of the Commander-in-Chief of the U.S. Central Command (CENTCOM, responsible for the Gulf region) submitted in conjunction with the FY 1995 budget cycle, expresses U.S. concerns about Iran's conventional military modernization program and its attempts to develop weapons of mass destruction. The Department of Defense is giving special attention to Iran's growing naval capabilities, especially the two Kilo class submarines it has received from Russia thus far. During the latter stages of the Iran-Iraq war, Iran used its naval forces to attack merchant shipping and U.S. naval forces. U.S. defense officials believe that the mine laying and torpedo launching capabilities of these submarines will allow Iran to interdict regional shipping lanes covertly.[35] U.S. forces in the Gulf, about 10,000 - 15,000 troops at any given time, are primarily there to deter a resurgent Iraq and to conduct operations consistent with U.N. Security Council resolutions on Iraq. U.S. defense officials note, however, that U.S. forces in the Gulf can be used against Iran, if need be. With several air and missile strikes on Iraq since the Persian Gulf war, the United States has shown it can also use standoff ship-based weapons to hit targets in the Gulf region with precision.

Though confident it can minimize the threat from Iran's submarines, the United States is taking some specific military steps to deal with the subs. Before Iran took delivery of its first Russian submarine in 1992, the United States reportedly sent its own submarines into the Persian Gulf to survey the acoustic properties of the waters in which the Iranian vessels will be operating. In addition, the U.S. Navy reportedly has fitted its warships in the Gulf with torpedo decoy equipment.[36]

---

[35]Draft of the 1994 posture statement of the Director of Naval Intelligence, submitted for the FY 1995 budget cycle. p. 14. Office of Naval Intelligence, 1994.

[36]Iran Sparks Off a Boat Race. Middle East Economic Digest, April 29, 1994. p. 15.

As a subset of its military posture, the United States is developing policies and equipment to militarily counter any weapons of mass destruction Iran, or other adversary states, might develop. The Defense Department's "counterproliferation" initiative is intended to prepare U.S. forces in the event U.S. non-proliferation efforts fail. The counterproliferation initiative was unveiled on December 7, 1993 by then Secretary of Defense Les Aspin. Elements of the initiative include development of new defenses against ballistic missiles;[37] better intelligence on weapons of mass destruction threats; special munitions to destroy mass destruction weapons production or storage facilities; sensors capable of locating mobile missile launchers or biological weapons, and other devices.[38] Such systems are expected to be in place by the end of the decade. The Defense Department reportedly plans to spend $400 million per year on new technology associated with the initiative, beginning in FY 1996.[39] The Administration has tried to implement its new approach multilaterally; at a meeting in June 1994, NATO defense ministers agreed to set up defenses against weapons of mass destruction. Some arms control advocates have criticized the counterproliferation approach as an abandonment of more traditional non-proliferation measures aimed at curbing the spread of weapons of mass destruction.

Building Strategic Alliances

The Administration has looked to regional states to help contain Iran, just as it has looked to its allies in Europe and Japan to impose economic sanctions on Iran multilaterally. NSC staff member Martin Indyk has said the United States can "draw on the support and friendship of the critical regional powers -- Egypt, Turkey, Israel and, of course, Saudi Arabia"[40] to establish a broad balance of power in the region. On a visit to the Middle East in May 1994, Assistant Secretary of State for the Near East Robert Pelletreau, referring to the Persian Gulf states, said it is important to build a strong and cohesive collective defense...so that Iran can see clearly that nations will defend themselves against any potential aggression."[41] In the immediate aftermath of the Persian Gulf war, the United States signed formal defense agreements with three Gulf states -- Kuwait, Bahrain, and Qatar. It signed a similar pact with the United Arab Emirates on July 25, 1994. (An existing facilities access agreement with Oman was renewed in October 1990.) The defense pacts provide for U.S. arms sales, training, and prepositioning of some U.S. equipment. These pacts give the United

---

[37]A major new mobile anti-missile system under development is the Theatre High Altitude Area Defense System, or THAAD.

[38]Gertz, Bill. Aspin Outlines Threat of Arms Proliferation. Washington Times, December 8, 1993. p. 4; and Lippman, Thomas. If Nonproliferation Fails, Pentagon Wants "Counterproliferation: in Place. May 15, 1993. p. A11.

[39]Starr, Barbara. Proliferation the New High Ground for USA. Jane's Defence Weekly, May 14, 1994. p. 1.

[40]Middle East Policy Council. Symposium on Dual Containment. p. 3.

[41]Ersan, Inal. U.S. Says Sanctions on Iraq to Be Renewed. Reuters, May 11, 1994.

States a forward presence against Iraq, but might also be useful to help the Gulf states defend against Iran.

Improving equipment and provision of advice is a major part of the U.S. program in the allied Gulf. Several of the Gulf states, particularly Saudi Arabia, Bahrain, and the United Arab Emirates, are planning to allocate some of their shrinking procurement budgets to upgrade their naval capabilities, in part to counter Iran's acquisitions of diesel submarines from Russia.[42] Saudi Arabia and the UAE are expected to lease U.S. FFG-7 frigates, which are well suited to anti-submarine warfare (ASW). The U.S. Navy is currently studying Bahrain's request to receive a U.S. FFG-7 as an excess defense article.[43] All three of these countries are building up their helicopter-based ASW capabilities and Oman reportedly is fitting some of its new warships with systems to better detect Iranian submarine movements. U.S. Central Command (CENTCOM) has also been working with the Gulf states to better integrate their defenses and invest more resources in their joint "Peninsula Shield" force, based in Saudi Arabia. The GCC states decided in December 1993 to triple the size of the force (from 9,000 to about 25,000), upgrade its air defense networks, reform its command structure, and add air and naval elements to it. U.S. defense officials report that progress in implementing these measures has been very slow.

U.S. defense pacts and close informal relationships with the Gulf states have won broad support in Congress and the policy community. These relationships enable the United States to monitor Iranian activities and deter aggressive action without a heavy U.S. presence in the Gulf. However, there has been longstanding concern that close relations with the United States could engender greater hostility to these countries on the part of Iran and Iranian supporters inside the Gulf states. Many question whether the Gulf states are militarily strong or cohesive enough to provide sufficient counterweight to Iran. The Gulf states have traditionally tended to try to accommodate rather than antagonize their adversaries and they may not always be willing to cooperate with U.S. efforts to contain Iran. It is also open to question whether Israel, which is geographically far from Iran and burdened by its own substantial security concerns, is available to help the United States balance out Iran. Similarly, Egypt is geographically distant from Iran and it and Syria have been unable to reach agreement with the six GCC states to implement a collective defense plan envisioned in the March 1991 "Damascus Declaration" of the eight countries. Turkey has generally tried to maintain good relations with Iran and there is considerable opposition within Turkish leadership circles to cooperating with U.S. efforts to contain Iran.

Though Egypt is outside the Gulf, Egypt and the United States perceive an emerging threat to that country from Iran's new submarine fleet. Egypt fears that Iran might try to deploy its subs in the Red Sea, using naval facilities of Iran's ally, Sudan, as a base. In part to counter this possibility, Egypt wants to purchase one of

---

[42]Country (Saudi Arabia) to Buy Submarines to Guard Gulf, Coastlines. Agence France Presse, April 14, 1994. This report quotes the Saudi deputy Defense Minister as saying Saudi Arabia would like to purchase its own submarines. Other Gulf states are reportedly interested in frigates or anti-submarine warfare systems to deal with Iran's submarine fleet.

[43]Bahrain became eligible to receive U.S. excess defense articles under the FY 1994 defense authorization act (P.L. 103-139).

two U.S. diesel submarines, using its $1.3 billion in FMF grants from the United States.[44] However, some U.S. officials are concerned that the $800 million for the two subs might crowd out other Egyptian acquisition programs. The United States also is leasing two frigates to Egypt and providing ten upgraded helicopters suited for ASW as excess defense articles. The helicopters will be able to drag sonar submarine detection devices through the water and drop depth charges and torpedoes if hostile subs are encountered.

Counter-Terrorism

In its report on worldwide terrorism or for 1993, the State Department said that "Iran remains the world's mot active and most dangerous state sponsor of terrorism, through its own state agents and the radical groups it supports."[45] Clinton Administration officials maintain that combatting terrorism, such as that sponsored by Iran, remains one of the Administration's highest priority global issues and several agencies have taken steps to improve their counter-terrorism capabilities. In 1991 the Federal Bureau of Investigation, which generally handles domestic terrorism, reportedly created a special section within its counter-terrorism office to focus on the terrorist threat from Iran.[46] The State Department contends that its proposal in 1993 to combine its Office of Counterterrorism with the bureau for Counternarcotics would have strengthened the hand of the Coordinator for Counter-terrorism within the Administration, but the proposal was not approved in the conference report on the FY 1994 State Department authorization bill (P.L. 103-236). The Central Intelligence Agency's Counter-terrorism Center reportedly has been adding to its staff detailees from other agencies.[47] The CIA center was created in 1986 after the hijacking of a TWA jetliner the previous year by pro-Iranian terrorists.

As in its other efforts to contain Iran, the Administration has tried to work multilaterally to limit Iranian terrorism. In testimony in 1993 before the Senate Judiciary Committee, the acting Coordinator for counter-terrorism said that the United States was working with its allies (the Group of Seven industrialized nations) and with other governments to ensure that there is a collective response to Iranian

---

[44]One on One: Interview with Field Marshal Hussein Tantawi, Egypt's Minister of Defense. Defense News, June 20-26, 1994. p. 54. Egypt plans to procure the diesel submarines from the Ingalls Shipyard, which would need to subcontract part of the submarines (the hulls) abroad. (The United States no longer makes diesel submarines.) Such offshore procurement would require congressional authorization. The House report on the FY 1995 foreign operations appropriation (H.R. 4426), passed by the House on May 25, 1994, supports Egypt's purchase of the submarine(s) and the needed offshore procurement. (H. Rept. 103-524).

[45]Department of State. Patterns of Global Terrorism: 1993. Department of State Publication 10136. Released April 1994. p. 1.

[46]Thomas, Pierre and Lippman, Thomas. U.S. Steps Up Efforts to Combat Terrorism. Washington Post, November 7, 1993. P. A1.

[47]Ibid.

terrorism.[48]   Secretary of State Christopher reiterated the U.S. call for such a multilateral approach in the aftermath of the bombings of Israeli and Jewish installations in Argentina and London in July 1994. He said he had directed the State Department's counter-terrorism experts to review their procedures and mechanisms to look to improve international counter-terrorism efforts and coordination.[49]

The multilateral approach has had mixed success, in part because the allies of the United States have seen benefits in accommodating Iran. The Administration felt that Germany had set back the U.S. attempt to forge a common approach on Iranian terrorism when it received Iran's minister of Intelligence, Ali Fallahian-Khuzestani, on an official visit during October 6-7, 1993. Fallahian's ministry is the lead Iranian body involved in the assassination of Iran's opponents abroad. The United States publicly criticized Germany for receiving Fallahian, contending that it undermined U.S. attempts to isolate Iran. In expressing U.S. displeasure, Secretary of State Christopher presented Germany with U.S. intelligence about Iran's support for international terrorism. The German Foreign Ministry has said the visit was arranged by German intelligence officials without the Ministry's approval. The Administration also protested a December 1993 decision by France to return suspected Iranian terrorists to Iran rather than extradite them to Switzerland for trial.

---

[48]Department's Efforts to Combat International Terrorism. Text of the statement of the Acting Coordinator for Counter-Terrorism, Laurence Pope, before the Senate Judiciary Committee, April 21, 1993, in U.S. Department of State Dispatch. Volume 4, No. 17. April 26, 1993. p. 300.

[49]Testimony of Secretary of State Christopher before the House Foreign Affairs Committee. Federal News Service, July 28, 1994.

SAUDI ARABIA: POST-WAR ISSUES[*]
Alfred B. Prados

Background and Analysis

CURRENT ISSUES

Arab-Israel Conflict

Saudi Arabia has supported Arab positions on the Palestinian question and strongly endorses Muslim claims in the old city of Jerusalem, which is the third holiest site in the Islamic religion. Saudi media strongly criticized legislation (S. 1322) passed by Congress on October 24, 1995, to move the U.S. Embassy in Israel from Tel Aviv to Jerusalem. Saudi Arabia has played a minimal military role in Arab-Israeli wars, and Saudi leaders generally have favored a peaceful solution to the Arab-Israeli conflict. In July 1991, Saudi Arabia supported President Bush's call for an Arab-Israeli peace, paid the costs of the opening session in Madrid in October, and subsequently has attended some of the multilateral Middle East peace talks that address regional issues. On November 7, 1995, a Saudi official condemned the assassination of Israeli Prime Minister Yitzhak Rabin, stating that "this act was directed against the peace process," and the Saudi Foreign Minister subsequently sent condolences to Mrs. Rabin. According to a statement by the Saudi Minister of Information, following a series of bombings in Israel in February and March 1996, King Fahd condemned "all forms of violence and terrorism regardless of the source or the justifications" and said "the peace process should re-tart quickly towards achieving its goals." Foreign Minister Prince Saudi bin Faysal attended the "Summit of Peace Builders" conference held in Egypt on March 13 at the invitation of President Clinton and Egyptian President Mubarak to further the peace process and counter terrorism in the Middle East.

Saudi-PLO Relationships. Saudi Arabia, like other Arab states, recognizes the PLO as the legitimate representative of the Palestinian people. Saudi financial aid to the PLO, which amounted to an estimated $1 billion from 1980 to 1990, ended after the Iraqi invasion of Kuwait as a result of PLO support for Iraq. The Saudi Government did continue to provide the PLO with the proceeds of a tax on the income of

---

[*]Excerpted from *CRS Issue Brief*, Order Code IB93113.

Palestinians residing in the Kingdom, and reportedly has conveyed private donations of approximately $15 million a year to the PLO.

There have been reports of Saudi assistance to the PLO's rival organization, the fundamentalist Hamas, particularly after the Saudi-PLO rift that began in 1990. Israeli sources have claimed that Saudi Arabia provided Hamas with around $10 million during the period 1991-1992, and a Saudi defector made similar accusations in June 1994. In its report entitled *Patterns of Global Terrorism, 1994*, the State Department noted that Hamas receives funding "From private benefactors in Saudi Arabia" but does not estimate amounts involved. Those who credit reports of Saudi-Hamas ties cite Saudi alienation from the PLO and possible Saudi affinities for Hamas' Islamic fundamentalist beliefs; however, the Saudi leadership generally disapproves of the more militant organizations, whether fundamentalist or radical secularist.

The Israeli-PLO Declarations. Despite Saudi resentment of PLO Chairman Yasir Arafat for siding with Iraq during the Gulf war, King Fahd welcomed the Declaration of Principles signed by representatives of Israel and the PLO on September 13, 1993, as "a historic step toward peace." At a conference of prospective donors organized by the United States on October 1, 1993, Saudi Arabia pledged $100 million to support the Israeli-Palestinian peace plan during the first year; a press report of March 12, 1995 quoted U.S. officials as saying that the Saudis had fulfilled this pledge. Saudi Government assistance to the West Bank and Gaza following the Israeli-PLO accord probably will be channeled to the internationally sponsored funding groups rather than directly to the PLO. However, on June 12, 1994, a PLO official announced that Saudi Arabia had granted $10 million to his organization, presumably part of the above pledge, and in February 1995 the press reported an additional Saudi payment of $7.5 million to the Palestinian police. The Saudi Foreign Minister welcomes the Israeli-Palestinian redeployment agreement of September 28, 1995, as a "positive" step.

Arab Boycott of Israel. In July 1991, Saudi Arabia endorsed an Egyptian proposal to lift the Arab boycott of Israel in return for a freeze on Israeli settlement activity in the occupied West Bank and Gaza. On September 26, Shaykh Fahim bin Sultan al-Qasimi, the Secretary General of the Gulf Cooperation Council (GCC) (presumably reflecting Saudi views), was quoted as saying it would be premature to terminate the boycott until Israeli withdrawal from Arab territories has taken place. On September 30, 1994, however, the six GCC states (including Saudi Arabia) decided to terminate their enforcement of the so-called secondary and tertiary boycotts of Israel, while retaining the ban on direct dealings with Israel. (The secondary boycott blacklists companies that deal with Israel; the tertiary boycott blacklists subsidiaries of such companies or other companies that deal with them.)

Security in the Gulf Region

Saudi Arabia was a key member of the allied coalition that expelled Iraqi forces from Kuwait in February 1991. Most Saudi military forces were committed to the allied effort; a senior Saudi army officer (Lt General Khalid ben Sultan) acted as commander of the Joint Arab-Islamic Force, which was a principal component of the coalition; and Operation Desert Storm was staged from Saudi territory. The joint GCC force known as Peninsula Shield, comprising 10,000 personnel drawn from the armed forces of the six GCC states, is also under Saudi command. Plans to expand this small force have been under discussion since the Gulf war. Saudi Arabia remains an important factor in post-war security planning for the Persian Gulf region, both through bilateral arrangements with the United States and through regional security cooperation.

During a visit to the Gulf in march 1995, U.S. Secretary of Defense William Perry praised Saudi Arabia as "an island of stability in a sea of trouble in the Gulf region." King Fahd, on his part, said that "full implementation [by Iraq] of all Security Council resolutions is essential for the security and stability of the region."

In the past, Saudi and other Gulf leaders preferred that U.S. military forces remain "over the horizon" and confined mainly to the small naval Middle East Force based in the Persian Gulf, with a few exception: U.S. Air Force use of the Dhahran Air Base until 1962; the brief deployment of U.S. F-100 fighter aircraft to Saudi Arabia in 1963 to resist Egyptian incursions during the Yemen civil war; and the reflagging and escorting of Kuwaiti ships by U.S. naval units in the late 1980s during the Iraq-Iran war. Agreement to the large scale deployment of U.S. and allied forces to Saudi Arabia and other Gulf states during the Iraq-Kuwait crisis represented a major shift in Saudi policy. Among the U.S. military forces remaining in the Gulf region (averaging about 20,000 personnel at a given time), several contingents are in Saudi Arabia, including U.S. Air Force units involved in enforcing a no-fly zone over southern Iraq and U.S. Army units involved in air and missile defense. The press has reported approximately 5,000 U.S. military personnel in Saudi Arabia as of early November 1995, plus a number of U.S. contractor personnel working with the Saudi Armed Forces and National Guard. U.S. firms providing such assistance include BDM/Vinnel Corporation (1,000 employees), Hughes Aircraft company (500), Booz-Allen & Hamilton Inc. (200 employees), Raytheon Corporation, McDonnell-Douglas Corporation, an General Dynamics corporation. So far, Saudi Arabia has been reluctant to conclude a prepositioning agreement like those reportedly signed with other Gulf states. Press reports have indicated that the United States and Saudi Arabia are using a 1977 training agreement [see below] as a framework for a broader program of military cooperation between the two countries. During his March 1995 visit, Secretary of Defense Perry said the two countries agreed that continued U.S. access to Saudi bases and ports "is the key to quick, forceful response to aggression."

A bomb that exploded at a U.S.-operated training facility for the Saudi National Guard on November 13, 1995, has created further concerns among Gulf leaders over threats from local elements opposed to a western military presence. The explosion, which occurred at the Office of the Program Manager for the Saudi Arabian National Guard program in Riyadh, killed seven persons (including five U.S. citizens -- one military and four civilian or retired military) and injured 60 others, including 37 U.S. citizens. U.S. officials described the explosive device as a 45-kilogram (100 lb) bomb filled with semtex. President Clinton vowed an "enormous effort" to find the perpetrators and sent an FBI team to join Saudi authorities investigating the crime. The United States and Saudi Arabia have offered rewards of $2 million and $800,000, respectively, for information leading to the arrest of those responsible. On February 4, media reported that a Saudi national suspected of the crime was turned over to Saudi authorities by Pakistan, where he had been hiding. Subsequently, four Saudi nationals were arrested, and confessed to the crime on Saudi state television on April 22.

The bombing was condemned by the six-member Gulf Cooperation Council, the secretarial of the Arab League, the European Union, and several Arab governments. Three little-known groups -- the "Tigers of the Gulf," the "Movement for Islamic Change," and the "Combatant Partisans of God" -- have claimed responsibility. The "Movement for Islamic Change" reportedly had circulated a previous warning that all non-Muslim western forces in the Arabian Peninsula should leave by June 28. Following the explosion, a caller from the "Tigers of the Gulf" told a news organization that his organization would continue such actions if the Americans do not depart. On January 31, 1996, the U.S. State Department warned U.S. citizens of "new and disturbing reports that additional attacks may be planned against institutions identified with the United States and its interests in Saudi Arabia." Subsequently, on April 21, the Saudi Minister of Interior stated that his government cannot rule out further attacks. In their televised confession, the four Saudis charged with the crime said they were planning to carry out similar operations before their arrest. They also said they had been influenced by two Saudi exiles active in Islamic fundamentalist movements. (One of the two exiles denied the allegation and maintained that he condemns violence.)

Arms Transfers to Saudi Arabia

Saudi Arabia has emerged in recent years as the largest arms purchaser in the Third World. During the period from 1987 through 1994, the Saudis bought $75.9 billion worth of military equipment (in current U.S. dollars), accounting for nearly 30% of all Third World arms agreements during the above eight-year period. Of this amount, $34.5 billion represent U.S. sales, and $41.4 billion came from all other sources. For the four most recent years, 1991-1994, however, the U.S. share of $20.2 billion as about twice the share of all other suppliers combined ($10.0 billion).

U.S. Arms Sales. The United States is currently Saudi Arabia's leading arms supplier. Total value of arms agreements with Saudi Arabia from 1950 through March 31, 1993 was $71.8 billion, of which $17.9 billion represent contracts signed since the beginning of fiscal year 1991. This recent increase in Saudi arms purchases from the United States was due in large measure to the Persian Gulf crisis and its aftermath. As the table shows, approximately 19% of the value of U.S.-Saudi arms contracts were for lethal equipment (i.e., weapons, ammunition, and combat vehicles, aircraft, and ships); the largest portion (29%) went for support services (repair, rehabilitation, supply operations, and training). Another major component of the Saudi program has been construction of military bases and facilities, accounting for the largest share (31%) through 1990 and the second largest share (24%) for the entire period. This decrease in the percentage share of construction is attributable both to the completion of many military infrastructure projects by 1990 and to a greater emphasis on combat equipment to enhance Saudi defensive capabilities since the Iraq invasion of Kuwait.

	TABLE 1. U.S. ARMS TRANSFERS TO SAUDI ARABIA (amounts in $billions unless otherwise indicated)[1]					
Category	1950-1990		1991-1993[3]		1950-1993	
	Ordered[1]	Pct.[2]	Ordered	Pct.	Ordered	Pct.
Weapons and ammunition	8.384	16%	5.317	30%	13.700	19%
Support equipment	8.541	16%	4.956	28%	13.497	19%
Spare parts, modifications	4.578	9%	2.609	15%	7.187	10%
Support services	15.835	29%	4.624	26%	20.459	29%
Construction	16.486	31%	0.421	2%	16.907	24%
TOTALS	53.823		17.927		71.751	

[1] Amounts represent agreements, not deliveries. A total of $46.765 billion had been delivered as of March 31, 1993.
[2] This column shows the percent of total arms transfers constituted by each of the five categories shown in the left-hand column.
[3] Includes FY1991, FY1992, and first 6 months of FY1993. It does not include a $9 billion order for 72 F-15S fighter aircraft signed in May 1993.

Successive U.S. Administrations have entered into military sales agreements with Saudi Arabia because of its prestige in the Arab world, its importance as a major source of oil, and its vulnerability to threats from neighboring states supported in the past by the former Soviet Union. Heightened threats from Iran in the late 1980s and subsequently from Iraq provided rationale for an expansion of the arms supply relationship, and some observers believe further ales are needed to redress a continuing gap between Saudi weapons inventories and those of potential adversaries.

Also, the Saudi arms market has helped maintain the U.S. industrial base and create jobs at a time of economic stress.

Some critics doubt that Saudi forces can absorb large quantities of advanced military hardware and voice concerns that such equipment could fall into the wrong hands in the event of external invasion or a radical change in the Saudi regime. Many are particularly concerned that arms being sold to Saudi Arabia might be used one day against Israel. Others doubt that Israel is seriously threatened by Saudi Arabia, but oppose sales to Arab countries technically at war with Israel and fear that enhancement of Saudi air and missile capabilities could increase the costs to Israel of a future conflict. Another concern is that continuing arms sales to Saudi Arabia undermine efforts to restrain the flow of advanced weaponry to an already heavily armed Middle East.

Some observers predict that arms sales to Saudi Arabia will decrease in the next few years partly because the Saudis have already ordered much of the equipment they wanted after the Gulf war and partly because of straitened finances (see below). Between January and April 1994, senior Saudi and U.S. officials agreed on a plan to restructure $9.2 billion in Saudi purchases of U.S. Arms reportedly through stretching out payments, delaying equipment deliveries, and limited borrowing.

Third Country Sales. Saudi Arabia, on its part, has shown a long-standing preference for U.S. equipment because of its high quality and the reliability of U.S. logistical support. Nonetheless, the Saudi Government has bought significant amounts of equipment from other countries, notably Britain and France, when the United States has been reluctant to sell such equipment or has been unable to offer price and availability terms sought by the Saudis. In the mid-1980s, following congressional opposition to selling additional fighter aircraft to Saudi Arabia, Britain and Saudi Arabia concluded a memorandum of understanding code-names "Al-Yamamah" which established a multi-billion dollar procurement program (approximately $30 billion according to a press account) including advanced Tornado jet fighter aircraft, followed by a 1988 addendum covering further procurement. France signed contracts worth between $1 and $1.5 billion with Saudi Arabia, covering the sale of four frigates and two replenishment ships, and the maintenance and renovation of Crotale and Shahine air defense missiles. In August and September 1995, the French firm Giat Industries conducted tests of the Leclerc tank in Saudi Arabia, which is reportedly considering purchasing 200 Leclercs. In 1988, the Kingdom also concluded a controversial purchase of approximately 30 intermediate range CSS-2 surface-to-air missiles from China, in what has so far been its only major arms acquisition from a communist state. With the exception of the Chinese missile sale, the U.S. Administration has not objected to these third country purchases by Saudi Arabia, although some U.S. contractors have deplored the diversion of lucrative military equipment sales to foreign suppliers.

Saudi External Aid

With its oil wealth and its commitment to supporting Islamic causes and moderate policies abroad, Saudi Arabia has been one of the world's leading donors to developing countries since the early 1970s. Total Saudi aid from 1973 through 1991 was over $60 billion, and 1991 aid ($3.7 billion) represented 1.5% of gross national product (GNP), one of the highest ratios in the world (the United Stated donated 0.2% of GNP). A total of 70 developing countries have received Saudi aid, including 38 in Africa, 25 in Asia, and 7 in other regions. Principal recipients have been friendly but poorer Arab states like Egypt, Syria, and (until recently) Jordan, together with various Arab and Muslim resistance groups: for example, the Afghan resistance groups (mujahedin) both during and after the Soviet occupation; the anti-Marxist Nicaraguan resistance (Contras) during the 1980s; Palestinian groups, as noted above; and Bosnian Muslims. (According to a statement by the King and the Crown Prince on May 22, 1994, Saudi Arabia has given a total of $106 billion in aid to Islamic countries and $14.6 billion to other developing countries, presumably since mid-century.) In addition to financial aid, Saudi Arabia contributed troops (678 in October 1993) to the former U.N. force in Somalia.

Bosnia. Bosnian Muslims have received at least $120 million in official Saudi aid plus another $235 million in private donations from wealthy Saudis. Before the December 1995 Dayton Peace Agreement, which stipulated withdrawal of foreign forces from Bosnia, Saudis formed the majority of a group of 400 volunteers from Persian Gulf countries training and fighting with Bosnian Muslims. On February 2, 1996, a *Washington Post* article, quoting unnamed Saudi officials, alleged that Saudi Arabia funded a $300 million covert operation to supply weapons to the Muslim-led Bosnian Government with the knowledge and tacit cooperation of the United States. A State Department spokesman denied that the United States was in any way involved with the reported program, bud did not say specifically whether or not the United States had knowledge of it. A Saudi spokesman said he could not confirm the report.

Trade Relationships

Saudi Arabia is the largest U.S. trading partner in the Middle East. For 1994, Saudi exports to the United States are estimated at $8.0 billion and imports from the United States at $6.4 billion. Comparable figures for the nearest Middle East competitor, Israel, were $5.2 billion in exports and $4.2 billion in imports. To a considerable extent, this high volume of trade is a result of U.S. oil imports from Saudi Arabia and U.S. arms exports to that country.

The Saudis buy significant amounts of U.S. commercial equipment as well. On October 26, 1995, U.S. and Saudi officials announced that Saudi Arabia had signed a $6 billion contract ($7.5 billion by some estimates) to purchase 61 U.S. commercial aircraft (5 Boeing 747s and 23 Boeing 777s; 29 McDonnell Douglas MD-90s and 4 McDonnell Douglas MD-11 freight aircraft), with deliveries over the period 1997 to 2002. Tentative agreement had been reached on the sale in February 1994, but financial constraints delayed final action for almost two years. On August 7, 1995, King Fahd said local Saudi capital would be used to finance the aircraft purchase. In addition, AT&T won a $4.1 billion contract to upgrade the Saudi telecommunications system in May 1994. One member of the Saudi royal family owns a 23.6% stake in the EuroDisney recreational park, although he had agreed to reduce his holdings to one half that of the U.S. Walt Disney company in five years.

Since 1974, a U.S.-Saudi Joint Commission for Economic Affairs has sponsored a wide range of bilateral cooperative activities in the economic sphere. On April 28, 1995, then U.S. Secretary of the Treasury Lloyd Bentsen and then Saudi Minister of Finance Muhammad Aba al-Khayl signed an agreement to extend the joint commission until the year 2000, and opened the first session of a U.S.-Saudi Business Council.

Oil Production. With the world's largest proven oil reserves (estimated at 261.2 billion barrels in January 1994), Saudi Arabia produced an average of 8.23 million barrels per day (bpd) in 1995. Approximately 6 million bpd are exported. Remaining production is allocated approximately as follows: 900,000 for domestic needs; 600,000 to cover payments on a long-term British arms purchase program; 300,000 for expansion and improvement of the two holy mosques; and 200,000 for a strategic oil reserve program. Formerly the largest foreign supplier of oil to the United States, Saudi Arabia took second place to Venezuela in 1995, although Saudi Arabia leads in crude oil supplies to the United States. In 1995, 17.0% of U.S. oil imports and 7.6% of total U.S. oil consumption came from Saudi Arabia. Corresponding figures for Venezuela were 18.7% of oil imports and 8.4% of total U.S. consumption. Comparative figures appear in Table 2.

TABLE 2: OIL CONSUMPTION AND IMPORTS (in millions of barrels per day)			
Category	1993	1994	1995
Total U.S. Consumption	17.237	17.718	17.605
Total U.S. Imports	7.618	8.054	7.908
Imports from Saudi Arabia	1.414	1.402	1.342
Imports from Venezuela	1.300	1.334	1.477

The United States and Saudi Arabia have cooperated on major issues of oil production and pricing, although there have been some differences in their positions. The United States welcomed the Saudi decision to increase oil production from approximately 5 million to 8 million bpd in August 1990, to compensate for loss of oil exports from Iraq and Kuwait after the Persian Gulf crisis erupted. For the past few years, the Saudis have sought to stabilize prices at a level which they and their customers will find acceptable. During 1992, there were press reports of informal U.S.-Saudi agreements to adjust prices to levels that would create economic conditions beneficial to the Reagan and Bush Administrations; both U.S. and Saudi officials denied reports of any collusion on oil pricing. King Fahd's appointment of a new, dynamic oil minister on August 2, 1995, may presage internal reorganization of the Saudi oil sector and greater emphasis on promoting the country's under-utilized gas industry.

Problems in Commercial Transactions. Complaints have arisen within the U.S. business community over commercial disputes that have resulted in hardships for U.S. companies doing business in Saudi Arabia and for their employees. In a letter of May 27, 1992, to a congressional subcommittee, the U.S. Department of Commerce identified 17 major unsettled cases (some of them 8-10 years old) involving 14 American firms with claims of approximately $500 million in Saudi Arabia. The Department also testified that "the Kingdom's system of commercial regulation lacks an effective internationally accepted mechanism to resolve disputes with foreign firms." In some cases, Saudi clients have refused to pay U.S. contractors; on occasion, Saudi officials allegedly have intimidated U.S. businessmen and employees through detention or denial of exit visas in an effort to force U.S. companies to complete additional work not originally contracted for or not reimbursed by Saudi clients. Some U.S. employees claim to have suffered serious injuries resulting from ill treatment during detention.

Saudi representatives state that they have a grievance board that successfully handles over 90% of all contractual disputes; moreover, they point to instances in which U.S. companies have not cooperated wit Saudi contract resolution procedures. In April 1992, the Saudi Embassy in Washington provided the Department of Commerce with two lists, respectively, enumerating 15 complaints cited by Saudi companies against U.S. companies, and 22 U.S. corporations that had failed to appear before the Saudi grievance board. The National U.S.-Arab Chamber of Commerce, though acknowledging some difficulties in commercial relationships, noted that during the 12 months prior to May 1992 over 40,000 export-related transactions took place between 6,000 U.S. companies and Saudi customers and that the great majority of these transactions involved little or no difficulty. The Chamber also noted recent Saudi steps to alleviate problems in commercial relationships, including a measure to enforce protection of intellectual property rights.

U.S. employees submitting claims for losses or injuries sustained in Saudi Arabia have encountered jurisdictional problems. Such persons in general have been unwilling to seek redress through Saudi mechanisms for conflict resolution, because of their fear of returning to Saudi Arabia or their lack of confidence in the impartiality of Saudi institutions. In one case (Nelson v. Saudi Arabia), a U.S. citizen alleging disabling injuries inflicted on him during imprisonment in Saudi Arabia lost a case before the Saudi grievance board because he was unwilling to testify in Saudi Arabia. His subsequent attempt to bring suit against the Saudi Government through the U.S. court system failed as a result of a March 1993 decision by the U.S. Supreme Court that U.S. courts lacked jurisdiction in this case, because his injuries were not related to a commercial activity in the United States. Members of Congress have criticized the U.S. executive branch for not doing enough to uphold the rights of U.S. employees caught in contractual disputes. According to the State Department, senior U.S. officials have raised these issues with the Saudi Government and have exerted efforts to resolve commercial disputes.

On July 27, 1994, the Department of Commerce informed the Chairman of the then House Foreign Affairs Committee as follows (the Department of Defense provided similar information to the President of the Senate on September 16, 1995): (2) Only three of the 17 cases cited in the Commerce Department's letter of May 27, 1992 remained unresolved (in two of these cases, the plaintiffs had accepted partial payments awarded by the Saudi Grievance Board). (2) Five out of 8 disputes mentioned in a subsequent letter of June 30, 1993 from the Department of Defense had been resolved. Of the six unresolved cases, according to the Department of Commerce, three are under review by agencies of the Saudi Government and one is being handled by the U.S. Federal Deposit Insurance Agency. Two cases remain unresolved: Gibbs and Hill, Inc. vs. Royal commission for Jubail and Yanbu; and Harbert International Construction, Inc. vs. Ministry of Agriculture.

Human Rights and Democracy

According to the State Department's annual report on human rights practices for 1994, principal human rights problems in Saudi Arabia include "the torture of prisoners; incommunicado detention; prohibitions or restrictions on the freedoms of speech, press, and religion; systematic discrimination against women; and strict limitations, and even suppression, of the rights of workers and ethnic and religious minorities." The report also notes frequent abuse of Saudis and foreigners of both sexes by official protectors of moral behavior (the "religious police") and unofficial vigilante groups. Of particular concern to Westerners are pervasive restrictions on women's activities and an injunction against the practice of other religions throughout the Kingdom. This injunction has been applied not only against non-Islamic faiths but also at times against the Shi'ite Muslim community in Saudi Arabia, estimated at 500,000 persons mainly in the Eastern Province. Reports in October 1993 indicate that the Saudi Government has moved quietly to ease some restrictions on Shi'ites. Application of the death penalty (frequently by beheading) has increased; press sources report that, as of October 16, a total of 192 persons had been executed in Saudi Arabia in 1995, many of them for drug offenses, as compared with 53 in 1994 and 85 in 1993.

Though committed to enforce Islamic tenets in Saudi Arabia, the government has moved to restrain militant Islamic fundamentalist groups, particularly since the brief seizure of the Grand Mosque in Mecca by an extremist Islamist group in 1979. In November 1992, a group of conservative Saudi religious figures signed a petition to King Fahd demanding a more vigorous application of Islamic prescriptions. In May 1993, a group of militant Islamists formed a "Committee for the Defense of Legitimate Rights" to eliminate "injustice" and defend Islamic law. The government promptly suppressed the movement and dismissed or arrested its founders. Some Saudis supported the government's rejection of the Committee's call for stricter Islamic legislation. Others sympathized with the Committee's effort to stop human rights abuses by the Saudi Government, including indefinite detention and mistreatment by police.

In mid-September 1995, media reports described demonstrations by a hitherto unknown organization known a the Battalions of Faith, and some sources said over 1,000 persons had been detained by Saudi authorities. On September 26, the Saudi Minister of Interior acknowledged the arrest of 100 Muslim militants accused of plotting seditious activity, and additional arrests brought the total number of detainees to 157. On October 16, the Saudi Press Agency announced the release of 130 of the detainees, while 27 -- including two outspoken Islamic religious figures -- remained in custody.

Recent political reforms promulgated by King Fahd appear to represent a limited move toward democracy and protection of individual freedoms. The "main law" announced by the King on March 1, 1992, bans arbitrary arrest, harassment, or entry of individual homes without legal authority and specifies privacy in telephone calls and mail. On August 26, 1993, in a message to King Fahd carried by the Saudi Press Agency, President Clinton welcomed the recently appointed consultative council "as an important step to widen popular participation in the government, which conforms with your history and traditions." On August 2, 1995, King Fahd appointed a new 28-member cabinet which contains a number of western-educated technocrats, although most key ministries remain in the hands of the Saud family; also, he announced that ministerial appointments normally will be limited to four years instead of an indefinite period. Commentators believe the measures will be popular among younger Saudis who have grown skeptical over the immobility of government and lack of new blood. On the other hand, King Fahd has said that free elections are not suitable for his country; he stated on March 30, 992 that elections "do not fall within the sphere of the Muslim religion, which believes in the *al-shura* (consultative) system and openness between ruler and his subjects and which makes whoever is in charge fully answerable to his people."

Other Issues. On April 16, 1996, during the annual Muslim pilgrimage season, Saudi authorities allowed a Libyan aircraft bringing pilgrims to the Islamic holy places to land in Saudi Arabia and return to Libya, in violation of U.N. Security Council resolutions that ban air travel to and from Libya. (A similar incident took place during the 1994 pilgrimage season.) A statement by the U.N. Security Council on April 18, supported by the United States, cited Libya's dispatch of an aircraft as a violation of Security Council resolutions; without specifically mentioning Saudi Arabia, the statement reminded all countries of their obligations to enforce these resolutions. Saudi officials maintain that they are obligated to welcome Muslim pilgrims during the annual pilgrimage season, regardless of their means of conveyance.

BACKGROUND TO U.S.-SAUDI RELATIONS

As the birthplace of the Islamic religion in 622 A.D. and as the home of Islam's two holiest shrines, the Arabian Peninsula has always occupied a position of special prestige within the Middle East. With the establishment of Arab empires based in Damascus and Baghdad, the peninsula gradually lost its political importance and sank into disunity. In the 16th century, much of the Arabian Peninsula came under the nominal rule of the Ottoman Empire; however tribal leaders effectively controlled most of the region. During this period, an alliance developed between an influential eastern tribe, the House of Saud, and the leaders of a puritanical and reformist Islamic group known as the Wahhabi movement. During the first quarter of the 20th century, a chieftain of the Saud family, Abd al-Aziz ibn Abd al-Rahman (later known as Ibn Saud) overcame numerous rivals with the support of his Wahhabi allies and succeeded in unifying most of the Arabian Peninsula under his rule, with the exception of Yemen in the southwest and the small, then British-protected principalities along the eastern coast. On September 23, 1932, Abd al-Aziz proclaimed the establishment of the Kingdom of Saudi Arabia, which he ruled until his death in 1953. Four of his sons have succeeded him: Saud (1953-1964), Faysal (1964-1975), Khalid (1975-1982), and the present King Fahd, who acceded to the throne in 1982.

On November 30, 1995, Saudi officials announced that King Fahd, who suffers from several ailments including diabetes, was admitted to a hospital for tests, following what U.S. officials reportedly described as a stroke. Though released from the hospital on December 7, the King left government business to Crown Prince Abdullah, who attended annual GCC conference in Oman on December 3. On January 1, 1966, King Fahd issues a decree addressed to the Crown Prince in which he stated that "we entrust you in this decree to take over management of government affairs while we enjoy rest and recuperation." A U.S. State Department commented that "In terms of the kingdom [of Saudi Arabia] and its governance, we think it's in good and stable hands." On February 13, King Fahd presided over the weekly Saudi Cabinet meeting for the first time since his illness, and on February 21 he announced that he was resuming his duties. In a message to Crown Prince Abdullah, the King announced "the end of the effect of our order of January 1" and expressed his appreciation to the Crown Prince. Some diplomats have speculated that the King may continue to delegate some duties.

Some observers believe these developments have put to rest the question of succession in the Saudi monarchy. Prince Abdullah, a half brother of King Fahd, has served as Crown Prince throughout King Fahd's reign; however, some commentators in the past have speculated that other members of the royal family (including full brothers of King Fahd) might challenge Prince Abdullah's position as heir apparent in the future. King Fahd's designation of Prince Abdullah as de facto acting head of state during the King's recent illness suggests a consensus in the royal family to back Prince Abdullah as successor if King Fahd should pass from the scene. With regard to policies, various sources describe Prince Abdullah as more traditional and conservative than King Fahd, less oriented toward the western world, and more inclined to emphasize Saudi ties with the Arab World. Most observers believe, however, that any changes under Prince Abdullah would be more of style than substance and that he is committed to a strong U.S.-Saudi relationship and to the core policies that Saudi leaders have pursued in the past.

Oil and national security concerns have combined to produce a close and cooperative relationship between the United States and Saudi Arabia. Since the award of the First Saudi oil concession to a U.S. company in 1933, both states have had an increasing interest, respectively, in the marketing and acquisition of Saudi petroleum supplies. As regional threats multiplied in the latter half of the century, mutual concerns over the stability of Saudi Arabia and other moderate regimes in the Arabian Peninsula engendered a significant degree of defense cooperation.

Economy and Aid

Economic Conditions. Oil is the dominant factor in the Saudi economy, accounting for 37% of GDP, 75% of budget receipts, and 90% of exports in 1993; however, much more of the GDP is derived indirectly from the oil industry. Despite immense oil revenue, increasing state expenditures, the oil glut of the early 1980s, and the collapse of oil prices in the mid-1980s have put governmental fiscal assets in deficit since 1982, and since 1987 the government has begun to borrow. Added strains resulting from the Persian Gulf crisis of 1990-1991 caused the deficit to rise to approximately one sixth of GDP. External debt was estimated at $30 billion at the end of 1994; however, Saudi Arabia remains a net creditor in world financial markets. As of 1994, foreign assets managed by the central banking authority were estimated at $50 billion (down from $127.7 billion in 1981). Saudi monetary officials estimate that only 10-15% of the $50 billion is readily available, with the remainder earmarked to guarantee the currency or letters of credit. Besides the official $50 billion portfolio, the State Department estimates a $15 billion fund for autonomous government institutions (pension, development, and social insurance) and $19.7 billion worth of foreign assets in the commercial banking system.

Lowered oil revenues, an expanding population, and recent Gulf war costs of $44 billion (including $16.9 billion contributed to the United States to help defray expenses) have placed additional burdens on the Saudi economy. On January 1, 1994, King Fahd announced that the 1994 budget would be cut by 19% to S.R. 160 billion ($42.7 billion), down from S.R. 197 billion ($52.5 billion) for 1993. Since the projected 1994 income of $42.7 billion was the same as the spending target, the budget deficit theoretically was to have been eliminated for the first time since 1982; however, subsequent reports indicated a deficit of $10.7 billion in 1994. On January 1, 1995, the Government announced another budget cut of approximately 6% for 1995, with spending down from S.R. 160 billion ($42.7 billion) to S.R. 150 billion ($4 billion). On January 1, 1996, Crown Prince Abdullah, in the name of King Fahd, announced a $40 million budget for 1996, unchanged from 1995, with an estimated deficit of S.R. 18.5 ($4.93 billion), slightly higher than the estimated deficit in 1995 because of a decrease in projected revenues. In 1995, the Saudi Government imposed some austerity measures including raising the costs of utilities (electricity, water, and communications facilities) and reducing subsidies in an effort to increase revenues and cut spending. In announcing the 1996 budget, Prince Abdullah promised to continue these measures "as an important step toward balancing the budget and stressing the strength of the national economy."

Aid Relationships. For some years, Saudi Arabia received very limited income from oil production and was a recipient of small amounts of U.S. financial aid during World War II; in 1951, the United States extended further assistance under development and military aid programs. Economic aid ended in 1959, as oil income rose from $57 billion in 1950 to over $300 million in 1958 and $663 million in 1965. Military aid continued through 1975, but was limited to a small international military education and training program, with the exception of two brief periods in the late 1950s and late 1960s when Saudi Arabia faced threats from radical neighbors. Total U.S. aid to Saudi Arabia from 1946 through its termination in 1975 amounted to $328.4 million, of which $295.8 million was military and $32.6 million was economic assistance. Approximately 20% of total aid was in the form of grants and 80% in loans, all of which have been repaid.

Defense and Security

Although Saudi forces acquired experience during the Gulf war and are undergoing further upgrading through a large-scale program of arms procurement (see below), both Saudi Arabia and its five smaller Gulf neighbors remain vulnerable to future external aggression. On one hand, both the Iranian and Iraqi armed forces suffered major personnel and equipment losses during the 1980-1988 Iran-Iraq war and Operation Desert Storm, respectively, and neither is in a position to offer an immediate threat to the GCC. On the other hand, as shown in Table 4 (last page), the combined forces of Saudi Arabia and its GCC allies are outnumbered in important categories by those of Iraq and Iran, even after the losses sustained by both countries in recent wars.

Although the United States and Saudi Arabia are not linked by a formal defense treaty, a series of informal agreements, statements by successive U.S. administrations, and military deployments have demonstrated a strong U.S. security commitment to Saudi Arabia. Three agreements, negotiated in 1951, 1953, and 1977, cover Saudi procurement of U.S. military equipment and the assignment of a U.S. Military Training Mission in Saudi Arabia. Beginning with the Administration of Franklin D. Roosevelt, U.S. Presidents and senior officials periodically have stated a U.S. commitment to the integrity and stability of the Saudi Kingdom. Among the more recent of these were the following:

-- a statement by President Jimmy Carter on January 23, 1980 (the Carter Doctrine) that "An attempt by any outside force to gain control of the Persian Gulf Region will be regarded as an assault on the vital interests of the United States of America and such an assault will be repelled by any means necessary, including military force";

-- a statement by President Ronald Reagan on October 1, 1981 (the Reagan Corollary) in which he committed the United States more specifically to the defense of Saudi Arabia, saying that "...there's no way that we could stand by" and see Saudi Arabia "taken over by anyone that would shut off that oil"; and

-- a statement by President George Bush on August 8, 1990, following the Iraqi invasion of Kuwait, that "The sovereign independence of Saudi Arabia is of vital interest to the United States."

-- a statement by Secretary of State Warren Christopher on February 21, 1993, citing the "shared commitment" of the United States and Saudi Arabia to peace and security in the Gulf." He added the "President Clinton's commitment to the security of friends in the Gulf, like that of every President since Franklin Roosevelt, is form and constant."

THE GOLAN HEIGHTS[*]

Clyde Mark

U.S. Policy Toward the Golan Heights

United States policy toward the Golan Heights has remained constant since June 1967; first, that the Golan Heights is occupied territory subject to U.N. Resolution 242 and the principle of exchanging territory for peace; second, that the United States does not recognize Israel's 1981 unilateral action annexing the Golan; and third, that the future status of the Golan Heights should be negotiated between Syria and Israel. The United States disapproved of Israel's extending its law and administration over the Golan Heights, which had the practical effect of annexing the territory. At a press conference on December 17, 1981, President Ronald Reagan said: "...we do deplore this unilateral action by Israel, which has increased the difficulty of seeking peace in the Middle East under the terms of U.N. Resolutions 242 and 338."[1] The next day, December 18, 1981, the Department of State's spokesman said: "We continue to believe that the final status of the Golan Heights can be determined only through negotiations between Syria and Israel..."[2] In 1991, the Department of State responded to a question from the Europe and Middle East Subcommittee of the House foreign Affairs Committee that the State Department believed that: "...the future of the Golan Heights involves a number of sensitive issues for both Israel and Syria, that these concerns must be fully addressed in a final resolution, and that they can only be resolved by negotiations within the framework of United Nations Security Council Resolutions 242 and 338."[3]

---

[*]Excerpted from *CRS Report 95-308 F.*

[1]News Conference of December 17, 1981, as reported in *Public Papers of the Presidents of the United States*. Ronald Reagan. 1981. Washington, U.S. Gov't. Print. Off., 1982, p. 1163.

[2]Statement by spokesman Dean Fischer, Dec. 18, 1981, Department of State Bulletin, Vol. 82, No. 2058, January 1982. p. 60.

[3]U.S. Congress. House of Representatives. Committee on Foreign Affairs. Subcommittee on Europe and the Middle East. *Developments in the Middle East*, November 1991. Hearing, Nov. 20, 1991. 102nd Cong., 1st session. Washington, U.S. Gov't. Print. Off., 1992. p. 65.

Status of Israeli-Syrian Negotiations

For both Syria and Israel, attending the U.S.-Soviet sponsored Madrid Peace Conference in October 1991 had the pragmatic effect of extending an indirect form of mutual recognition and accepting the other's right to exist.[4] The two nations have continued the bilateral talks begun at Madrid with a series of meetings between diplomats and military officers in Washington, but Syria (and Lebanon) has refused to participate in the multilateral talks until there is substantial progress toward a bilateral settlement.[5] U.S. leaders, including Presidents Clinton and Bush, Secretaries of State Baker and Christopher, Assistant Secretaries Pelletreau, Djerejian, and Murphy, and special envoy Ross, have met with Syrian and Israeli leaders in Damascus, Jerusalem, and Washington to facilitate the peace talks, serve as messengers between the parties, and act as mediators offering compromises to resolve disputes. Syria and Israel deny the persistent rumors that the two nations are conducting secret negotiations similar to the 1993 Oslo talks between Israel and the PLO.

Israel repeatedly labels "security" as its first priority, and insists that any agreement and any arrangement that may emerge from the negotiations must provide Israel with security. Syria agrees that security is a primary priority and that it must be assured that Israel will no longer pose a threat to Syria. Following are some of the several points that remain at issue between Israel and Syria, and a summary of the Israeli and Syrian positions on each of the issues.[6]

SOVEREIGNTY

Israeli Position

The Israeli government position on sovereignty over the Golan Heights is not clear. On the one hand, Israel extended its law and administration over the territory, an act that could be interpreted as annexation and therefore an act intended to establish Israeli sovereignty over Golan. But on the other hand, Israeli leaders have stated that they recognize Syrian sovereignty over the Golan Heights and are willing to withdraw Israeli forces and claims of sovereignty from the area in exchange for peace.[7]

---

[4]See: *Syrian-U.S. Relations*. CRS Issue Brief 92075, by Alfred Prados, updated periodically.

[5]See: *The Middle East Peace Conference*, CRS Issue Brief 91137, by Carol Migdalovitz, updated regularly.

[6]For a discussion of points at issue between Syria and Israel, see: Moore, James W. "An Israeli-Syrian Peace Treaty: So Close and Yet So Far." *Middle East Policy*, Vol. III, No. 3, 1994: 60-82.

[7]For example, Foreign Minister Peres said on July 14, 1994: "In the past, the Israeli Government recognized Syrian sovereignty over the Golan Heights..." The Foreign Minister was referring to the action of the National Unity Government in 1967, and apparently implying that Israel continued to concede sovereignty to Syria. Reported by a Foreign Ministry Spokesman and retrieved electronically from Israel Foreign Ministry files. See also: FBIS, *Near East and South Asia, Daily Report*, July 14, 1994 and July 15, 1994.

The Israeli people also are divide on the issue of sovereignty over Golan. One group of Israelis supports the 1981 annexation and wants continued Israeli sovereignty over the Golan Heights for various reasons. One reason offered by some Israelis is that Israel should retain sovereignty over the Golan Heights because of its strategic value; continued Israeli occupation would deny Syria the opportunity to bombard Israel from the escarpment and afford Israel surveillance avenues to monitor Syrian military traffic from Damascus. Another reason offered by some Israelis for retaining the Golan is that the Golan Heights was part of traditional Israel[8] and part of the Palestine Mandate following World War I,[9] and should remain part of Israel for historical/religious reasons. Other Israelis believe the Golan should be retained because the region is populated with Israeli settlements, or because it is an important part of the Jordan River watershed.

Another group of Israelis believes that whatever the reasons offered for keeping the Golan, the benefit to be gained from surrendering Israeli claims of sovereignty, peace with Syria, is well worth the costs. These Israelis discount the strategic advantage of retaining the Golan in an age of missiles, believe that satellites have replaced observation posts for early warning, insist that the few Israeli settlers can be moved to other areas, and may be skeptical of biblical or historical arguments. The views of the present Israeli Government appear to be closer to this group.

Syrian Position

Syria claims sovereignty over the Golan Heights based upon its traditional control of the area and the Mandate boundaries drawn in 1920 and 1923.[10]

Israeli Withdrawal

United Nations Security Council Resolution 242, passed in November 1967 following the June 1967 war, lists two guiding principles; first, "Withdrawal of Israeli armed forces from territories occupied in the recent conflict," and second, an end of war.

---

[8]According to Jewish tradition, Moses assigned the Golan area, called Bashan, to the tribe of Manasseh (Joshua XIII, 29-31 and Deuteronomy III, 13). the historian Josephus Flavius reported that the region was the site of battles between the Romans and the Jews prior to the fall of the second Temple in 70 A.D.

[9]See "Territorial Claims" section, below.

[10]See "Territorial Claims" section, below.

Syrian Position

Syria insists that Israel withdraw from all of the Golan Heights occupied in 1967, and that Syria will take steps toward normalizing relations with Israel after the Israeli withdrawal. Although some observers of the Middle Eastern peace process search for signs of compromise in the Syrian position, such as suggestions that Syria could allow Israel to retain a small strip of the Golan, or that Syria would permit Israel to retain control over selected sites for military early warning posts, or that Syria should "lease"[11] part of Golan to Israel, the Syrians have demonstrated little inclination to relax their demand for full Israeli withdrawal. Most Arabs believe U.N. Resolution 242 means that Israel has to withdraw from all occupied territories.

Israeli Position

The present Israeli government has stated that it would withdraw from the Golan Heights in exchange for a peace treaty and the normalization of relations between Israel and Syria. The beginning of a withdrawal process should coincide with Syria signing a peace treaty, recognizing Israel, and establishing "normal" relations. But the Israeli government position does not mean necessarily that Israel would withdraw from all of the Golan in a single move. The government holds that the depth of withdrawal, all or partial, is the subject of the negotiations. In addition to the question of depth, the Israelis will consider possible stages or phases of withdrawal, and the timing of the withdrawal process.

In response to Syrians and others who maintain that Israel must withdraw from occupied territory under U.N. Resolution 242, some conservative Israelis, most of whom oppose any withdrawal from Golan, argue that 242 did not say withdrawal from all territory, and that Israel met its obligations under 242 when Israel withdrew from the Sinai Peninsula in 1982 under the 1979 peace treaty with Egypt. Some conservative Israelis would accept a partial withdrawal providing Israel could maintain a militarily advantageous position on the Heights.

The Likud opposition has called for a referendum on an Israeli withdrawal before any withdrawal takes place. The Labor Government has agreed to hold a referendum on withdrawal, but has offered no other details about when the referendum would be held, on what issues, or if the results would be binding on the Government.

TIMING OF THE WITHDRAWAL

One recurring suggestion in the peace talks is that Israel withdraw from the Golan in stages or phases over a period of years rather than withdraw all at once. In theory, a staged withdrawal temporarily would allow Israel to continue occupying part of the Golan Heights to ensure early warning capabilities, and would provide Israel with time

---

[11]Syrian President Assad criticized Jordan's King Husayn for leasing some of the disputed territory along the Wadi Araba to Israel in the October 23, 1994 peace treaty. Reuters, Oct. 27, 1994.

to gain confidence in Syria's intention to adhere to a peace treaty. The phased withdrawal would, in theory, still ensure Syria that Israel would withdraw.

Israeli Position

Israeli leaders have stated that they want a phased or staged withdrawal, and that the minimum time for a first stage should be 3 years.[12] During the first phase, Syria can take steps, such as establishing diplomatic missions, and opening trade, commerce, tourism, and other relations, that will demonstrate Syria's peaceful intentions.

Syrian Position

Syrian leaders have stated that they want an Israeli commitment t a full withdrawal before they discuss other aspects of the withdrawal.[13] From recent indications, it appears likely that Syria would accept a staged withdrawal, providing the phases were short, and were defined and not open ended.

PEACE TREATY

Syrian Position

Although hesitant in the past, Syrian leaders have stated that they will sign a peace treaty with Israel. Recently, President Assad said that Syria wants "full peace in return for a full withdrawal."[14] President Assad went on to explain that full peace meant a "normal" peace such as exists among mot nations of the world.

---

[12]See, for example, reports of Prime Minister Rabin's statement to the press on Sept. 8, 1994, reprinted in FBIS, *Near East and South Asia, Daily Report*, Sept. 8, 1994.

[13]Assistant Secretary of State for Near East Edward Djerejian told a House subcommittee in October 1992 that the Syrians did not see the necessity for interim agreements. U.S. Congress, House of Representatives. Committee on Foreign Affairs, Subcommittee on Europe and the Near East. *Developments in the Middle East.* Hearing. Oct. 1, 1992. 102nd Cong., 2nd session. Washington, U.S. Gov't. Print. Off., 1993. p. 28.

[14]Minutes of a conversation between U.S. Congressman Tom Lantos and Syrian President Hafiz al-Assad in Damascus in early January 1995; as reported in the Israeli newspaper *Yediot Aharonot*, Jan. 16, 1995, reprinted in FBIS, Jan. 17, 1995.

Israeli Position

Israel wants demilitarized zones with force and weapons limitations specified for each zone. The demilitarization regimen, according to the Israelis, would include all of southern Syria, and would move mot Syrian armed forces north of Damascus.[15]

Syrian Position

Syria would accept balanced demilitarized zones on both sides of the boundary, but would not accept demilitarizing all of southern Syria as Israel proposes.[16]

PEACE KEEPING FORCE

A peace keeping force could be an early warning or detection group that would report possible violations to the two sides, a monitoring force that would patrol the border to report violations, a deterrent force that would act to protect the victim of a violation, or a defensive force that would act to stop a violation. UNDOF presently stationed on the Golan is a monitoring force. (See section on UNDOF in Appendices.)

Syrian Position

Syria accepts a peace keeping or peace monitoring force on the Golan Heights as part of an overall settlement. It is not clear if Syria would accept a monitoring, deterrent, or defense force, or if Syria would accept a U.S. component in the force. It appears likely that Syria would want the peace monitoring force under United Nations auspices.[17]

Israeli Position

Israeli leaders have stated that they want a peace monitoring force stationed on the Golan Heights between the two countries, but they do not want a deterrent or defense force. Israel would welcome U.S. participation in the force. It is unlikely that Israel would want the force under U.N. auspices.[18]

---

[15]Gold, Dore. U.S. Forces on the Golan Heights and Israeli-Syrian Arrangements. Jaffee Center for Strategic Studies, Tel Aviv University, Memorandum No. 44, August 1994: 8-9.

[16]Gold, U.S. Forces on the Golan Heights, op.cit., p. 10. Bacevich, et al. *Supporting Peace.* op. cit. p. 14.

[17]Bacevich, et. al., *Supporting Peace, op. cit., p. 19-22.*

[18]Bacevich, et. al., *Supporting Peace, op. cit., p. 19-22.*

BOUNDARIES

Israeli Position

Israel wants some changes in the 1949 Armistice Line, such as moving the boundary between Syria and Israel eastward further up the slopes to place Israel on the high ground equal to Syria. Israel fears that leaving the boundary where it is, at the bottom of the slopes, will allow the Syrians to re-establish gun emplacements among the Heights that would threaten Israeli positions in the Huleh Valley and the Galilee. Israel also wants to retain control over the 1948-1967 demilitarized zone. Some Israelis advocate that Israel maintain a presence on the Golan Heights to act as an early warning outpost and to ensure that Syria does not move troops and equipment back to the region. The proposal apparently would require that Israeli enclaves, observation posts, or security positions, be established in the Golan area for a predetermined period of time, such a 25 years.[19]

Syrian Position

Syria prefers to eliminate the demilitarized zones and return to the boundary as demarcated in 1923 by the British and French.[20] The Armistice Line of 1949 paralleled the French-British boundary except for the creation of the demilitarized zones.

Appendices

PHYSICAL DESCRIPTION

The Golan Heights (Jawlan in Arabic, called the Syrian Heights by the Israelis) is a plateau in the Lebanon-Israel-Syria boundary area ranging in height from 9,000 foot (2,814 meters) Mr. Hermon in the north down to an average 1,200 feet (approx. 400 meters) in elevation along the Yarmuk River in the south. Lake Kinneret (also known as Lake Tiberias or the Sea of Galilee) at the southwest corner of the Golan Heights is 600 feet (200 meters) below sea level. The northern half of the Golan is mountainous, including the foothills of the Hermon massif, and the southern half a more level plateau. The Golan is approximately 40 miles (65 kilometers) from north to south and varied in width from 7 to 16 miles (12 to 25 kilometers) east to west. The Golan plateau overlooks the southern reaches of the Biqaa Valley in Lebanon to the north, the Syria plain (Haran or Hawran district) between the Lebanon mountains and the Jabal al-Duruz (Druze mountain) to the east, the hills of northern Jordan and the Jordan River valley to the south, and the Jordan River, Huleh Valley, and Lake

---

[19]Gold, U.S. Forces on the Golan, op. cit., p. 11-12.
[20]See "Territorial Claims" section, below.

Kinneret of Israel's Galilee region to the west. The western side along the Jordan-Hulah-Kinneret boundary is a sheer escarpment and the eastern side facing Damascus and the Haran is a gentle slope, declining west to east. East of the Haran beyond the Jabal al-Duruz is the Syrian desert.

The Golan Heights is approximately 675 square miles (1,750 square kilometers). In 1967, Israel occupied about 482 square miles (1,250 square kilometers) of the Golan Heights. In the 1973 war, the Israeli counter-attack into Syrian territory occupied another 326 square miles (845 square kilometers), but Israel withdrew from that territory plus an additional 39 square miles (100 square kilometers around the city of al-Qunaytirah)[21] as part of the 1974 disengagement agreement. At present, Israel occupies about 444 square miles (1,150 square kilometers) of Syrian territory.

The Haran, including the Golan Heights, is a fertile area with rainfall adequate for orchards, grains, vegetables, and grazing. In the past, the region was the "bread basket" for Damascus to the north. The Banyas River, from the Banyas spring, and the Dan River are the primary rivers rising on the Golan, although two other rivers, the Hasbani and the Yarmuk, flow along the edges of the Golan and derive their sources from the surrounding highlands. The Banyas, Hasbani, and Yarmuk are the primary tributaries of the Jordan River. It is estimated that one-third of the water in Lake Kinneret comes from run-off from the Golan Heights; Kinneret is Israel's primary reservoir.

The 130,000 Syrians who lived in 139 small villages and towns on the Golan Heights became refugees when Israel invaded in 1967.[22] Israel bulldozed most of the villages after the 1967 war. About 12,000 Syrians mostly Druze, remained on Golan despite the Israel occupation. The first Israeli settlement on the Golan was established in Late July 1967. At present, about 16,000 Syrians live in 5 towns, and 15,000 Israeli Jews live in 35 settlements.

A military force holding the Golan enjoys a military advantage of looking down from the escarpment over Israel's Hulah Valley, and down the sloping plain that leads northeastward to Damascus. The summit of Mr. Hermon (Jabal al-Shaykh in Arabic) at the northern end of the Golan offers good early warning surveillance points for monitoring troop movements between Damascus and Golan. The Mt. Hermon summit presently is in the UNDOF zone, but the Israelis maintain surveillance points on the Mt. Hermon massif.

HISTORICAL BACKGROUND

Israel had claimed over the years that Syrian armed forces indiscriminately fired down on Israeli settlemtns in the Hulah Valley from the vantage points on the Golan Heights. Syria claimed tht it was retaliating for Israeli attacks and defending its territory and the demilitarized zones from Israeli encroachment.

---

[21]Various spellings: Kunaytra, Quneitra, Kunaytrah, etc.

[22]Muslih, Muhammad. "The Golan: Israel, Syria, and Strategic Calculations." *Middle East Journal*, vol. 47, No. 4, Augusmn 1993: 611-632.

Shortly after Israel declared its independence on May 14, 1948, Syrian forces attacked Israel's Degania settlements at the southern end of Lake Kinneret. The attacks failed but a second Syrian attack against the Israeli settlement at Mishmar Hayarden on the Syrian-Palestine border between Kinneret and Lake Hulah was successful, and Syria controlled the town an the roads along the Jordan River. The first truce in June 1948 ended the fighting temporarily. The Israelis counterattacked in July 1948 but were not able to drive the Syrians out before the second truce temporarily ended the fighting. An Israeli offensive in October 1948 successfully drove the Lebanese and Palestinian forces out of the Galilee area of what is now northern Israel but the Israeli attacks on Syrian forces at Mishmar Hayarden failed. The third truce on October 21, 1948 ended the war in the north.[23] The Armistice Agreement signed between Syria and Israel on July 20, 1949, created demilitarized zones of those areas evacuated by Syrian and Israel forces as they withdrew to the previous boundary line between Syria and Palestine.[24] Mishmar Hayarden, scene of fighting during the war, was divided by a demilitarized zone line.

On June 5, 1967, the Israeli air force destroyed about one-third of the Syrian air force in the first hours of the war. There were a few air battles and ground skirmishes until June when 8 Brigades of Israeli armor and infantry attacked 8 Brigades of Syrian forces[25] on the Golan Heights. By the end of June 10, the collapsing and retreating Syrian force left Israel in control of 482 square miles of the Golan Heights.

On October 6, 1973, Egypt and Syria launched coordinated attacks against Israel, Egypt moving its third army across the Suez Canal and Syria sending three armored divisions against the Israeli defenses on the Golan Heights. Some 4,500 Israeli soldiers fell back but held the Golan against 45,000 Syrians until October 15 when Israeli reinforcements drove the Syrians off Golan and back along the highway to Damascus. After the October 24 cease-fire, Israel held more of the Golan Heights than it had before the war, but surrendered the 1973 gains in the Disengagement Agreement of May 31, 1974, negotiated by U.S. Secretary of State Henry A. Kissinger.

United Nations Disengagement Observer Force (UNDOF)

As part of the 1974 Disengagement Agreement, the United Nations created the U.N. Disengagement Observer Force (UNDOF) to monitor the Golan Heights cease-fire. The UNDOF patrols an irregularly shaped zone of separation that roughly parallels the Syrian-Israeli cease-fire line. The separation zone is on the Syrian side of the cease-fire line. Parallel to the separation zone are two strips, one on each side of the separation zone, each 6 miles (10 kilometers) wide. Israeli and Syrian forces are limited to 75 tanks and 6,000 men in their respective zones. Parallel to these first

---

[23]There are a number of sources on the early wars: see for example, Dupuy, Trevor N. *Elusivd Victory, the Arab-Israeli Wars*, 1947-1974. New York, Harper and Tow, 1978.

[24]Moore, John Norton, ed. *The Arab-Israeli Conflict*. Vol. III, Documents. Princeton, Princeton University Press, 1974. p. 410.

[25]Gold, U.S. Forces on the Golan Heights, op. cit., p. 6. Gold cites *The Six Day War* by the Israeli General Staff and *Elusive Victory* by Trevor Depuy.

limited force zones is a second 6 mile (10 kilometer) wide zone, one on each side of the separation zone, in which both Syria and Israel are limited to 450 tanks and a specified number of artillery pieces. In addition, both Syria and Israel have agreed not to place surface-to-air missiles closer than 16 miles (25 kilometers) from the separation zone. UNDOF's authorized strength is 1,250 men; at present, there are about 1,130 peace keeping troops from Austria, Canada, Finland, and Poland, and a contingent of U.N. Truce Supervisory Observers (UNTSO).[26] UNDOF's annual budget is about $36 million, and the mandate is renewed every six months.

EXTENDING ISRAELI ADMINISTRATION OVER THE GOLAN

On December 14, 1981, Israeli Prime Minister Menachem Begin called an emergency cabinet meeting to approve a draft law that would extend Israeli "Law, jurisdiction, and administration" over the Golan Heights. The 120-seat Knesset passed the cabinet approved bill the same day, December 14, 1981, by a vote of 63-17. The law had the practical effect of annexing the territory to Israel although the Israeli action did not formally annex the Golan. On December 17, 1981, the U.N. Security Council unanimously passed Resolution 497 that denounced Israel's illegal action and called upon Israel to rescind the annexation. No other country has recognized Israeli sovereignty over the Golan Heights.

TERRITORIAL CLAIMS

Some Israelis and some Israeli supporters claim that Golan, or parts of it, was part of the Palestine Mandate promised to the Jews as a national home under the Balfour Declaration of 1917.[27] According to these Israelis, Britain ceded part of the Golan Heights, which should have been part of the Jewish national home, to France as the Mandatory power for Syria. Many Israelis believe Israel should retain the Golan Heights as part of historical Israel. The Israeli claim that part of Golan was included in the Palestine Mandata promised to the Jews may be based on the description of the temporary boundary between British Mandata Palestine and French Mandata Syria signed in 1920.[28] The area in question is within a rough triangle formed by the town

---

[26]UNTSO was formed in May 1948 to monitor ceae-fire arrangements between Isrel and Syria, Lebanon, Jordan, and Egypt. At present UNTSO is compoed of 224 officers from 19 countires, including 17 offiers rom U.S. Armed Forces. Some UNTSO offices are attahed to UNDOF on the Golan Heights.

[27]The Balfour statement said "...the establishment in Palestine of a national home for the Jewish people..." without defining Palestine, national home, or Jewish people. The first indication of the Golan Heights relation to Palestine is in the 1920 French-British boundary agreement, and the first definitive demarction of the boundary is in the 1923 Anglo-French treaty. See footnotes 39 and 40 below.

[28]United Kingdom. Franco-British Convention of December 23, 1920, on Certain Points Connected with the Mandates for Syria and Lebanon, Palestine and Mesopotamia. Miscellaneous No. 4 (1921), Command Paper 1195. London, H. M. Stationary Office, 1921. Also see: Gilbert, Martin. Jewish History Atlas. Revised Edition. New York, acmillan, 1976. p. 86.

of Banyas, the northern point of Lake Kinneret, and the western edge of the town of Qunaytirah.

Syrians and Syrian supporters counter that Golan traditionally has been part of Syria. In the more recent past, the Syrians point to the Ottoman Turkish boundaries that placed Golan within the Sanjak of Haran in the Vilayet of Damascus, as part of Syria. Syrians also point out the 1920 British-French agreement was temporary, and that the Banyas-Kinneret-Qunaytirah triangle was erased in the final demarcation of the line between Palestine and Syria drawn by the British and French in 1923.[29] The current boundary line follows the French-British line of 1923.

SELECTED READINGS

Asher, Jerry. *Duel for the Golan: the 100-hour Battle that Saved Israel*. 1st ed., New York, W. Morrow, 1987. 288 p.

Bacevich, Andrew, Michael Eisenstadt, and Carl Ford. *Supporting Peace, America's Role in an Israel-Syria Peace Agreement. Report of a Washington Institute Study Group*. The Washington Institute for Near East Policy, 87 p.

Ben-Meir, Alon. The Israeli-Syrian Battle for Equitable Peace. *Middle East Policy*, v. 3, no. 1, 1994: 70-83.

Bier, Aharon. The Golan Heights. Jerusalem, *Israel Digest*, 1974. 47 p.

Center for Security Policy, U.S. Forces on the Golan Heights. Printed in: *Commentary*, Vol. 98, No. 6, December 1994: 74-88.

Cohen, Saul G., The Geopolitics of a Golan Heights Agreement, *Focus*, v. 42, summer 1992: 15-18.

Cohen, Saul B. *The Geopolitics of Israel's Border Question*. Tel Aviv, Jaffee Center for Strategic Studies, c1986. 124 p.

Davis, Uri. *The Golan Heights Under Israeli Occupation*, 1967-1981. Durham City, England, University of Durham, Centre for Middle Eastern and Islamic Studies, 1983. 60 p.

Elagab, Omer Yousif, *The Law of Belligerent Occupation Versus the Law of Annexation of Territories: A Case Study of the Golan Heights, Development and Peace*, v. 6, spring 1985: 118-128.

Gold, Dore. *U.S. Forces on the Golan Heights and Israeli-Syrian Security Arrangements*. Jaffee Center for Strategic Studies, Tel Aviv University, Memorandum No. 44, August 1994. 61 p.

Ilan, Zvi. *The Golan was Always Jewish*. Tel-Aviv, World Zionist Organization, Dept. of Organization and Education, 1969. 20 p.

Israel Defense Forces. *The Golan Heights* [Tel Aviv, Israel], [1981], 36 p.

---

[29]United Kingdom. Agreement beween His Majesty's Government and the Frensh Government Respecting the Boundary Line between Syria and Palestine from the Mediterranean to El Hamme. Treat Series No. 13 (1923), Command Paper 1910. London, H. M. Stationary Office, 1923. See also: Gilbert, *Jewish Historical Atlas*, op. cit. p 69, 84, 86. The Golan Heights area is within the boundaries of the Hauran Sanjak of the Vilayet of Damascus under the Ottoman Turks, 1516-1918.

James, Alan. *The U.N. on Golan: Peacekeeping Paradox?* Oslo, Published in cooperation with the project on peace keeping operations at the Norwegian Institute of International Affairs, [1986] 46 p. (Also appeared in: International relations, v. 9, May 1987: 64-84.)

The Meaning of Golan. *Near East Report*, Vol. 25, December 25, 1981: 233-238.

Miller, R. Reuben, The Golan Heights: an Obsolete Security Buffer, *Mediterranean Quarterly*, v. 4, spring 1993: 121-128.

Pa'il, Meir, The Golan Heights in Exchange for Peace: a Military Plan, *New Outlook*, v. 34, Apr.-May 1991: 12-15.

Shalev, Arye. *Israel and Syria: Peace and Security on the Golan.* Boulder, Westview Press, 1994.

Silverstein, David. *Strategic Heights, American Targets: Why U.S. Troops Should Stay off the Golan. Policy View*, The Shalem Center-National Policy Institute (Jerusalem), No. 4, September 11, 1994. 18 p.

Golan Heights

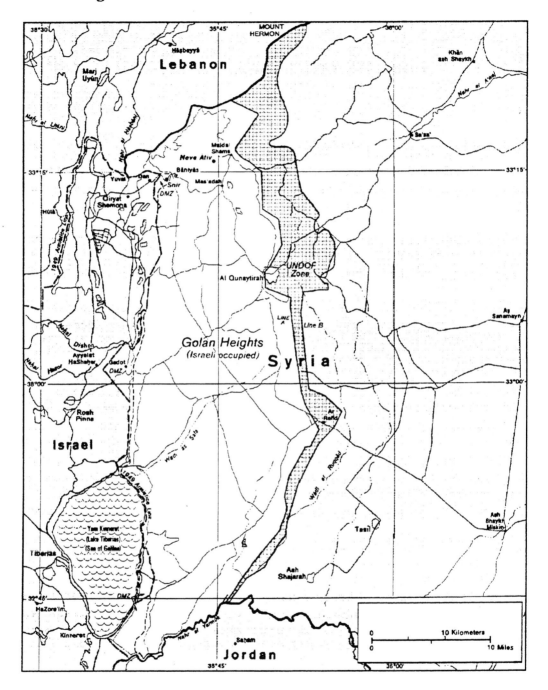

Jordan: U.S. Relations and Bilateral Issues[*]

Alfred B. Prados

Background and Analysis

U.S.-Jordanian Relations and the Gulf Crisis

Development of Bilateral Relations

Although the United States and Jordan have never been linked by a formal treaty, they have cooperated on a number of regional and international issues over the years. Several factors have contributed toward U.S. interest in Jordan. First, throughout much of its history, Jordan has been a pro-Western, modernizing country that has adopted moderate policies on most regional issues. Second, the country's stable political leadership and talented population have given Jordan considerable importance in the Middle East political scene. Third, Jordan has made significant contributions to regional stability and economic development in the Persian Gulf area; during the 1970s and 1980s, Jordan provided the small, oil-rich but newly independent Gulf states with military advisors, instructors, engineers, skilled workers, and technical specialists. Fourth, because of its large Palestinian population, its former role on the West Bank, and its extended border with Israel and the occupied territories, Jordan is pivotal in the search for a solution to the Arab-Israeli conflict.

From Jordan's standpoint, U.S. support has been an important factor in helping Jordan deal with serious vulnerabilities, both internal and external. Jordan's small size and lack of major economic resources have made it dependent on aid from Western and friendly Arab sources. Jordan's unique population composition has created chronic internal security problems. Palestinians comprise an estimated 55-70% of the population, and include just over a million registered refugees, of which 220,000 reside in camps. Although significant numbers of Palestinians have acquired a stake in Jordan's economy, many continue to regard their stay in Jordan as temporary, and some are at most lukewarm in their support of the Jordanian regime. Jordan's

---

[*]Excerpted from *CRS Issue Brief*, Order Code IB93085.

geographic position, wedged between Israel, Syria, Iraq, and Saudi Arabia, has made it vulnerable to the strategic designs of its more powerful neighbors, but has also given Jordan an important role as a buffer between these potential adversaries.

Gulf Crisis and Its Aftermath

The Iraqi invasion of Kuwait precipitated a serious crisis in U.S.-Jordanian relations. Although Jordan condemned the invasion, it refused to join the allied coalition and strongly opposed the presence of western forces in the Gulf. Reports that Jordan had moved or allowed the movement of supplies to Iraq in violation of U.N. Security Council resolutions heightened criticism of Jordan both in U.S. Administration and in Congress and led to temporary suspension of U.S. aid to Jordan. Saudi Arabia, Kuwait, and to a lesser extent other Gulf states ostracized Jordan for its stand during the crisis.

The crisis dealt a major blow to Jordan's already troubled economy: a brief influx of some 860,000 international refugees in transit from Kuwait and Iraq; loss of income from tourism; termination of $450-$500 million per year in subsidies from Gulf states; loss of remittances from Jordanian expatriate workers, some 325,000 of whom returned from the Gulf, thereby burdening the trained economy further. Unemployment soared to 30%. The World Bank originally projected the annual loss to Jordan's economy as a result of the Gulf crisis at $1.5 billion; press estimates of the total loss to Jordan's economy as a result of the international embargo range as high as $9 billion (see *Christian Science Monitor*, October 13, 1993, p. 3).

Nonetheless, Jordan's economic situation has improved significantly since reaching its lowest point during the Gulf crisis. The return of Jordanians from the Gulf caused an expansion in construction. In May 1994, the International Monetary Fund approved a load to support structural adjustments in the country's economy, and in June Jordan reached agreement with the Paris Club to reschedule over $1.2 billion in debt, and individual lender nations have offered other relief (see below). In March 1995, Jordanian officials said the country's budget would be balanced by 1998; however, they noted that payments on the country's rescheduled debt will fall due in 1996 and further rescheduling will not be possible.

JORDANIAN ISSUES OF U.S. INTEREST

Bilateral relations began to improve in late 1991 and 1992, as Jordan joined the Arab-Israeli peace talks and began to tighten its enforcement of U.N. sanctions against Iraq. Several issues of bilateral interest face the two countries in the post-Gulf War period.

Stability of the Regime and Succession

MILESTONES IN DEVELOPMENT OF JORDAN AS A STATE

1921 State of Transjordan established as British mandate under Prince (later King) Abdullah of the Hashemite family

1946 Transjordan received independence; became Hashemite Kingdom of Jordan

1950 Jordan annexed the West Bank territory (one fifth of former mandate of Palestine) after establishment of Israel

1951 King Abdullah assassinated; succeeded by son, King Talal, who abdicated the following year due to illness

1953 Hussein ibn Talal, son of previous King, formally enthroned upon reaching constitutional age (18 years)

1965 Hassan ibn Talal, younger brother o King Hussein, designated as Crown Prince and heir apparent

1967 Israel occupied West Bank during six-day Arab-Israeli war

1970 Civil strife, in which Jordanian government forces defeated Palestinian guerrilla groups

1974 Arab summit conference recognized Palestine Liberation Organization as sole representative of Palestinian people, implicitly rejecting a Jordanian role on West Bank

1988 King Hussein officially severed Jordan's relationship with West Bank

Ever since it gained independence, the stability of Jordan has rested to a considerable extent on the twin pillars of the Hashemite monarchy and the small but well trained armed forces. King Hussein, on the throne since 1953, is the world's longest ruling head of state and has dominated the Jordanian political scene throughout his reign. Despite periodic challenges to his regime and some health problems (including cancer surgery in August 1992), he enjoys a high degree of legitimacy as head of a prestigious dynasty, the loyalty of the armed forces, and widespread respect as a strong and energetic leader with extensive experience in governing his country. The King is supported by an experienced cadre of family members, senior public officials, and military officers -- both active and retired -- who share his views on Jordan's regional role and could provide a basis for continuity in the future.

In 1965, the King's youngest brother, Hassan ibn Talal, was appointed Crown Prince and heir to the throne. A dynamic administrator and prolific writer, Prince Hassan has overseen Jordan's economic development programs since 1971. King Hussein's oldest son by an Arab mother, Prince Ali, was designated as successor to the Crown Prince in 1974. (A constitutional requirement that both parents of the heir apparent be of Arab nationality removed the King's oldest son, Prince Abdullah, a brigadier general in the Army, from the line of succession.) In a speech on November 15, 1994, the King reaffirmed Crown Prince Hassan as his successor; however, he appeared to open future succession more widely by stating that after Hassan, the descendants of a common Hashemite ancestor (Hussein's great grandfather) would meet and select one of their number as king. Observers sometimes speculate about the

future of Jordan and the nature of U.S.-Jordanian relationships in the absence of King
Hussein; however, under an orderly process of succession, bilateral working
relationships are likely to continue.

Experiments in Democratic Reform

In November 1989, Jordan embarked upon a new era of democratic reform,
holding elections for a lower house of parliament for the first time since 1967.
Subsequent elections were held on November 8, 1993, and this time political parties
were permitted. The fundamentalist Islamic Action Front (IAF), the political party
of the Muslim Brotherhood, won 16 seats (down from 23 in the previous parliament),
in addition to several more seats (estimated from 2 to 5) won by independent
supporters of the IAF, giving Islamists a bloc of 18 to 21 votes, as compared with 33
in the previous house. In addition, supporters of left-wing nationalist lists won 7 seats
(some commentators think the nationalist bloc could muster as many as 12 votes).
Remaining seats were won largely by independents with moderate to conservative
views and in some cases tribal affiliations. For the first time, voters elected a woman
candidate to parliament (one of three women to run). The King subsequently
appointed a 40-member Senate on November 18, including several former cabinet
officials and members of parliament. Initial results of municipal elections held on July
11, 1995, indicated a setback for the fundamentalist IAF, which has complained of
official interference in the voting.

Jordan's recent moves toward creating a freer and more pluralistic political
system are in harmony with U.S. goals of encouraging greater democracy, as
articulated by both the Clinton Administration and Members of Congress. At the
same time, the growth of democracy in Jordan has led to parliamentary pressure on
the Jordanian Government to oppose women U.S. regional goals. Some of the more
powerful groups in the present parliament such as the Muslim Brotherhood have
condemned the Jordanian-Israeli peace treaty and parliamentary deputies from the
IAF block boycotted President Clinton's address to the Jordanian parliament
following the treaty's signature on October 16, 1994. Arab nationalist groups,
including Palestinians, oppose the enforcement of sanctions against Iraq, although
pro-Iraqi sentiment in Jordan has diminished. Security measures in Jordan reportedly
have been tightened since early 1995, and some commentators have expressed
concern that the King may feel it necessary to slow the pace of democratization in
Jordan in an effort to forestall attempts by the opposition to resist implementation
of the terms of the Jordanian-Israeli peace treaty. A report prepared by the
committee on civil liberties of the Jordanian parliament in September 1995 said
government policy since the October 1994 peace treaty with Israel "has visibly
affected the ceiling of public freedoms." The Jordanian Government rejected this
charge. On March 2, 1 Jordanian human rights agency cited a "clear, tangible
deterioration" in human rights.

On February 4, 1996, King Hussein appointed a new cabinet headed by the former
Foreign Minister Add al-Karim al-Kabariti, who will also serve as Foreign Minister
and Minister of Defense. In his previous role as Foreign Minister, Prime Minister

Kabariti was closely associated with steps by King Hussein to normalize relations with Israel, to reorient Jordanian policy away from the Iraqi regime of President Saddam Husayn, and to improve relations with Saudi Arabia and other Gulf states. Commentators have suggested that the King wanted a cabinet with younger, more dynamic ministers and wanted to replace several previous ministers who had been resistant toward the new directions in the King's regional policies. On March 4, the new cabinet received a vote of confidence from the lower house of parliament (57 in favor; 17 opposed).

Jordan's Role in the Peace Process

Peace Agreements. Jordanian-Israeli negotiations have constituted the most successful phase of the current Arab-Israeli peace process inaugurated during the Bush Administration in late 1991. Negotiations gathered momentum in 1993, with the signature on September 13 by Jordanian and Israeli representatives of a "common agenda" for further negotiations with the stated goal of achieving a "just, lasting and comprehensive peace." In 1994, Jordan and Israel reached two milestone agreements: a Declaration of Non-Belligerency singed in Washington on July 25, followed by a full-fledged peace treaty signed on October 26 at a ceremony on the Israeli-Jordanian border attended by President Clinton. The peace treaty provides for recognition by each party of the other's sovereignty, borders, and political independence; demarcation of borders; full diplomatic relations; agreement on water sharing; and cooperation in economic, scientific, and cultural fields. The 120-member Israeli parliament ratified the treaty by a vote of 105-3, with 6 abstentions on October 25. On November 6, the 80-member Jordanian lower house of parliament endorsed the treaty by a vote of 56-23, with one absentee. On November 9, Jordan's royally appointed Senate endorsed it by a vote of 33-0, with one abstention and 6 absentees, and ratification became final with the King's signature on November 10.

Normalization with Israel. Since the 1994 treaty, King Hussein and Israeli leaders have moved quickly to implement the terms of their agreement. Embassies were established in the two countries in late 1994. On February 9, 1995, Israel completed the return to Jordan of approximately 131 square miles of territory, mostly south of the Dead Sea but also including a small enclave along their northern border, with a provision to lease back several small parcels of land to Israeli farmers under a 25-year renewable agreement. During the year that followed, Jordan and Israel concluded 14 agreements to normalize economic and cultural links between the two countries; the last four agreements were signed on January 18, 1996. Highlights of the 14 agreements included the following: (1) a civil air agreement (May 1995) regulating long-range Jordanian flights through Israeli airspace; (2) a follow-on transportation agreement (January 16, 1996) regulating air, sea, and land transport links between the two countries; (3) and a trade agreement (October, 25, 1995), which reportedly will give Jordan tariff cuts of up to 50% while a limited list of Israeli goods will get reductions of 10%, with an additional 5% reduction in two years. Under the civil air and transportation agreements, direct flights between the cities of Amman, Jordan and Tel Aviv, Israel at a cost of $70 per ticket began on April 7, 1996. Among the other agreements were accords on tourism, security and crime control, health and environment, agriculture, energy, transportation, post and telecommunications, and scientific and cultural exchanges.

King Hussein was one of two Arab heads of state to attend the funeral of the late Israeli Prime Minister Yitzhak Rabin in November 1995. Jordan condemned the series of bombings in Israel occurring in late February and early March and during a meeting with President Clinton on March 7, King Hussein said "we must do everything we can to put an end" to this violence. King Hussein leaders of 26 other countries at the "summit of Peace Builders" conference held at Sharm al-shaykh, Egypt on March 13 at the invitation of President Clinton and Egyptian President Husni Mubarak, to discuss ways to further the peace process and counter terrorism; Jordan was also represented at a follow-on conference in Washington on March 28-29. On April 15, King Hussein expressed concern over the renewed outbreak of strife involving Lebanon and Israel and said the escalating violence in Lebanon is "threatening the peace process in the Middle East." Jordan became more critical of the Israeli campaign against targets in southern Lebanon after Israeli artillery strikes on killed 102 Lebanese civilians sheltering in a U.N. base on April 18; on April 25, Jordan voted for a U.N. General Assembly resolution condemning Israeli attacks against civilians and calling on Israel to pay reparations (the United States voted against the resolution).

Resistance to normalization with Israel continues in some Jordanian circles, particularly among Islamist groups, parts of the Palestinian community, and the influential trade and professional organizations representing some 80,000 engineers, doctors, lawyers, journalists, and writers. In February 1995, a bloc of Islamist and left-wing nationalist members of parliament were able to delay passage of government sponsored legislation to repeal three laws: a 1973 law that imposed a death sentence (never executed) on Jordanians who sell land to Israelis and two 1950s-era laws that banned personal contacts and commercial dealings with Israelis. The repeal legislation, however, did pass in July 1995 by comfortable majorities in both houses of parliament (51-21 in the lower house on July 27, and 30-3 in the Senate on July 21). On March 17, 1996, a prominent Jordanian Islamist who is head of the 35,000-member engineers union was sentenced to three years' imprisonment for publicly accusing King Hussein of betraying his country to Israel. On April 17, during Israel's campaign in Lebanon, Jordanian deputies from the opposition IAF called on the government to abrogate the peace treaty with Israel. Among mainstream Jordanians, there is some disappointment that the treaty so far has not brought many tangible economic benefits to them.

Multilateral Talks. In addition to their bilateral negotiations with Israel, Jordanian representatives have participated in the other phase of the U.S.-Russian sponsored peace talks, namely, the multilateral talks dealing with regional issues. These issues include environment, water, economic development refugees, and arms control. On September 20, 1995, representatives from Israel, 11 Arab states, and 5 external countries met in Amman, Jordan, to make arrangements for establishment of a regional conflict prevention center in Jordan with branches in Qatar and Tunisia. On October 29-31, 1995, Jordan hosted a Middle East/North Africa economic conference attended by 1,500 government and business leaders representing over 60 countries. Attendees discussed a number of development projects and agreed to establish a Middle East Development Bank to be headquartered in Cairo with an initial authorized capital of $5 billion.

The West Bank and East Jerusalem. The treaty does not address the status of the West Bank territory, which was annexed by Jordan in 1950 but occupied by Israel in 1967, nor does it address the status of East Jerusalem (except as noted below); both issues are subjects of Israeli-Palestinian rather than Israeli-Jordanian negotiations. Although King Hussein severed Jordanian ties with the West Bank in 1988, Jordan remains involved in Palestinian issues for several reasons: Jordan's large Palestinian population, its continuing involvement in supporting some West Bank institutions, the preference on the part of some Israeli leaders (particularly in the governing Labor Party) for a Jordanian role in a future Palestinian settlement, and Jordan's continued role in protecting and maintaining the Islamic holy places in East Jerusalem.

Palestinian leaders have taken exception to Article 9 of the treaty, which states that Israel "respects the historical role of the Hashemite Kingdom [of Jordan] in the mosques of Jerusalem" and "will give high priority to the Jordanian historic role in these shrines." PLO Chairman Yasir Arafat has asserted that "sovereignty over Jerusalem and supervision of Jerusalem is for Palestinians." King Hussein has said that Jordan will continue its role in protecting and maintaining the Islamic holy places in Jerusalem to assure that there is no vacuum in Muslim control of these sites. On November 1, 1994, however, Crown Prince Hassan issued the following clarification which indicated Jordanian willingness to relinquish its role to Palestinians when the issue of Jerusalem is fully resolved: "In the final status, when responsibility is transferred in full to the Palestinians, this responsibility (for the sites) will be transferred in full to those concerned." On December 14, 1994, following a meeting with Arafat, King Hussein said Jordan would remain the custodian of the holy places in Jerusalem "until we transfer it to its people" [presumably Palestinians]. In early May 1996, the King reportedly said the holy places in Jerusalem should be outside any sovereignty; on May 12, he reportedly expressed the view that the Arab eastern part of Jerusalem belongs rightfully to the Palestinians, but that the city should be a symbol of Palestinian-Israeli peace and Arab-Israeli peace.

Enforcement of Sanctions Against Iraq

Jordan's earlier ties with Iraq, a long-standing irritant in U.S.-Jordanian relations, have deteriorated dramatically since the Gulf crisis and its immediate aftermath. Since 1992, Jordan has gradually tightened enforcement of U.N. sanctions against Iraq. Subsequently, the United States and Jordan reached an agreement (which became effective on August 24, 1994) to replace U.S. Navy searches of Red Sea shipping bound for Jordan with a less intrusive land-based monitoring regime, including verification of cargoes and manifests by the insurance agency Lloyds Registry of London. In December 1995, Jordanian officials announced that Jordan had intercepted a shipment of 115 Russian-made missile guidance systems destined for Iraq valued at $25 million, as well as "dangerous chemicals" bound for Iraq, although the Iraqi press dismissed the reports as a CIA fabrication. On March 7, 1996,

Jordanian officials said Jordan had seized spare parts and equipment for military fighter planes bound from Poland to Iraq; Poland denied that it had authorized the shipment, and an Amman-based Iraqi trader allegedly involved in the transaction said the shipments contained spare parts for Polish-made helicopters used in spraying pesticides for agricultural purposes.

Jordan has continued to import between 60,000 and 75,000 barrels per day of oil from Iraq, pointing out to the U.N. Sanctions Committee that it has no other source of oil because of the cessation of Saudi oil shipments in 1990. Jordan reportedly buys Iraqi oil under the following terms: 25,000 barrels of Iraqi crude oil per day at market prices, minus $1 per barrel for trucking costs that are borne by Jordan; another 25,000 barrels per day of Iraqi petroleum products at market prices; and the remainder at undisclosed concessionary terms. According to the Jordanians, money does not actually change hands: payments for oil have been credited against previous Iraqi debts to Jordan (reportedly $310 million) and against the costs of food and medicine which Jordan is allowed under pertinent U.N. resolutions to ship to Iraq on humanitarian grounds. Costs of these supplies have been estimated at $400 million per year (some estimates are higher). On August 23, 1995, King Hussein estimated Iraq's debt to Jordan at $1.1 billion, which may include both the basic debt of $310 million and an undetermined amount of supplies shipped to Iraq. Some analysts are skeptical of these figures, pointing out that a large portion of Iraq's debt should have been liquidated after several years of oil shipments to Jordan.

On January 22 1996, it was reported that under a recently renewed Jordanian-Iraqi trade protocol, Jordan will cut its exports to Iraq from over $400 million in 1995 to approximately $200 million in 1996. Jordanian officials advanced economic reasons for the change: Jordan's Minister of Trade stated that his country could not afford to keep making large payments to local traders to send their goods to Iraq while Iraq maintains a high level of debt to Jordan. Some observers believe deteriorating relations between the two countries contributed to the Jordanian decision to cut exports to Iraq. Nonetheless, it was announced on December 30, 1995, that Iraq signed an agreement to provide 4.4 million tons (roughly 88,000 barrels per day) of oil to Jordan during 1996.

Support for Iraqi Opposition. On August 10, 1995, in a move that foreshadowed further cooling of Jordanian-Iraqi ties, King Hussein granted political asylum to two high-ranking Iraqi officials, sons-in-law of President Saddam Husayn, who apparently defected after a power struggle within Saddam's inner circle. Although the two officials unwisely returned to Iraq in February 1996 (and were promptly murdered), Jordan has welcomed additional Iraqi defectors; one-time Armed Forces Chief of Staff Lt. General Nazar Khazraji fled to Jordan on March 21, and former Director of Military Intelligence Wifaq al-Samarra'i (who had first received asylum in Syria) moved to Jordan in early April. Since August 1995, statements by King Hussein have been increasingly critical of the Iraqi regime. In late November, the King reportedly met with Iraqi opposition leaders in London and on December 16, he called for a meeting of Iraqi factions opposed to the present regime to discuss national reconciliation and chart a new direction for the country. On March 25, an Iraqi opposition group known as the Iraqi National Accord opened an office in Amman. On April 1, Jordan's Prime Minister described Iraq under the present regime as "a big prison."

The two countries have stopped short of a complete break. Jordanian officials, including King Hussein, have said Jordan will not end its trade links or close its borders with Iraq. On September 7, 1995, shortly after granting asylum to the two defecting relatives of the Iraqi President, King Hussein (in response to a query by a journalist) denied any intention to seek a leadership role in Iraq (which members of his family had ruled prior to 1958). Iraq, on its part, has been slow to register its anger over the Jordanian decision, presumably because Jordan constitutes Iraq's principal trade and travel link to the outside world; however, Iraqi statements concerning Jordan have become increasingly critical, and in January 1996 there were press reports of Iraqi harassment of Jordanian travelers in Iraq. As in the case of normalization with Israel, however, King Hussein's altered policy toward Iraq to some extent has outstripped Jordanian public opinion, particularly in those parts of the business community that have developed close ties with Iraq over the years.

Relations with Gulf States. Jordan's growing hostility to the Iraqi regime has led to a warming trend between Jordan and its former Gulf allies, who had been alienated by Jordan's tilt toward Iraq during the 1990-1991 Gulf crisis. As late as 1994, King Fahd of Saudi Arabia and other Saudi officials pointedly refused to receive King Hussein while the latter was making a pilgrimage to the holy city of Mecca. Relations began to improve in 1995 after King Hussein granted political asylum to two high level Iraqi defectors and reportedly made them available to the Saudi intelligence chief for debriefing. In January 1996, the Saudi Foreign Minister visited Jordan in the highest level contact between the two countries since the Iraqi invasion of Kuwait, partly to help plan for a fence-mending visit to Saudi Arabia by King Hussein. The visit, which took place on February 10, proved partially successful from Jordan's standpoint; the King was received by Saudi Crown Prince Abdullah, who had been functioning as acting head of state during King Fahd's recovery from a recent illness. Some commentators describe the failure of King Fahd to receive King Hussein as a "smooth snub," since King Fahd reportedly chaired a cabinet meeting shortly after Hussein's departure; others believe the visit still represented a significant breakthrough in reestablishment of Saudi-Jordanian ties.

Elsewhere in the Arabian Peninsula, Kuwait's Crown Prince and Prime Minister, hitherto strongly resentful of Jordan's stand in 1990, has also spoken of the possibility of better relations. On November 16, 1995, Bahrain returned its ambassador to Jordan, as did Saudi Arabia. (Jordan has already largely restored its previous ties with Qatar and Oman.)

U.S. Reactions. President Clinton praised King Hussein's decision to grant political asylum to the initial Iraqi defectors in August 1995 as "an act of real courage" and promised U.S. protection if Jordan is threatened as a result of this incident. During the last two weeks of August, between 2,000 and 3,000 U.S. Marines and up to 4,000 Jordanian troops conducted a previously scheduled joint exercise in Jordan, and the United States undertook several other precautionary measures, including the movement of additional naval and air assets to the region and the acceleration by two months of a previously scheduled joint exercise with Kuwait. On

February 6, 1996, U.S. Secretary of Defense William Perry indicated that the United States and Jordan are cooperating in actions "to accelerate the demise of the present regime in Iraq," but said he was not able to discuss the details of those actions. According to press reports of February 16, the U.S. Central Intelligence Agency suggested that Jordan agree to the installation of a radio station for broadcasts directed against the Saddam Husayn regime. On April 12, U.S. fighter aircraft began a two-month deployment to Jordan to conduct combined training with Jordanian crews and to assist in enforcing a no-fly zone over southern Iraq imposed by the United States and its allies in 1992 (see below).

Alternatives and Implications

In the aftermath of the Gulf war and the peace treaty with Israel, several alternative scenarios could develop in Jordan. The first would be continued movement toward democracy under the present regime. There is much evidence that the King favors this course. The political experience since the parliamentary elections of 1989 and 1993 has been generally positive. The King has succeeded in opening the political system to a wide spectrum of Jordanian opinion while restraining any extreme steps by the religious right or the nationalist left. Externally, Jordan has survived major diplomatic isolation and economic loss brought on by the Gulf crisis, and conditions have improved on both fronts. The course of events following the 1994 peace treaty with Israel will continue to confront the King with sensitive decisions; so far, however, opposition groups are still working within the present Jordanian political system.

Under a second scenario, Jordan might return to a more restrictive political system in Jordan. In addition to him commitment to fostering democracy, the King has long been dedicated to preserving the basic integrity and institutional character of the state that his grandfather built. On at least two occasions -- when threatened by a radical nationalist coup d'etat in 1957 and by a potential takeover of the country by armed Palestinian guerrillas in 1970 -- the King, backed by the armed forces, has moved decisively to reestablish order at the expense of democratic experiments previously under way. It is arguable that the country's institutions today are stronger, more durable, and more able to absorb political pressures than they were in 1957 or 1970 and that the current situation is far less threatening. On the other hand, the combination of domestic economic hardships, an uncertain peace process opposed by many Jordanians, and a strong and aggressive Islamist movement could create new challenges that the King might feel compelled to preempt through returning to a more autocratic system of government.

A third scenario would involve a fundamental change in the character of the Jordanian state. This could come about in a number of ways: emergence of a strongly Islamist government that would exclude other groups from participation in national political life; a close alliance with a neighboring patron (Iraq or Syria) that would exert control over Jordanian policies; disappearance of the monarchy; or replacement of the present Jordanian state with a Palestinian entity. These scenarios, though not likely in the short term, could become more plausible if the country's governmental, economic, and military institutions should suffer serious erosion.

These developments will be of importance to U.S. policy makers. The growth of democratic institutions in Jordan under the leadership of King Hussein and this successors would serve long term U.S. interests. At times, however, the democratic process in Jordan would complicate bilateral relations as groups opposed to specific U.S. objectives gained a more influential voice. U.S. relations with a more autocratic Jordanian regime less susceptible to internal public opinion might be smoother in the short term, but could threaten U.S. interests in the long term by reversing democratic development, polarizing political groups in Jordan, and undermining the durability of the Hashemite regime. Radical changes in the character or configuration of Jordan would be of even greater concern. Almost any successor to the Jordanian state as it is now constituted would present the United States and its allies with a less stable and more threatening regional environment.

Fiscal Year (FY)	Economic Assistance			Military Assistance		Totals
	ESF*	Food	DA**	FMF***	IMET****	
1991	35.0[a]	0	0	20.0[a]	1.25	56.25
1992	30.0[b]	20.0	0	20.0[b]	.6	70.60
1993[c]	5.0	30.0	0	9.0	.5	44.50
1994[d]	9.0	15.0	4.0	9.0	.8	37.80
1995	7.2	15.0	6.7	7.3	1.2	37.40
1996	10.0	15.0	7.9	30.0	1.6	64.50
1997[e]	10.0	15.0	5.8	30.0	1.6	62.40
Totals[f]	106.2	110.0	24.4	125.3	7.55	373.45

U.S. Aid to Jordan since the Gulf Crisis ($ in millions)

*   Economic Support Fund
**   Development Assistance
***   Foreign Military Financing
**** International Military Education and Training

a   Suspended in April 1991 under P.L. 102-27; released in early 1993
b   These funds were released in late July 1993
c   Restrictions on FY1993 funds waived by Presidential Determination 93-39 on September 17, which also permits U.S. Government to spend an addition $5 million on other centrally funded programs that may benefit Jordan
d   FY1994 funds were released under Presidential Determination 94-11 signed January 13, 1994, waiving restrictions under P.L. 103-87
e   Tentative allocations based on Administration request
f   These totals do not include: debt forgiveness subsidies ($99 million in FY94; $275 million in FY95), $100 million in drawdown authority from U.S. military equipment stocks (FY96), and $0.3 million ($300,000) in de-mining assistance

Subject Index